The Accidental Citizen-Soldier
By Young Chun

Contents

Preface

"AMBER ALERT! AMBER ALERT![1] The base is under indirect fire!"

All around me, soldiers in various states of battle readiness are pouring out of the B-huts and scrambling toward the main bunker in the compound. My K2 rifle slapping hard against my hip, I fight against the dark current of shadowy figures toward the squad B-hut to grab my Kevlar and helmet before joining the throng heading to the bunker.

I blindly claw through the darkness for a seat on one of the wooden benches that line the walls. A tense silence hangs heavy in the confines of the cramped bunker. The only sounds are an occasional grunt or cough and the crunching of gravel under fidgeting, booted feet.

"Chun! Where the hell is Private Chun?!"

Shit.

Hunched over, I creep through the narrow tunnel to the far entrance, where the major is calling for me. I can make out the silhouette of his face by the silvery moonlight streaming in through the entrance. He grabs me and pushes me halfway out the entrance.

"Stand here and tell me what's going on, got it?"

"Yes, sir," I respond uneasily. Standing where I am, I'm no longer protected from indirect fire by the thick sandbag walls of the bunker. I can hear the Giant Voice fine from just inside the entrance, but I know there is no reasoning with the major once he's given an order. I only pray that today's attack is like yesterday's—a single rocket fired in the middle of the night—and not the beginning of a prolonged battle.

"AMBER ALERT! Each unit is to conduct reconnaissance. Sweep your areas and report to 4209."

"What did they say?" the major asks, peering out from the darkness.

"Uh… they said to c-conduct…." My mind falters. What was the Korean word for reconnaissance?

"Well? Spit it out."

I subconsciously take a small step farther out of the bunker, wondering which is the lesser of two evils, to get physically wounded by a rocket blast or

---

[1] Amber Alert: A status given over the Giant Voice alerting soldiers on Bagram AB of some sort of danger, usually in response to a rocket attack. Not to be confused with the alert for missing children. (Definitions of military expressions and Korean words can also be found in the glossary in the back of the book.)

to continue to get emotionally blasted by Korean officers.

"They said to… check the compound."

Luckily, the major is sharp and orders the commander of the 2nd Construction Company to send out a squad to conduct reconnaissance.

Once the Giant Voice has called off the Amber Alert, I return to the squad B-hut, where everyone has already passed out on their cots. I'm in a somber mood as I pull out my notebook and pen and start writing letters of farewell to my mother and brothers.

The next day, the unit visits the 109th Engineers to survey the damage. I see Sergeant Luvaas talking with Captain Koepke and stray from the group to join them. They're looking at the blast crater, and I'm surprised by the size of it.

"Any casualties?" I ask.

"Two wounded, but nothing serious," Captain Koepke responds, grinning.

"It's much smaller than I thought," I remark. It's a bit smaller than a pitcher's mound.

"Yeah," Luvaas says. "It's not the blast that'll kill you. The rockets are only four inches wide. It's the shrapnel that'll get you."

"The shrapnel will shred through the walls of a B-hut like paper."

"Damn."

"You don't have to worry too much. There haven't been any KIA since we've been here. At least from rockets."

"Yeah, they're not very accurate. These guys lean them up against a pile of rocks and set a long fuse and run away."

I feel slightly better as I walk back to the compound but not completely reassured. Sure, the possibility of my meeting an early end by rocket attack is infinitesimally small, but one thing I've finally come to accept is that awful, unimaginable things with a very low probability of happening tend to happen to me. I've already had a near brush with death a couple of weeks earlier simply because I happened to be the first interpreter off the plane. And there I was, an American forced to serve two years in the Korean Army, deployed on an American air base in the middle of Afghanistan.

I used to not believe in luck. Most of the calamities in my life have been a result of awfully stupid decisions, but I admit that I'm beginning to consider the possibility that there's something more. There is randomness in life, and the majority of people fit within a normal standard deviation, but the bell curve also produces winners and losers. For example, if you were to flip a coin ten times, probability tells us that you'd most likely get five heads and five tails or something relatively close to that. But on one end, you'll have people who'll flip ten heads and people who'll flip ten tails at the other end. It's far from common—basic statistics tells us a normal person would have to flip 10,240 coins to get there—but it's possible. If heads are events that turns out favorably and tails are the opposite, I'd say that the person who gets ten tails deserves to say he has bad luck even if it is only a random occurrence of chance.

This story is my ten-tails story.

The story begins much earlier, in a completely different setting. It's the fall of 2002 in Seattle, and I'm sitting in front of a Fujifilm photo processor. Not one of those new Frontier Digital Labs they have at the other branches, the ones that you sit in front of and it feels like you're at the console of a space shuttle. This is a dinosaur, a relic from a bygone age, sputtering and spilling its photo-chemicals in the throes of death, held together with superglue and duct tape.

My boss, Rebecca, a red-haired hipster barely an adult at eighteen, walks over and picks up the finished sets and drops them in the paper boxes.

"I'm taking off," she says as she places the finished boxes in the outbox.

"Have a good night," I say over my shoulder, the same as I've said night after night in this godforsaken place.

She punches out, slings her bag over her shoulder, and walks out the door.

These times when I'm alone holding down the fort, after Rebecca and the two high-school stoners I call my co-workers have called it a day, these are the times I begin to think about what has become of my life. During the day, I am a machine, mindlessly adjusting the cyan-magenta-yellow of hundreds of amateur nature shots and washed-out family vacations. But after dusk, when I'm alone in the shop, I find it hard not to think.

Five years at the University of Washington and this was the best I could do. I had not known that this would be my best option once I finally declared myself an Art major. I had considered a degree, any degree, to be the end goal and figured things would work themselves out from there. Of course now, trying to explain the flexibility of the expression "one hour" to disgruntled customers and trying to "add on" a pack of Fuji film on every transaction for a twenty-five cent commission, I realize my folly.

I finish printing the remaining rolls of film and shut down the printer, turning off the neon KITS CAMERAS and setting the alarm before scurrying

3

out the door and locking up.

The drive home is uneventful, marked only by thoughts of which fast food place I should stop by to grab some dinner.

I'm met by our pug when I step through the door and tread quietly through the hall, hoping to make it up the stairs to the refuge of my room without having to hear the disapproving clucks and barbs of my mother.

I know I'm a disappointment. My older brother Charlie has two Master's degrees and is working out on the East Coast, and my younger brother Jason is working in finance, driving around in a fancy car and living in a posh condo downtown. Burdened by credit card debt and the loans I took out to pay for my worthless degree, I had no choice but to stay at home.

I'll never be able to give Mom the life I want to give her, a life of comfort with no worries about how she'd have to pay for groceries. I can't even get her to stop worrying about me. She sacrificed her entire adult life in raising and later supporting three boys as a single mother, and she is still burdened by her good-for-nothing middle son long after she should. When I tell her that one day I'm going to buy her a house, her reply is always, "Just move out."

I'm at the bottom of the stairs and I hear voices in the living room. We have guests. She has guests.

"Young? Young Jin?"

I walk out to the living room and see familiar faces. It's Debbie's mom and older sister. Debbie was one of my best friends from my childhood in Chicago.

Debbie's mom asks what I'm doing for a living.

"I work at a one-hour photo."

Even without looking, I already know my mother is embarrassed. She doesn't have to say anything. I'm sure they already broached the subject before I got home. I know by the looks I got when I walked in the living room. I don't ask but I'm also sure Debbie has turned out to be a doctor or lawyer, something respectable.

I stew quietly in my shame as they continue chatting, stew until Debbie's mom turns back to me.

"Have you ever thought about teaching English in Korea?" she asks. "A friend's son did it and saved a lot of money."

"You should think about it," my mom chimes in.

This has been rehearsed. They've tried to make it seem natural but I know a trap when I'm caught up in one.

"I'll think about it," I answer and excuse myself from the awkward conversation.

4

I've never considered it. I often saw ads for teaching jobs in Korea in the back of the Daily, the UW student newspaper. TEACH ENGLISH IN KOREA. All caps, shouting from between ads for egg donors and caretakers. A line of dollar signs. It was always there. I'd skip over it, asking myself, *Why would anyone go to a foreign country just to teach English?*

Lying on my bed, listening to the muffled voices in judgment floating up toward my room, I actually begin to consider it. I wasn't planning on considering it, but I'm in a contemplative mood. I make a mental list of pros and cons and reach a conclusion.

Hell, why not? Can my life get any worse than it is?

Two months and nearly sixty applications later, I'm on a Singapore Airlines flight direct to Incheon International Airport. The *hagwon*[2] has paid for the ticket and had it mailed to my address. The universe is waiting with my answer.

It is said that the stars align when you come across uncharacteristically good luck. If the same applies to bad luck, I can now identify the ones that came together to throw me in the Army. But the thing about stars, they're hundreds and thousands of light years away and unless you spend a great deal of time looking at them, you never really know where they are.

The first star aligned at my birth. I was born on December 17, 1978, 7:21 p.m., at the Burnham City Hospital in Champaign, Illinois, as Young Jin Chun. The second of three sons, I was the only one to not be given an English name. I later asked my mother why she hadn't, and she said, "I don't know. I guess I thought Young was an English name."

Shakespeare would argue that there isn't much in a name, but the fact is that when most people see or hear my name, they assume that I can't speak fluent English or that I just got off the boat. When I moved to Seattle in middle school, the school apparently didn't bother to check my academic records, taking one look at my name and putting me in remedial English classes. When I started looking for a job in Korea, even the dodgy recruiters didn't want to help me because my name was "too Korean." In 2003, this would be very important because the government was able to link the name on my passport with the

---

[2] *Hagwon:* A privately run after-school academy. Korean children spend much of their time after school in these academies to get ahead in their studies as early as kindergarten. I had one kindergartener who consistently had nosebleeds due to stress and fatigue. These places are where most of the English teaching ads will take you.

name on a problematic document, which was the beginning of the end.

The second alignment is a big one, maybe the biggest one of all since none of this would have happened without it. The family register, or *hojeok*, is the basis of citizenship in Korea. When I was very young, I once saw the actual, physical Chun family register, a small and ancient notebook with yellowing pages and bound with string, hundreds of names printed in Chinese characters. Of course, these days, everything has become computerized.

My first month in Korea, before I could start working, I had to go to Immigration to apply for a visa. I had painstakingly prepared my stack of documents and approached the counter when my number flashed on the display. The officer took my papers without a word and started typing furiously on the computer. The expression on his face went from mild perturbation to surprise and confusion, and finally to suspicion.

"You can't get a visa," he said. "You're a Korean citizen." I was dumbfounded. Not only had I been born and raised in the States, even my parents didn't have Korean citizenship. He pointed out my name on the family register and sent me on my way. On my way back to the *hagwon*, I pored over the register. It was true. There was my name, but the information was horribly wrong. The document had my birthplace recorded as some place west of Seoul, a place I had never been to or even heard of. Charlie's name was there, too, and instead of Providence, Rhode Island, his birthplace was recorded as mine, Champaign, Illinois.

I called my mother and she was as surprised as I was. I called my father and he was shocked as well. "Your grandfather must've reported your birth," he guessed, but I looked at the register and it said that my grandfather died several months before I was born. It was a mystery, but the fact remained that someone had my birth recorded on the family register and either died or forgot about it.

The third star aligned when my parents separated and eventually divorced. When I first got my draft papers in the mail, I went down to the Military Manpower Administration in Suwon with a co-worker to translate for me. I had my mother send me every single document she could get her hands on to show that, aside from a short stay in elementary school when my father's business brought us to Korea, I've lived in America my entire life. That stack of papers was my entire life in the form of my birth certificate, report cards, progress reports, transcripts, diplomas, and even class and yearbook photos. I handed my case worker the stack and she said, "This isn't necessary. It says here that you've lived in Korea since 1988."

Korea is a patriarchal society, and it used to be that children would typically live with the father in the event of a divorce. After the divorce, my father decided to stay in Korea. He's not Korean, at least not legally, and has stayed since then on a resident visa. So even if I hadn't seen my father since the divorce, I was considered as living with him in Korea in the eyes of the government.

The thing about stars aligning is that, in its very nature, it's about timing. I've been told that from the late 1990s up until 2002, the Army was actually very selective about new recruits. It was after the Asian Financial Crisis, and young men couldn't find jobs, so they decided to do their military service en masse. But in 2002, the year that I came to Korea, a young celebrity raised a furor when he made rounds of the talk-show circuit, proudly announcing that he was going to do his military service at a time when many celebrities assumed it was their privilege not to go. He eventually went back on his word, giving up his Korean citizenship and his military obligation with it. The public was outraged and regulations were tightened severely, I assume to catch the privileged who would use all sorts of means to dodge the draft. Unfortunately, I was caught up in that net.

Not to say that it was pure bad luck. I had a lot to do with it. I should have looked into teaching in Korea before I left. But even if I had read any kind of warning, it wouldn't have set off any bells since I hadn't known that I had another citizenship at the time. I've noticed that after I went to the Army, the US embassy in Korea updated its page to lengthen the section about the dangers of dual citizenship. I don't know whether it was because of me, but I'd like to think I made a small difference.

I naturally went to the embassy as soon as I found out that I was being drafted. Hollywood had taught me that all I needed to do was pass those gates and everything would be okay. It was my right as an American to get into trouble; it was my rich Uncle Sam who would bail me out. Instead, I was tossed a phonebook and told to sort it out on my own. I'll be honest; it hurt. It felt as if I was being sold into slavery by my own parents.

I actually had an out, and this is the part of the story I hate sharing because this story never had to happen if I hadn't been such a moron. My first nine months at the *hagwon* were uneventful. I had found out I had Korean citizenship in my first month, but somehow I hadn't managed to associate this new identity with the military obligation. I didn't give it a second thought. It only meant that I had to go to Japan to apply for a work visa for my time in Korea. I had only been an American—or so I thought—and this new knowledge didn't have any bearing on who I was or how I thought.

But in September, I used my vacation days to go back home to Seattle. I didn't choose to travel around Asia although I hadn't been anywhere outside of the US and Korea if you don't count Tijuana and Vancouver. I just wanted to go home even though my contract ended in three months. I didn't come to Korea to learn the language or culture or even to travel. It was only to chip away at some of my debt so I could figure out what to do with my life. I had considered working on a fishing boat in Alaska, but considering I couldn't swim, Korea seemed like the safe bet.

It felt good to be home. It was as if I had never left but better because I had been missed. I wasn't getting nagged at home, and I had stories to tell when out with friends. For some reason, I was reminded of the minor fact that I had Korean citizenship so I headed to the consulate with my mother to have it revoked. "He can't revoke his citizenship," the clerk told my mother. "He's past the age limit for doing it." I shrugged and made to go. The workings of the Korean government made very little sense to me, but just as learning of my second citizenship had little impact on me, learning of the inability of revoking it was inconsequential.

"Isn't there anything he can do?" my mother asked.

"Well, he can at least apply for an exemption from military service," the clerk offered. "Not that it's likely he'll get it."

I didn't see the need, but I filled it out to give my mother peace of mind. I didn't give it another thought as I spent my last few days at home or when I boarded the plane back to Korea. Little did I know that the document would get processed, alerting the Korean government of my existence.

It was only a week or two before I got my draft papers in the mail along with a Notice of Suspension of Departure from the Ministry of Justice.

I couldn't leave the country. At least not legally. I entertained various ways to dodge the service, but they were mostly half-baked. I was a drowning man clutching at straw. There were not many lifelines available, and they all turned out to be nothing substantial. The audience and phone calls were of no help. For a while, my most plausible plan of escape was to travel south to Busan and try to find a boat to take me to Japan. If I couldn't hire a boat, I'd resort to buying a rowboat and rowing across the Korea Strait myself in the way of Tenente Henry in Hemingway's *A Farewell to Arms*. It was a crazy plan, but it was my only plan. I was desperate.

As my time began to run out and I began to seriously consider stealing

8

away to Japan under the cover of night, a co-worker presented me with something more reasonable. Her husband was an American soldier stationed at the base in Yongsan, and she had gotten in contact with a recruiter who said he could get me out of the country on a military transport on the condition that I joined the US Army. I agreed.

I knew very little about the Korean Army, but what little I had heard was awful. Twenty dollars a month pay, frequent beatings, inhumane living conditions. Enlisting as a GI stood out in stark contrast—a living wage, job training, respect. There was a strong possibility I'd be shipped out to a war zone after I was done with training, but I figured it was worth it. At least I'd be able to communicate and eat food I could actually stomach. While I was in the service, there was an article about my plight in the Seattle Post Intelligencer. "He's more Big Mac than kimchi," it said. While I dislike the analogy, I admit it was true.

I rushed through the recruitment process, got sworn in as a Specialist in front of an officer and the Stars and Stripes, was issued my military ID and orders, and headed to Osan Air Base for my flight to Fort Jackson.

Whenever I've met someone who has heard of my story, I've been asked if it's true that I was caught at the airport. I simply nod and leave it at that because it's not untrue and the actual facts are complicated. I was caught at an airport, the airport on Osan Air Base, and even though I wasn't using my passport but my military ID and orders like any other American soldier, red flags popped up on the immigration officer's computer, and I was detained until my plane left, after which I was sent on my way back to Seoul. I went to see my recruiter on the Yongsan base; he said a simple sorry and asked for my ID back. I was an American soldier for one day.

I didn't have the time to revisit the plan to escape to Japan. It was January 27, 2004. My date of induction into the Korean Army was two days later.

Boot Camp

Jeungpyeong, North Chungcheong Province, Korea
37th Division, Recruit Training Battalion, 2nd Company
29 January 2004 - 6 March 2004

D-729 (29JAN04): The 11:15 to Jeungpyeong

Inside the bus, the radiators furiously pump concentrated gusts of dry heat at my feet and nowhere else. I wrap my coat tighter around me, nestling my hands in the shelter of my armpits. I'm making this trip with only the clothes on my back. Where I'm going, I won't need anything else. I won't even need the clothes.

The bus is mostly empty. A few elderly folk scattered through the length of the carriage loll in their seats, occasionally fidgeting or coughing dry, hacking coughs. Everyone else must be going with their families. A television set high and to the right of the driver flickers soundlessly, the cable-news anchor reporting in words that can't be heard. I turn my gaze to the window, melt a small section in the icy frost with my fingers, and watch the countryside pass by.

Whirr, whirr, whirr, badum, badum, badumm, whirr. The bus somberly hums a dirge as it lumbers down the lonely country highway.

I face my fate unaccompanied but not entirely of my own accord. What choice do I have? The alternative is to be prosecuted for treason in a foreign land and thrown in prison with relatively hardened felons for three full years. I'd be a piece of meat thrown to the lions. In a country like this, even hardened felons are fiercely patriotic.

"Jeungpyeonggibnida. Jeungpyeong."

Jeungpyeong. This is my stop.

I step off the bus and it leaves me behind in a black fog of diesel exhaust. I survey my surroundings from where I stand. I'm at a small intersection with a bus stop, a gas station on one corner and a small diner on the other. It's a little past noon and I have some time, so I make my way to the diner and take a seat at an empty table.

The few other tables are occupied by groups of mostly three, my future comrades and their parents. The young men are downcast and slurp their soups vacantly, their eyes in the bottom of their bowls. They look like cancer patients, gaunt and pale with closely cropped hair. The mothers don't eat much; they gaze dolefully at their sons and occasionally place some food on their sons' plates with chopsticks. Eat more, they urge weakly. The fathers are carved from stone, stoically observing their sons, un-eating and un-speaking.

It is an awkward, oppressive silence that fills the room. I order my soup and choke down the steaming hot bowl, scald the damn butterflies in my

13

belly as fast as I can.

The path leading to the division is a winding, two-lane country road. I take in my surroundings, and the impression I get is simply one of flatness. The terrain itself is mountainous but covered by nothing but amber waves of shorn straw and dead grass. The country homes and farms are a jumble of concrete, curved roof tiles, and corrugated steel sheets. As I walk along the shoulder of the road, I marvel at the division's outer wall, which stands so high and imposing in relation to its surroundings, and am struck with the notion that it was built more to keep people in than to keep people out. It looms, brooding high over the road, everything a little more gray and dead in its shadow. I walk in its shadow.

The front gate of the base is even less welcoming, with long rebar spikes protruding from oil barrels and metal sawhorses painted yellow and black.

So these are the gates of hell. It has frozen over and can be found in North Chungcheong Province.

I stop, my feet reluctant to take the last steps through the gate. I take a moment to steel myself for what lies ahead. A deep, drawn-out sigh escapes my lips when I realize that I have no idea what lies ahead. As I pass underneath the arch, I overhear a mother's plea for mercy.

"Please take care of my son."

The officer at the gate offers her affirmations, but the rotten grins of the guards and drill instructors behind him say otherwise. They are the grins of wolves as they look out at untended flocks of sheep.

I follow the herd of people past a large, open field to a small, run-down auditorium. Inside is a sea of black, permed hair and unsightly comb-overs and garish faux-fur coats. They all face the front. I can't see above their heads, and so I distance myself from them, choosing to stand near the door. A lady catches sight of me and tells me to hurry up, get up there.

The crowd is pungent with the smell of cheap perfume. I jostle, elbow, and push my way up to the front; the crowd steadfastly watches the front, oblivious to my intrusion. I squeeze through the last of them into an opening where neat rows of metal folding chairs have been set up. A soldier, the brim of his helmet low over his eyes, grabs my arm and pushes me into the next available seat.

"Leg-*neun* shoulder-*neolbi pigo* hand-*eun jumeok jwigo* knee above-*e* put up."[3]

---

[3] "Place your feet shoulder-width apart, ball up your fists and place them on your

14

I look quizzically up into the grim face of the soldier, my mind trying to piece together the Korean for various body parts, unable to form anything remotely intelligible.

The soldier's teeth begin to clench, jowls twitching. I panic and look for help to the others sitting to my left and it finally registers. I copy their stances, feet shoulder-width apart and hands balled up into fists, resting on their knees. The remaining two seats beside me fill up and the soldier walks up to the stage and glares menacingly out at us.

Another soldier is at the podium and all the recruits sit still and listen. I don't understand what's going on or what's being said so I open my mouth when everyone else does but otherwise sit still.

The soldier leaves and an officer walks up to the podium and delivers a long-winded speech. I can't catch anything because I'm sitting in the back and the amps obscure his words. When he is finished, all of the recruits yell out something in unison and then the soldiers descend on us and herd us outside to stand in neat rows, four nervous young men to a row. Run, they order.

We run in formation for the first time and as we run, a few parents run alongside the road, waving and shouting to their children. "Be strong!" "We love you, son!" I don't mind so much when their shouts fade in the distance.

The floor of this auditorium is stone, cold and hard. It's about a seven-minute run deeper in the base, seven minutes deeper into the belly of the beast. The fanfare and superficial smiles and any semblance of warmth are gone. It has begun.

The three hundred of us recruits are sitting in rows of twenty each, cross-legged on the cold stone floor. One soldier hands out cheap dime-store pens that read Monami on the grip; two more hover off to the side, scrutinizing us while another soldier sits in a metal folding chair at the front and starts reading off names.

"Chun, Young Jin. *Jumindeungnokbeonho* [4] : seven-eight-one-two-one-seven…"

---

knees." Arms are not to be bent. This is the Korean soldier's position of attention while seated. I still do this on occasion when I'm feeling extremely uncomfortable and nervous.

[4] *Jumindeungrokbeonho*: Citizen Registration Number, a 13-digit number somewhat equivalent to a Social Security Number in the US.

I feel the gapes of my comrades as I walk up to get my paper. It's not because I'm an American. It's because, at 27 by Korean accounting[5], I'm old.

The first six digits of citizen registration numbers are a YYMMDD representation of birth date; the other registration numbers to that point all began with an eight and a middling second digit. I'm a good five or six years older than everyone else, most of them fresh out of high school or taking a break after their first year or two of college. In a society where age factors into strict hierarchical considerations, a good five or six years is an eternity.

"Don't make a mistake," the soldier that handed out the pens says as he returns to the front of the congregation. I don't hear the consequences but the message is clear. *Or you're in a shitload of trouble.*

The paper is a series of boxes, blank spaces to fill in personal information.

Address.

I take out a scrap of paper I had jotted down my aunt's address on and carefully copy it in the box.

Hoju.

Don't know what this is.

Hoju bongeoji.[6]

Don't know what this is, either.

I scan the rest of the paper and my head begins to hurt, blood throbbing in my skull. Damn. What to do, what to do. I look around me and all the other recruits are hard at work on their forms, pens racing across their papers. I look up at the guards. I consider asking them for help but decide against it. They must choose the training center soldiers by their menacing, granite faces.

Panic hits. Helpless and with no one to turn to, I regress to grade school habits. I straighten my back and start sneaking glances at my neighbor's paper out of the corner of my eye.

My neighbor's arm, clad in a thick, black North Face rip-off, is obscuring my view. I inch forward and forward again, little increments, baby steps. He's

---

[5] Age is calculated differently in Korea than anywhere else in the world. First, babies are considered a year old when they are born. I've been told it's because they count the time spent in the womb. In addition, they don't age on their birthdays but gain a year of age collectively at the beginning of the year. I was 25 (by Western accounting) at the time of my induction.

[6] *Hoju*: Head of the household. When my grandfather passed away, the title was passed on to my father as the eldest son. *Hoju bongeoji*: Base (residence) of the head of the household.

stopped writing. I look up and into his round face and make contact with two dark, threatening eyes under a thick, wild, furrowed brow. He shifts his paper farther from me, shielding it from me with his Michelin torso, giving me another threatening look over his shoulder for good measure.

Damn.

I look to my right but the kid is already giving me dirty looks intermittently as he works on his paper.

Fine, I'll get up and ask. Whatever happened to camaraderie, the bond between brothers who suffer together?

I make to stand up but my right leg has fallen asleep. I'm not used to sitting Indian-style, haven't been since kindergarten. Needles shoot from my hip down to my ankles and into my foot when I shift my 145 pounds onto it.

I limp down the row to the side, the needles jabbing into my leg with every dragged step, where the two soldiers are eyeing me, their stares hacking away at my self-respect.

"What?"

"I-I don't know."

"You don't know what?"

"Korean. I don't know Korean."

Before I left my aunt's house for the bus to Jeungpyeong, my cousin Sherrie told me not to worry. "As soon as they realize you can't speak Korean, they'll send you back. I heard it happened to someone I know."

Unlike the families of many other second-generation American children, English was the only language spoken in our home. My parents wanted us boys to achieve the American Dream, and learning two languages at once was only going to confuse us, they thought. When my father's work took us briefly to Seoul when I was ten, I went to an international school, and when we packed up for Seattle two years later due to the separation, I only knew how to say *Mollayo*[7]—"I don't know"—my go-to whenever someone tried to ask

---

[7] One incident from this period has stayed with me throughout the years and probably contributed to my aversion to learning Korean later in life. I was at home alone when the phone rang. I don't know what possessed me to pick up the phone, but the conversation went something like this (in Korean):
"Hello?"
"Yes."
"Oh. Is your father home?"
"I don't know."

me something.

My cousin's words gave me little hope. I already knew the Army didn't care. I had gone to the Military Manpower Administration in Suwon three months earlier for a physical examination. I went on threat of prison. A co-worker at the *hagwon* translated for me, "Failure to appear at the physical examination will result in imprisonment." In the waiting room, they gave me a booklet and pen and told me to fill the booklet out. I sat on a bench and opened the booklet.

Five hundred questions. Five hundred sentences followed by a yes or no selection.

1. I sometimes hear *hwancheong*.

Next.

2. Somebody *na-ege chemyeon-eul georeonoko* work *hage hago itdaneun geo-seul* feel *jeok itda.*.

3. *Aein-i byeonshinhamyeon bobokhal geoshida.*

I skip ahead to see if I can understand anything.

57. My *yeonghon* sometimes my body *ddeonanda*.

286. When I see women use *mulgeon*, I *heungbunhanda* (*seutaking, saenglidae, ripseutik*).[8]

I wasn't sure what any of them meant completely but I could guess for maybe seven questions. A person can run faster than lightning. There is a person around me who is trying to kill me.

It was a psych evaluation, I could deduce that much, but I couldn't guess the wrong answers even if I tried.

I picked up my booklet and walked back over to the woman who had given it to me.

"You don't know if your father is home?"

"I don't know."

"Did your father go somewhere?"

"I don't know."

A long pause, followed by, "Can you give your father a message?"

"I don't know."

"I'll call back later."

"I don't know."

Click.

[8] 1. I sometimes hear auditory hallucinations. 2. I have felt that somebody has hypnotized me into doing something (against my will). 3. If my girlfriend dumps me, I will take revenge. 57. Sometimes my soul leaves my body. 286. I get aroused when I see objects that women use (stockings, feminine pads, lipstick).

"What?"

"I-I don't know Korean."

She stared at me blankly for a second and then led me over to a separate pew. "Sit here."

I sat by myself quietly for about half an hour, pointedly looking unassuming and helpless, and when the half hour was over, they collected my booklet along with the others.

"Uh... I couldn't do it," I said when I handed over my pristine booklet.

The proctor simply gave me a disapproving cluck and walked away.

I didn't get it. I couldn't speak so I must be sane?

After stripping down to my shorts, I was administered a back x-ray, blood and urine tests, height and weight measurements, and put into a group of five and sent to a large room with desks lined against the perimeter of the room. Each desk was a station, but I didn't figure out until toward the end that each station was a specific medical department where recruits could plead their cases before a doctor. I have never seen, before or since, so many young men leaning on crutches, wearing back braces and clutching x-ray files, or sporting bad sewing needle-and-ink tattoos in one room.

It says a lot about the conditions of the Army when you consider the lengths these kids go in order to avoid their military obligations. The key is to have money and a connection to an unscrupulous doctor. Many popular singers and actors have avoided the service with excuses such as mental illness; dislocated joints; brain, heart, and liver disease; even tuberculosis and autism. You'd think that Korean variety shows would be tame considering how infirm all these people are, but when you turn on the television, there they are, running wacky obstacle courses in tight spandex jumpsuits.

The prospective recruit before me showed the doctor his tattoos, so I also went up and showed the doctor mine, a few relics from sloppy college mistakes. Word was that tattoos could get you an exemption from the service. When I reached the last table, I told the officer that I couldn't speak Korean. He nodded, jotted something down on a piece of paper, and gave me an indication to leave.

I thought that, with my language deficiency and the perceived gang affiliation kicker, [9] they'd apologize for the mix-up and send me home.

---

[9] Although they have been gaining a slight degree of popularity among ordinary civilians in Korea, tattoos were originally a sign that a person was a member of

At the end of the room stood a machine. When it was my turn, I stepped up to the machine and typed in my Citizen Registration Number. A voucher for the bus home slid out of a slot at the bottom as my result popped up on the screen: Class 3, Active duty. [10]

One of the soldiers says, "Wait," and walks away. The other ignores me and keeps watch over the recruits filling out their information sheets. The first soldier returns with another soldier, short and ruddy, with narrow eyes and a small head.

"Where're you from?" he asks in English. I can't place his accent; his voice is raspy and garbled, as if he's holding a handful of crabapples in his mouth.

"Seattle, sir."

"My name's In-su," he says with a smile. "I studied in Australia. Follow me."

He walks me over to the stage and patiently tries to explain what each thing is. He explains them, but there are some things I just don't get or don't know how to answer. "Skip it," he says each time.

It feels as if we've been holed up in the auditorium for hours. They've collected the personal information sheets, and I'm back among the mass of recruits on the floor. The cold of the auditorium floor seeps up through my pants to my ass and scrotum and I feel a constant need to piss.

We don't get to piss on our own. A couple ask and are told to wait. This is the beginning of our education. When we go, we go together. Every so often, they give the call for a bathroom break and I have to get up to take a piss every time.

---

organized crime. Prior to 2002, young men with tattoos were not allowed to perform military service.

[10] The classifications of recruits are from 1 to 7, with Class 1 given to those healthiest and most fit for service. The obligations of each classification are revised regularly. In 2003, the classifications were as follows.

Classes 1-3: Active duty

Class 4: "Recruit service" or "replenishment service" – recruits go through basic combat training and are then allowed to perform some kind of alternative service such as working at a local government office

Class 5: "Second militia service" – recruits do not go through basic combat training and are allowed to perform some kind of alternative service

Class 6: Exemption from military service

Class 7: Subject for re-examination

"Bathroom break."

It's getting dark out. We piss in a ditch just outside the auditorium, side by side, ten at a time. There are no lights outside, so we walk to the ditch by the light from the auditorium. Steam from the piss rises from the bottom of the ditch in a thin line of fog, quickly dissipating in the cold January air. There are so many of us, it's like a fog machine tuned to emit thirty-second bursts every minute or so.

When everyone has returned to the auditorium and has sat down, they tell us to stand.

"Tall people up front, short ones in the back. Move."

I stand in the back, as far back as I can. I thought that Koreans were supposed to be short, but there are only a handful out of the three hundred that are shorter than me.

They line us up, fifteen deep, moving back through the lines to make sure we are sorting ourselves correctly by height. The Australian grabs my arm and moves me into a line and then grabs another recruit and stands him in front of me. "Stay here."

They separate us into groups of four lines each. This is my *sodae, il sodae.* 1st Platoon, I guess, having brushed up on Army units and rank designations in the months leading up to this day.

Once we are in twenty lines, five platoons, they give us numbers—I'm Forty-four—and lead us out of the auditorium and into the black of night.

We walk along a rocky path down past bare, concrete buildings, an occasional lamppost casting its orange hue along the way. The path curves to the right and down a slight decline, past a wider one-story building to a three-story barracks. It seems as if we're walking the path we followed after the initial ceremony, but everything looks different in the dark. We enter the barracks and walk up a dark, musty concrete stairwell to the third floor. There is a barred gate at the entrance to the corridor. We wait as they unlock the gate and soon after stop again inside the gate.

"Trainees 1 to 16, Squad Room 1." The Australian walks the sixteen members of 1st Squad into the first room on the right. I'm confused. Wasn't I supposed to be in the Australian's squad? We move on.

"Trainees 17 to 36, Squad Room 2." Another soldier, stocky with wire-rimmed glasses, leads the twenty members of 2nd Squad into the room across the hall.

"Trainees 37 to 58, Squad Room 3." The last soldier, skinny with dark, smooth skin and squinty eyes, takes us into our room. The rest of the three hundred file on down the hall.

The squad room is a small, bare room, roughly thirty feet by twenty feet for twenty-two men, with rusty steel lockers which rest against either wall, perched on raised floors on either side of the narrow, concrete path which bisects the room.

There are only twenty lockers and there are twenty-two of us. The four recruits at the far end of the room have to share their lockers. This also means that there will be less space to sleep.

"Sit," the soldier orders, and we sit on the edges of the raised floors. "You're to call me Squad Leader Lee Seul-gi. You're my squad." There is something disconcerting about the way he flashes his white teeth when he smiles.

He goes over some basic protocol for the room which I don't understand. I sit and feign understanding so as not to stand out. My plan is to wing it and just copy my neighbors until I get the hang of things. It didn't work earlier because I'm still rusty but I have no other option.

Squad Leader Lee pulls out the bedding from underneath one of the lockers on the right.

"Listen well. I'm only going to explain this once. *Maeteuriseu* first, *mopo* and *podan* over the *maeteuriseu* folded in half, pillow toward the center, and *chimnang* over it like this."[11]

We pull out our bedding and lay it out on the raised floors like we were instructed.

"Lie down on your backs."

We lie down on our backs.

"Lights out."

Click.

I lie there in my sleeping bag, shoulder to shoulder with my squadmates, and I stare up at the ceiling in the dark. Not too long afterward, the others drift off, some snore. I hear the sound of chains against metal and the occasional echo of booted footsteps down the hall, but otherwise it's deathly silent.

I stare at the ceiling, dumbfounded, exhausted, confused. I stare at the

---

[11] *Maeteuriseu*: mattress, a foldable, 2-inch thick foam pad; *mopo*: wool blanket; *podan*: a thin blanket made of synthetic material, *chimnang*: sleeping bag

little holes in the plastered tiles in the ceiling, little black stars in a scummy, off-white sky, and the thought that echoes throughout the chaos of my mind is one: What the hell am I doing here?

When I was in college, I was in a bad car crash. It was a near head-on collision, and the laws of physics dictated that my tiny Subaru GL would be compacted by the American-made van that plowed into me. It is said that your life flashes before your eyes in those moments, but all I remember was a blinding white nothingness and then lying in my seat, thinking, "What the hell just happened?"

That's how I feel right now, lying in the darkness of this squad room. This past day, this past year has left me disoriented, as if I've been spun around in circles in a twister. I can't wrap my head around where I've ended up. One thing is certain—this isn't Kansas. I'm not even sure if this is Korea.

After lying in my car for a few moments, I decided to get out of the car to get a grip on where I was. I had to force the door open and, even though I was in an intersection I passed through daily, I couldn't grasp my surroundings. What was left of my car was in a ditch. Was that ditch always there? There were people standing in the street with horrified looks on their faces. One of them approached me with an outstretched hand and said, "Sit back down." It was then that I noticed the blood spurting out of my elbow. I looked at it curiously. It didn't hurt at all. I had had a concussion and was still in shock.

My mind is numb, cloudy. I try to answer the question but it's utter chaos inside my head and my concussed brain cannot process any of the memories or information into something rational. I have an idea that I was supposed to go to the Army but I don't understand why. I know that this is the Army but I don't have a clue where I am.

I look around me and see the dark lockers looming overhead and can make out the rows of sleeping figures around me, and it's all surreal because I've never been in a place like this, in a situation like this, ever before.

Those were hard days after I returned home from the emergency room. I was battered and bruised, the right side of my face a purplish, scabby mess and my neck locked in place. Weeks afterward, I was still squeezing little shards of windshield out of my forearm. But the worst of it wasn't physical.

When I was laid out on the stretcher waiting for the ambulance to take me to the hospital, the police officer on the scene started writing me up for reckless driving. He didn't bother asking for my side of the story even though it must've been clear that I was the one whose car was hit.

"Come on, officer," the paramedic pleaded. "Give the kid a break."

The officer ignored the paramedic's pleas, tearing off the ticket from his pad and handing it to the paramedic to give to me later.

Coming from a low-income family, I couldn't afford car insurance or health insurance, which meant that I had to pay for repairs on the van that hit me and hospital bills for the four hours I was in the ER on top of the $500 fine for reckless driving.

What can be done in those situations but to suck it up and tighten your belt? I moved out of my shared apartment on University Avenue and back into my room at home. I quit my job teaching kids to start waiting tables again, something I told myself I was done with, and found two more part-time jobs for the weekends. I spent hours every day on the bus, which was the only time during the day I could hit the books. I made minimum payments on my debt, and when I couldn't, I took out emergency loans from school, saying it was for tuition, which wasn't a lie since the money I was going to use toward tuition was now going toward other obligations. And when that wasn't enough, I put the payments on one of my Visa cards or my American Express card or my Discover card or my Mastercard. It was a tough life, but it wasn't too bad once I figured out how to make it work.

But from the first night until then, the days were dark. I remember lying in my bed that first night, my face pulsing and my neck stiff and sore and my arm wrapped up tightly. I was still slightly loopy—it's hard to say whether it was from the drugs or the shock—but I could feel the weight of all that had transpired and that had yet to transpire pressing down on my body. There is no future in the dark, no path ahead. You are just left wondering exactly how you ended up where you are and hoping that it's nothing but a bad dream.

D-728 (30JAN04): Waking up to a Nightmare

I'm awakened at 0630 by the blaring of a scratchy, crackly rendition of reveille, a pre-recorded bugle belching a bright yet stiff Wake Up. I open my eyes. In the near darkness, I see the black holes in the scummy tiles in the ceiling. I hear booted footsteps running down the corridor. I hear the click of the lights, am blinded by fluorescent white, and get my morning greeting.

"Get up, crazy bitches!"

Yesterday wasn't a nightmare. It had to be a nightmare but it wasn't. In a sense, it was and still is. A waking nightmare, infinitely worse than a sleeping nightmare because at least the nightmares that come in the night come with the promise of reprieve in the morning. Infinitely worse because I know exactly when the morning will come and know that it's still two years off, less one day.

"You're not going to get up quickly?" Squad Leader Lee says through gritted teeth, a threat and not a question. He's heading for a recruit down the line who hasn't grasped the gravity of the situation in his sleepiness. The poor kid is used to sleeping in and saying, "Five more minutes, Mom."

Squad Leader Lee is not his mother. Squad Leader Lee yanks the pillow from underneath the recruit's head, the suddenly unsupported head thudding hard and dull against the mat. Lee flings the pillow across the room, recruits ducking and dodging to avoid the compact missile. The small pillow is packed tight with small, hard plastic tubes and has weight. Lee jumps up onto the raised floor and picks the dazed recruit up by the scruff of his neck.

Everybody gets up. If they weren't awake before, they are now.

"Hands at your sides, *balggumchi* together, feet at forty-five *do*!"[12] Once we're properly at attention, he makes us salute three times, yelling out the prescribed catchword "*Chungseong!*" with each salute.[13] He orders us to fold our bedding before storming out of the room. "You have three minutes."

The thin foam mat needs to be folded three times, the wool blanket in half lengthwise and three times the other way and placed on top of the mattress to the left, the sleeping bag rolled up and tied up with the strings and placed on top and to the right, the small, stiff pillow placed on top of the blanket and all of it pushed under the locker. In three minutes.

Everything is done in a panic. Even though he's left the room, I feel the specter of his presence hovering over me. Fold, fold, fold. Roll, roll, roll. Tie and primp and line everything up. My fingers are like sausages that were boiled too long and it feels as if I have the only set of bedding in the room that is misshapen and will never fold up nicely and line up without a pair of

---

[12] *Balggumchi*: Heels. *Do*: Degrees.

[13] *Chungseong* means loyalty. Every time a salute is delivered, it must be accompanied by the catchword. *Chungseong* is the standard for the Army although certain units have their own unique catchword. The catchword for the Marines is *pilseung*, meaning certain victory.

scissors.

This has to be a nightmare. I'm not caught in public in just my underwear and it certainly feels real, but sometimes a nightmare can be so vivid it seems real to the fear-addled brain and the only way to tell is if the events in the dream make sense. This has to be a nightmare.

While I'm tying up my sleeping bag, Lee storms back into the room, heaping on insults and threats until we've all got our bedding under our lockers and are ready and waiting on the edge of the raised floors.

"Put on your shoes, sons of bitches. It's time for breakfast."

The mess hall is a long rectangular room with drab hospital-green walls and rusty steel tables and chairs in neat rows. The only décor is the posters on the walls, propaganda for the wait in line. The first is a picture of a field with red teardrop shapes falling in the foreground. "*Janbap* is the blood and sweat of your parents." The next is a similar picture but with green 10,000-won bills instead of drops of blood: "Throwing away food is throwing away *segeum* of the *jumin*."[14]

The line crawls along the walls in silence and measured steps. We have our steel trays tucked under our left arms and our sporks in our right hands, as instructed. The seating capacity of the room is seventy-two, and the line trudges forward only when the previous squads finish their breakfasts and leave their tables.

At the tables set up at the end of the line, a few recruits who were volunteered for kitchen duty sparingly scoop chow out of massive industrial-sized pots onto my tray. I follow the recruit in front of me to a table where five others are standing, waiting. Our party complete, we sit in unison and the others announce, "We will eat this meal well." I try to keep up but end up mumbling nonsense to maintain appearances. We eat in silence with one hand, the other below the table, resting on our knees.

I look at the food on my tray. Meager portions of rice and kimchi, a shallow helping of some kind of fish soup, and what appears to be a cutlet of some sort but with tiny fish parts—heads, fins, tails—poking through the breaded crust. It looks as if someone scooped out a netful of tetras from a fish tank and dumped them directly into a deep fryer. Even the thought that this will end up in my stomach makes me retch. I haven't been able to eat

---

[14] *Janbap*: Leftovers. *Segeum*: Taxes. *Jumin*: Citizens. All of the posters urge conscripts not to waste food.

seafood since middle school, not that I'm sure this qualifies as sea*food*. I had a traumatic experience when I tagged along with my mother when she was keeping the books at a fish-processing factory. The experience has been blocked from my memory but the trauma has remained as a social handicap in a country where conforming to a standard is the rule and that standard enjoys little eels ground up and dumped in soup.

"Eat your *shikpan* clean or I'm gonna kill you," Squad Leader Lee threatens, patrolling the mess hall. He hovers over our table for a moment to give us a hard glare for effect. Oh, the benefits that come with being in his squad.

I slice the cutlet in half with my spork, revealing the silvery gray inside a soggy crust. Little fish heads and fins and tails poke out through the cut. I hesitate, holding the half-cutlet in front of my mouth, until I make very uncomfortable eye contact with another *jogyo*,[15] a squad leader, assigned to clean tray duty.

I cram the half-cutlet in my mouth, chew as fast as I can, swallow, and promptly throw it all back up in my mouth. The fish bits are swimming in the sweet, burning bile between swollen cheeks. Tears form in the corners of my eyes. I look up, cheeks swollen with bile and eyes brimming with tears, and a *jogyo* is walking down the line toward me, what I imagine to be metal beads in his pant legs jangling with each step. I choke down the foul mouthful of breading and fish and chase it down with rice and kimchi, fighting the urge to regurgitate the already regurgitated fish bits.

I don't eat the other half of the cutlet at once. I've lost my courage. I cut it into smaller pieces and follow them immediately with the spicy, pickled kimchi to cleanse my palate and stuff the rice down without chewing to keep everything down like a cork. The five others have been waiting anxiously for me. When I put down my spork, we announce, "We ate this meal well," gain approval from another *jogyo*, rise, wait in another line, wash our trays and sporks while shuffling down the line in front of a long stainless trough of a sink, gain approval on the thoroughness of our tray and spork washing, and get back into formation outside the mess hall. Squad Leader Lee is waiting for us outside.

---

[15] *Jogyo* means assistant instructor but refers to any conscript whose Military Occupational Specialty (MOS) is the training of other recruits. All squad leaders are *jogyo*. They fulfill the role of drill sergeants although they can be of any rank. Squad Leader Lee is a corporal, the Australian is a sergeant, and the squad leader for 2nd Squad is a Private First Class.

"Walk *juljuri*.[16] When you get back to the squad room, don't say a word. If I catch you bitches talking, you're gonna die."

"Yes, sir!"

The rest of the day and the next are spent in being issued our new lives and giving up our old ones. If clothes truly make the man, the whole process is more than symbolic. Everything they issue gives me a sense of the person I'm expected to become.

3 sets *jeontu-bok*, active combat uniforms—two for everyday use and one for special occasions

2 pair *jeontu-hwa*, combat boots

1 *jeontu-mo*, battle cap[17]

1 field jacket

1 belt and buckle

2 blousing straps

1 set winter PT uniform—a bright, inmate-orange sweatsuit with navy trim

1 set summer PT uniform—camouflage short shorts and a bright green shirt

6 pairs of socks, thick wool and olive green

6 pair undershirts and underwear, olive green or fecal brown (another type of camouflage, I guess)

I pick up the skimpy butt-huggers and read the tag—TBM, The Brave Man.

2 sets of long-johns, cream-colored

2 pairs of gloves—one for hard labor and one for guard duty

1 *ggalggari*—a padded, collarless jacket to be worn under the field jacket

1 set earmuffs—a camouflaged headband that widens to cover the ears

1 mock turtleneck, olive green, the last of the cold-weather issue

---

[16] *Juljuri:* "One after another" or "in a row." Used often in the Army to mean "in formation."

[17] *Jeontu:* Battle or combat. The words *bok*, *hwa*, and *mo* mean clothing, footwear, and headwear respectively.

Squad Leader Lee teaches us how to fold each item as we get it. "Listen well, crazy bitches." We've all been given new names, our trainee numbers, but crazy bitch, *michinnyeon*,[18] is Lee's favorite term of endearment for us, his squad. "I'm only going to show you once. I should be able to open each of your *seorap* and see the same thing." The uniforms need to be folded so that our name tags will show, and our socks and even our undershirts and underwear all need to be folded into tight little balls that fit nicely into our shallow locker drawers.

1 toothbrush
1 tube toothpaste
1 disposable razor
1 bar bath soap
1 bar laundry soap
1 sewing kit
1 toiletry bag
2 hand towels, bright blue
1 handkerchief, flesh-colored
2 rolls toilet paper

Squad Leader Lee tells us to rip off exactly five squares of the toilet paper and to put them into the left butt pocket of our uniforms for "emergencies." The two rolls are to last us the two years, so five squares per trip to the head as well. I've never inquired into the toilet-paper consumption of other people, but five squares seem barely enough for a single wipe. And it's industrial one-ply.

1 Monami-brand ball-point pen
1 felt pen
2 notebooks—one cargo-pocket sized and one chest pocket-sized
1 journal
1 white plastic strip

He gives us time to write our trainee numbers on the white tag with the

---

18 The word *nyeon* is a derogatory term similar in meaning to "bitch." It is usually preceded with some sort of descriptor such as *michin* ("crazy") or *ssibal* ("fucking").

felt pen and sew it onto the breast of our uniforms. The Monami pen doubles as a ruler to place the tag and it must be sewn fifteen stitches across and six down.

1 cardboard postal box

"Take off your clothes and put all of your *sabok* in your box. Put on your green underwear and undershirts and your PT uniforms. Put all of your *geinmulpum*[19] in the box, too. You can only keep medications and photos. Everything else goes in the box. Begin."

I'm facing my locker, I've got my boxers off, my dick exposed and shrunken, when I hear a whisper from my left.

"Hey, you're American, right?" It's the recruit the Australian placed in front of me on the first day during the sorting. He's speaking in English but I wish he wasn't speaking at all because both of us are in a state of undress and, while Squad Leader Lee is at the other end of the room, we're not allowed to talk to each other. I don't want to get beat for talking, especially when I'm bottom half-naked.

"Yeah. You speak English?" I whisper back, soft enough so that Squad Leader Lee won't hear but loud enough so Forty-three doesn't come any closer.

"Yeah, I was studying at Rutgers before I came back to Korea. My name is Johnny."

"Look, Johnny, let's continue this after lights out."

"Oh, right."

When everything is packed, we pass around tape and tape up our boxes and use our felt pens to write our addresses on our boxes and take them out into the hall and stack them up neatly. I sit down on the raised floor, feeling uncomfortable in my PT uniform. It feels like I'm in somebody's borrowed clothes, someone I don't particularly like.

There it goes, my identity as Young, the individual, the civilian, the free man. I'm now *Sashipsabeon Hullyeonbyeong*, Trainee Forty-four.

Lights out. I lie shoulder to shoulder with Forty-three—Johnny—and Forty-five, the metamorphosis weighing heavy in my heart. I wonder how

---

[19] *Sabok*: A word that means one's own clothes, as opposed to a uniform. *Geinmulpum*: Personal belongings.

some of the others can find sleep so readily—blessed are they who can find sleep in the worst of circumstances—but there are also whispers in the darkness. I guess those who can sleep do and those who need to be comforted by interpersonal connection do so as well. I only wish for time in peace to make some sense of the chaos.

"Your name is Young Jin, right?" Johnny picks up where we left off earlier, interrupting my tormenting examination of the question of the previous night.

"Just Young."

"Can I call you *hyeong*?"[20] I guess he's feeling lonely.

"Sure."

"Where are you from?"

"Seattle. And Chicago. About half and half. You?"

"I was studying at Rutgers but my father forced me to come back to Korea." There's a hard edge to this sentence, a slight bitterness in his voice. "So I transferred to Yonsei University and he made me come here."

I let him vent for a few more minutes, mostly about his father and the injustice of his fate, but he's beginning to drag on. The injustice of it all. What is it about man that makes his problems so much bigger in his own eyes? All of us walking around with flies in our eyes. Are his problems bigger than my own? I'm actually having a little difficulty finding the injustice in his story. Are mine bigger than his? All I know is that my eyes are full.

The patience I afford him is because of his potential utility as a personal interpreter but the setting and the topic of discussion have drained what little patience I have left to afford.

"Hey, Johnny. I'm sorry but I'm gonna go to bed. I'm really tired."

"Oh, okay." The disappointment in his voice is now directed at me.

"Good night."

"Good night."

I close my eyes so he doesn't think I'm a complete asshole.

I hear Johnny sigh next to me. There's a lot of pain and frustration in that sigh, but I allow myself to ignore him. I've got my own problems to deal with.

---

[20] *Hyeong*: Literally, "older brother." The word is also commonly used as a term of affection between non-related males.

31

D-727 (31JAN04): Deaf, Dumb, and Mute

After breakfast and donating blood, the whole platoon is seated in our squad room, three to a row on both sides of the room. God, what I would give for a chair. Between my acute scoliosis and aversion to physical contact, I'm a ball of pain and frustration and there's nothing I can do about it. Squad Leader Lee is standing at the end of the room with clipboard in hand.

"We're going to be assigning additional duties. Everyone has to sign up for one."

He wears his battle cap low on his brow, obscuring his eyes. It makes him look cold and inhuman as he reads off the list of duties and selects volunteers.

"Bathroom duty. I'm in charge of this duty."

The room is tense. This is the first of what will certainly be many damned-if-you-do, damned-if-you-don't situations. The uncertainty leads to powerlessness. Signing up means spending even more time under Lee's direct supervision. It's only been a couple days, but from those brief and sporadic encounters with the other *jogyo*, it definitely seems as if he's the worst of the bunch. Poison, if it has to be taken, should be taken in small doses. But perhaps signing up for something no one wants to do will curry his favor. He's already begun to regularly abuse some of the more obvious targets, like Fifty, who's always got a jovial smile on his ample face perched on top of a perfectly round body—it must horribly irritate Lee, whose additional duty is to wipe the smiles from our faces—or Fifty-seven, who doesn't seem to get that we're in basic training. What to do? What to do?

Of the fifty-eight of us, six are brave or stupid enough to volunteer. Being neither brave nor entirely stupid, I don't raise my hand.

He gives the six his approval; it seems a smirk is as good as it gets, and I look at one of them nearest me and see a look of satisfaction on his face at the brownie points he just earned. He doesn't look familiar; he must be from 1st or 2nd Squad. In that case, he wouldn't understand the full extent of Lee's cruelty like those of us in his squad have. I've decided that, with someone like Squad Leader Lee, having brownie points is probably a small, passing matter and not worth having to clean up other people's shit for five weeks.

He goes through the duties—some I can understand; most I can't—and I start getting anxious because of the uncertainty of what will be left over.

"Cutting hair," he says. Finally, something I can understand and wouldn't

32

mind doing. I can give a mean fade.

I raise my hand. "*Sa-ship-sa… beon… hullyeon…*"

"What the fuck? Who are you?" It was only a matter of time before I showed up on his radar.

"*Sa-ship-sa… b-beon…*" I repeat, protocol requiring that I give my trainee number and name every time I'm called on, referred to, touched, or even looked at with intent.

"Are you fucking retarded?"

"*S-sa… sa-ship-sa… beon…*" I'm stuck in a hellish infinite loop. Now that I'm being threatened, my stutter is getting worse, only reinforcing his opinion. Yes, I'm retarded. I can't even say my own name.

"Oh, it's you. The American bastard."

"*S-sa-ship-sa…*"

"That's enough."

Thank God.

"You cut hair?"

"Y-Yes, sir."

"You can't cut hair," he scoffs. "You'll make everyone look like Yankees." He gives a cue to the rest of the platoon to laugh so they do. "Put your hand down."

I lower my hand and feel a numb heat spread across my face.

I certainly feel retarded. I guess it's the intended purpose of basic training, to break a recruit down completely so that they can accept without question, but it seems too effective in my case. Over the weekend, Squad Leader Lee instructed us in modes of walking. While swinging my arms forward to ninety degrees and backward to thirty is something unnatural and must be ingrained in my body through practice, the problem is that in doing so, I've forgotten how to walk at all. Left foot forward, left arm forward? Even toddlers know better.

I can't speak, I can't walk, I can barely eat without feeling the need to throw up on myself. What is happening to me?

I haven't seen the Australian since processing. The other *jogyo* were around during the issuing of our equipment and meal times, and the squad leader of 2nd Squad is standing at the front beside Squad Leader Lee. He only has two bars on his chest to Lee's three, and the difference in rank is clear by the way that Squad Leader Lee occasionally demeans him in front of us.

On that first day, the Australian placed Johnny in front of me in order to help me—that much I've guessed already—but with Lee as my squad leader, I can't talk to Johnny when I need to. I know that the Army is not a place to be babied, but I thought a minimum of concessions could be made for someone with such an obvious deficiency.

There's a trainee in 1st Squad who looks foreign, not fully Korean. The skin on his chubby face is a shade too pasty, his nose a little too large and hooked, his eyes a little too round with the distinctive Caucasoid eyefolds. But when he responds with his trainee number, his pronunciation is flawless, the timing of his response without the awkward pause that mine has. Whenever I have a chance, I examine his features. Is he Korean? Is he Caucasian? He must be Korean. I know that even half-blooded Koreans are exempt from the service because they make easy targets for discrimination. I must be looking for things that aren't there.

The others in my squad don't pay me much mind, but they don't pick on me, either. I guess I should be thankful for that. When I've had to salute a squad leader on my way to and from the head, I've heard muted laughter and snickers and mocking of my pronunciation of the salute call, *Chungseong*, from the second platoon squad rooms. I know I've been putting a sharp emphasis on the second syllable, saying *sseong* instead of *seong*, but I can't help it. I have a hard enough time paying attention to how I walk.

D-725 (02FEB04): The First of Many a Long Day

After reveille and the three salutes to start the day, the scratchy monotone booms out again over the P.A. "Recruits have ten minutes to report for morning call on the parade ground. Today's dress code is ACUs, battle caps, earmuffs, gloves."

Squad Leader Lee storms into the room on cue. The surprise of his morning greeting is gone but the fear and panic remains. My fingers are again flaccid sausages.

"Who are the sons of bitches that are still putting away their bedding?" he snarls. He's a rabid dog let loose to nip at our heels and the only way to avoid his fangs is to be faster than the rest.

I'm out of my PT uniform and am hurriedly putting on my uniform

34

pants. At the moment, I'm filled with a seething desire to kill the bastard whose idea it was to put button flies on these pants.

"Three minutes left. You aren't gonna hurry?"[21]

I have my uniform and jacket on and am on the floor, putting on my socks and blousing my trousers, my battle cap and earmuffs next to me.

"Put your boots on and sit on the edges." Squad Leader Lee is standing in front of the door, arms crossed and a scowl on his face. When all of my squad mates are ready and sitting on the edges of the raised floors with their boots on, he continues, "When the company is called, go outside and line up by platoon in front of the barracks. The last out one turns off the lights."

Squad Leader Lee runs out of the room and we wait in silence until the call to head outside is given over the P.A. Three hundred recruits stream out of the squad rooms and down the hall. There are chains wrapped around the handles of the door closest to first platoon and so we walk the length of the hall to the far doors.

When I walk through the first set of doors, I'm met with a cold blast of winter air that stings the exposed skin of my face. Through the second set of doors, I'm met with the pitch-black darkness of the pre-dawn morning. Squad leaders stand in the stairwell, waving lighted batons and barking at us to get a move on. The flow of soldiers curling around the barracks to the parade ground is like mountain rapids, recruits unceremoniously bumping into one another in the dark, wrapping and running around the ones who have slowed or stopped.

"*Il sodae*?" "First Platoon?" I ask figures in the dark until I find my platoon and my place in the squad.

When everyone is accounted for, Squad Leader Lee takes us down to the parade ground in formation. "One, two, three, four! Left... left...."

Three hundred recruits in the cold and darkness of a countryside February before dawn. A few halogen lamps tower above and slightly behind the podium where the instructors and squad leaders stand as shadowy figures with silvery outlines. We take roll by shouting out our trainee numbers into the dark sky back through the lines. When we sing the national anthem and recite the Service Creed, I'm thankful for my short stature, thankful that none of the squad leaders can see the one recruit in the back of the third of twenty lines who can't follow along. The squad leader appoints a standard and the

---

[21] *Bballi anhae?* A very Korean way of threatening someone, it's much worse than it sounds in direct translation. It basically means "Hurry up or else."

mass of recruits spread out to two arms' length from each other. A recorded voice counting from one to eight over and over again plays over the speakers as we begin calisthenics.

The squad leaders taught us the twelve exercises of the calisthenics over the weekend. Arms and legs, arms, neck, chest, flank, back and stomach, torso, arms and legs, full body, jumping, arms and legs, and breathing. I assume the *jogyo* would say that the exercises were designed by experts in some academic field or other but it would make more sense if they had been designed by mental patients or Japanese comic artists, my arms stretched out at weird angles or on hips and legs bent or stretched out or flung into the air with abandon.

The *jogyo* appoints a standard again and we gather together in formation. We are told to strip down to our undershirts and fold and place our jackets, *ggalggari*, and uniform tops on the ground next to us. Squad Leader Lee orders us to get ready to run, to clench our fists and bring them up to our chests, bending over slightly and grunting loudly in response. He gives the call and leads us around the parade ground in a brisk jog, leading us in battle hymns as we go. The thundering of boots on the pavement and the hoarse cries of recruits in song echo all around the parade ground.

Two laps later, we return to our spots, put our uniform tops back on, and the squad leader announces the end of call.

"Report to Auditorium No. 2 for morning cleaning."

We sweep and mop Auditorium No. 2 under the careful watch of a tac-iturn, stony-faced hulk of a *jogyo* and return to the barracks to wash up, sixty recruits from the first and second platoons clambering to use three sinks, have breakfast, and return to the parade ground for our first day of training.

The white lettering on the bookish, squinty-eyed captain's helmet reads *gyogam*.[22] It's not the *jogyo* that marks the helmets of the squad leaders. The recruits sit on concrete steps, the chill wind blowing softly through the ranks, and the *gyogam* stands in front of us, lecturing on things I don't understand. I pick up my pen to take notes but never apply pen to paper. I just sit and hope that nothing I miss will get me in too much trouble.

Afterwards, Squad Leader Lee takes the platoon to the far corner of the parade ground and drills us on walking and turning as a group. The language

---

[22] *Gyogam*: Drill instructor, officers who deliver lectures to recruits. They leave the discipline and punishment to the *jogyo*.

he uses is downright confusing. I know the Korean for left and right but he's not using those words. He's using words I've never heard before, words I wonder are even Korean, and I have no choice but to follow what the recruit next to me is doing as quickly as I can. It's been my strategy from day one, and while it may work for some things, I will make a mistake when an immediate response is required. We parade march endlessly forward, ears alert, waiting the call for the turn. The flawless turn to the right or left depends on using the right pivot foot. The change in direction is instantaneous to give the formation that crisp, ceremonious feel. At that pivotal moment, there's no way that one retard turning left instead of right while marching in formation, bumping into the recruit on his left, is going to escape Lee's watchful eye.

"Stop!"

Squad Leader Lee strides over and pulls me from the formation by the front of my field jacket.

"*Ssibal*. What are hell do you think you're doing?"

"I will do my best, sir." It's all I can say although this is already my best. There's no leeway for the deaf.

"Get back in line, *byeongshin*."[23]

My only comfort is that I'm not the only idiot who can't do things right. This is my first lesson from the Army, something I learned from the morning rush to get ready. In the jungle, you only have to be marginally faster, smarter, better than the worst of the herd to survive. I'm thankful for Forty, a goofy-looking kid with strong Mongoloid features, and Fifty-seven, a skinny kid with thick, bushy eyebrows. I'm thankful for them because no matter how much I screw things up, they screw up more frequently and sometimes before or with me.

I decide to revise my strategy, to not act with complete certainty. I'm a little less than a half-step behind all the time, but I can pick up the pace after the turn. I look slow-witted. The guy walking the other way gets abused.

"Again. Forward march!"

At lunch, we're standing in front of the mess hall by platoon. The *jogyo* use this time to drill us on protocol or teach us battle hymns. Again my height is proving useful. I take out my notebook and flip to the page with the right

---

[23] *Byeongshin* refers to a (physically) disabled person but is used to mean moron or idiot.

lyrics, using Johnny's wide frame to hide behind. These were supposed to be committed to memory over the weekend along with the Soldier's Creed, but even the simplest songs are rife with words I can't understand.

Taking out my notebook seems like a foolish move with all the squad leaders around, but faking it is only going to get me so far. I'm reading my notebook, singing every third word because I can't keep up, my head almost imperceptibly tilted downward, when I notice something in my peripheral vision. When three hundred men stand in formation, wearing the same clothes and doing the same things, any variation sticks out. I notice that I've stopped singing. It's because I can't believe what I see.

In the line to my left, Fifty-seven is not standing at attention like the rest of us. He's waving his arms and raising his legs and twisting on his ankles. He's practicing the drills from earlier. My first instinct is to get his attention and stop him but this isn't the time or place to be doing that. After lights out, maybe. Or in a locked bathroom stall.

I don't act on my instinct. My notebook open in my left hand, my lips mouthing what barely could pass as Korean, I know now is not the time to be worrying about others, especially others that will act as my buffer in the days to come.

The day's training is not over at dinnertime. After all the platoons have shuffled through the mess, we gather outside the barracks in formation and march up the hill to Auditorium No. 1 for *jeongshin-gyoyuk*, "mental education." From what I can gather, there's nothing of substance being taught. The *gyogam* is up at the podium, rambling on ad infinitum about something like why Korea needs an Army and to lessen its reliance on America. The recruits are crowded in the pews; we sit and are expected to pay attention, something that the *jogyo* are there to ensure.

We've been pushed around all day, and the fatigue and the lecturing has a soporific effect. Perhaps it's just me, because I can't understand much of the lecture beyond a word here and there, but it seems as if this is more mental training or willpower training or veiled torture-resistance training than education. At the peak of fatigue, I can feel my eyelids becoming heavy. My head feels like a bowling ball balanced on the end of a broomstick. The audience watches on, wondering when it will fall. And it's not just me. I see more than a couple recruits nodding off around me.

In front of me, a recruit has reached his mental limit and has surrendered

38

himself to sweet slumber, squad leaders be damned. I feel sleep taking over, too, until I notice a *jogyo* striding over to the slumbering recruit. The *jogyo* shakes the recruit awake. The recruit is startled and then fearful as the *jogyo* takes him off to the side and down the aisle to a small room next to the stage. What sort of punishment awaits him behind that door? The imagination is torture itself. I see recruits being led in but none returning. Has anyone come out of the room? I haven't noticed but my attention is impaired by sleep deprivation. Images of crude, rusty medieval torture devices dance in my half-consciousness.

The *gyogam* continues on, his passion for whatever bullshit he is spewing unfazed by the lambs being led to the slaughter before him. I hear the shuffling of feet behind me as another recruit is led away. The terror is there but the fatigue is gaining ground, so I take my pen and dig the pointy end sharply into my thigh. Streaks of pain shoot up my leg and I gain a short period of lucidity. The fatigue returns and I bring the pen down deeper into my thigh. At least the pen is good for something.

After the education, we return to the company, change into our PT uniforms, clean the squad room and the hallway, have evening call by squad in our rooms, and then it's lights out.

D-723 (04FEB04): Always Cold, Always Tired, Always Hungry, Always Abused

Time is a bitch. It has to be, making the sweet times short and the bitter as drawn out as possible. I feel as if I've been here for so long I'm beginning to forget what life outside was like. It's only the third day of actual training.

The first few days of training have passed without much variation. Army life is nothing if not monotonous. It's the monotony that's clouding my concept of time. Wake up at the same time; eat the same bland mush for breakfast, lunch, and dinner; drill all morning and afternoon; fight to stay awake through the same message at the nightly brainwashing; listen to the same complaints after lights out. The monotony is sucking the humanity out of me. Boot camp is a factory creating a horde of walking dead in uniforms. Last night, I pretended to sleep right at lights out to avoid listening to Johnny gripe about his lot in life and I overheard Forty-two telling him that the life of a soldier is this: always cold, always tired, always hungry.

I look at the calendar and realize how few days have passed and how many, so many more days are remaining. In the absence of hope, there is only desperation and resignation. The *jogyo* call it "adaptation." I wonder if there is a hell and if the people there eventually get used to it.

I don't know if I'll ever get used to this life, but the one saving grace is that practically every minute of the day from reveille to lights out is accounted for. I'm kept so busy and anxious and frustrated, it's like being slapped in the face constantly—eventually you get numb. Sometimes you just get slapped.

In the lull after lunch, thirty minutes reserved for "personal maintenance," the others are working at the creases in their bedding and I'm still trying to memorize the Soldier's Creed, something the others have committed to memory long ago. The difference between memorizing sentences and memorizing sounds.

I look up from my notebook to see Lee strolling into the squad room with a grin on his face. I freeze in fear. We've quickly learned that Squad Leader Lee's smiles are the candy offered by the kidnapper before he rapes you and buries your violated, dismembered corpse in the basement.

"*Michinnyeon*s with a sister, stand up."

Still adjusting to abject and immediate obedience, the guilty hesitate until they understand the gravity of the situation reflected in Lee's gritted teeth. One by one, recruits with sisters get up, stand at attention, and state their trainee number.

"All right. Take out pictures," he says slyly, the grin returning to his face. Working his way down the line, one by one, Squad Leader Lee inspects the pictures, adding commentary on their appearance and fuckability, which intensifies as he goes down the line. "Shit." "What's this?" "What the fuck?" When he gets to Fifty-seven, he's already in a bad mood; we are not a good-looking squad, which apparently extends to our families. Fifty-seven hasn't noticed this and I cringe.

"Picture," Lee orders, hand extended.

Fifty-seven is silent, looking straight ahead, trying to avoid Lee's stare.

"Picture, bastard."

Come on. Just give him the damn picture.

It's not that I don't understand Fifty-seven, but Squad Leader Lee is an absolute psycho. Just let him see the damn picture. Fifty-seven doesn't.

"Are you out of your mind?"

40

Lee explodes. He leaps up onto the raised floor and violently grabs the front of Fifty-seven's training uniform in his fist, giving him a few rough shakes before slapping him and shoving him into the corner.

"Stand up."

Fifty-seven gets up.

"*Ssibal.* Take out the picture. Right now."

Again, Fifty-seven is silent, shockingly insubordinate. I'm impressed. I didn't think he had it in him. He's a skinny kid and, from what I've observed, a little on the clueless side. He's a decent-looking kid, though, and I can see that Lee is expectant. Of course, the result of Fifty-seven's insubordination is getting shoved to the floor again.

Lee then yanks Fifty-seven's drawer free from the locker and upends it, emptying its contents onto the floor. Pens and notebooks and socks and underwear scatter across the linoleum. Lee bends down and sorts through the papers until he finds the picture among the mess.

"Not bad," he comments, scrutinizing the photo with lustful eyes. "Introduce me to her."

Fifty-seven is battered but still silent. It's clear that it's not a request. It's a command, another command he doesn't want to comply with. He has balls the size of watermelons but what good will it do him if he's dead?

"What, you think I'm not good enough for her?"

"No, sir."

"Introduce me."

"No, sir."

"Sonnuvabitch."

He grabs Fifty-seven again, shaking and slapping him until the PA calls him out to prepare for the next round of training. Saved by the bell.

Fifty-six and Fifty-eight help Fifty-seven pick up his things and put them back in the drawer. I have a newfound respect for the kid, for his brash stupidity if not for his bravery. Even the latter is something we've lost in the short time we've been here. I wonder if I would've done the same had I been in the same situation. Thankful I only have brothers and didn't have to make the decision, I return to my notebook and the Soldier's Creed.

The hunger in the Army is insatiable. It's with me all day long and meals do nothing to affect it. The hunger right after meals is just as strong as the hunger before. Having wrestled in middle and high school and grown up with constantly empty cupboards, I had forgotten what it was to feel the pangs of hunger, my body losing its natural urge to eat. I ate when it seemed like I should eat or when I felt languid. Yet boot camp has again taught me what it is to hunger. Always hungry. What they say is true.

Not that I've been eating much lately. I've been rejecting the things in the mess line I know I won't be able to keep down, which more often than not means that I'm eating nothing but rice and kimchi. I wonder how long I'll last on nothing but rice and kimchi with the rigorous training and brainwashing, but I'm not too concerned. Wrestling taught me that I can find some strength even without food or water. I don't know where it comes from, but it's there.

Despite the lack of nourishment, my stomach feels bloated and heavy, which does worry me. Sitting in front of my locker, I reach up and open up the compartment for my extra pair of boots, long underwear, and toilet paper. I stare at my two rolls of toilet paper. Two full rolls of toilet paper, minus five squares that are still in the butt pocket of my uniform. It's been over two weeks and I still haven't taken a shit.

I'm not the only one. Maybe it's the chow or the stress or something else but a good number of the squad is suffering from constipation. We're Army regulars but we're far from regular. It's gotten to a point where we refer to taking a trip to the head and leaving something solid behind as a "success."

I start to wonder how much shit the human body can hold before the digested rice and kimchi starts to fester. I feel sick. The intestinal walls can't take anymore and the foul, acidic juices start seeping through to the bloodstream. The poison begins to circulate throughout my body, down through my legs and neglected nether regions and up to my heart and lungs and arms and brain. I don't know if it can actually happen but it's making me sick.

Fifty walks in through the door. He's practically strutting. He has a smile as wide as his mouth and those big, puffy cheeks will allow.

"Success?" Forty asks in a whisper.

"Success," Fifty answers proudly as he passes by me on the way to his place on the other side of the room.

I'm sick and green with envy. I stare at the two rolls in my locker. Two pristine rolls.

The next person to walk through the door is Squad Leader Lee and he's not happy.

"Fuck!"

He now has everyone's attention and we watch in fear and knowledge of what's to come.

"What do you think you're looking at? *Eopdeuryeo,* crazy bitches."

Eopdeuryeo is the call for us to assume the position, a static push-up position, hands on the floor, shoulder-width apart, feet together, a straight line from head to foot. After Lee confirms that nobody is slouching, he leaves the room with a warning. "Let your knees touch the floor and you're gonna die."

Lee stops in at random intervals—five, three, ten minutes—to make sure we are being obedient and leaves every time with the same warning. "You're gonna die."

After the first few minutes, I'm no longer worrying about my obstinate bowels. I wonder how much shit I can take mentally and how the poison will affect me.

A few are daring to rest on their knees. No, you bastards, stay strong. I curse them not for being weak but because my already strained willpower falters even faster when I see how wonderful it looks to surrender, pain for pleasure although that momentary pleasure potentially heralds a world of pain. My biceps and delts and traps and glutes are on fire, burning from the inside, and my vision is blurry, a dark, furry ring along the periphery.

I look at Forty-five and he's having no trouble with it. It's the skinny kids who have no problem with this kind of physical exertion. Johnny on my right already has both knees on the floor. Maybe just a second, one sweet second of rest. I could just put my knee farthest from the door down.

"3rd Squad, get up."

My body doesn't want to respond but the last shred of willpower bolstered by the shock of Lee's sudden appearance and fear of punishment at his hands gives me the boost to hoist myself up to standing position with the grace of a wino. I fight the wooziness and stand at attention.

"Sit in rows on this side," he says, pointing to the raised floors on my side of the room. "It's time for education."

1st and 2nd Squads enter the room shortly and fill up the squad room to capacity. He lectures on guard procedures—all I understand is "Put your hands up" and "Move and I'll shoot" and "cigarette"—and while the pain in my arms, shoulders, upper back, and ass are subsiding, it is being replaced by a wrenching tightness in my lower back.

Squad Leader Lee has stopped talking mid-sentence. I follow his gaze to the door where the Australian is standing.

"Seul-gi. Follow me."

"Yes, sir!" Lee shouts and runs out the room like we have so often done at his call. I imagine a collective grin in the room at seeing the tables turned.

Unable to move without Lee's command, we wait in silence. A few of my squadmates take the opportunity for self-conscious stretches. I absent-mindedly pick at the creases in my pillow. Nobody dares to talk, even in whispers.

Squad Leader Lee curses under his breath as he charges back into the room. His face is showing the most emotion he has allowed himself to show but it's the only one we're familiar with—anger.

"Where was I?" he asks himself. "So when an officer shows up... *jotga-teun* bastard!" He starts cursing under his breath, unable to keep his composure. "1st Platoon, get up."

What ensues is a stream of punishments issued through gritted teeth. *Dwiro milchak. Apeuro milchak. Dwiro milchak. Apeuro milchak. Dwiro chwichim. Ireoseo. Apeuro chwichim. Jwaro gulleo, Uro gulleo. Jwaro gulleo. Uro gulleo. Ireoseo. Anja. Ireoseo. Anja. Ireoseo.* We back up flush against the far wall, rush forward and mush ourselves against the front wall, back again and forward again. We drop down on our backs, heads bumping against knees and feet and shins, get up, prostrate ourselves face down, roll to the left, roll to the right, roll to the left again and once more to the right, get up, crouch, get up, crouch, get up.

When Lee's anger has subsided and his thirst for punishment has been satiated, he stops ordering us back and forth and up and down, pauses, and walks out the door. The fifty-eight of us are left standing in the squad room, out of breath and bewildered.

I get the feeling that the sporadic and unwarranted punishments my squad has been subject to for the past week are mostly no fault of our own. While I'm sure a fair amount can be attributed to Squad Leader Lee's sadistic nature, we are also the outlet for his stress. It's too bad for 1st and 2nd Squads that they happened to be in the room this time.

D-720 (07FEB04): Confucius Must Be Rolling in His Grave

They've given us an hour to write letters. My squad mates unfold the tiny desks that are normally stored in the lockers, take out pads of paper and their trusty Monami pens, and start writing to loved ones. Having no one to write to, I sit cross-legged, facing my locker. I pinch a section of my pillow case with the first two fingers of my right hand and, holding the pillow steady with my left, I run my fingers down the length of the pillow, leaving a sharp but rapidly wilting edge. I line up the folded mattress with the support bars of the locker, adjust the folded blankets above it, the sleeping bag, and then the pillow case again for good measure, giving it another crease. I look at my watch. Three minutes down, fifty-seven to go.

"Forty-four!"

"Trainee Forty-four, Young Jin Chun!" I yell from my seat.

"Report to the administration office."

"Trainee Forty-four, Young Jin Chun!"

I hurriedly scoot to the edge of the linoleum, slip my feet into the knock-off Adidas slippers, parade march down the hall, arms swinging to 90 degrees, stop in front of the office to take a deep breath, and rap my knuckles on the door twice.

"Trainee Forty-four, Young Jin Chun! I came because I have *yongmu*."

"Enter."

I open the door, step inside, salute, "Trainee Forty-four, Young Jin Chun," wait for a response, close the door, and report to my platoon leader, a tall, skinny guy with a strong, hooked nose and curly hair, sitting on one of a pair of couches to the left of the door.

"Sit."

"Yes, sir."

He waits until I sit at attention before talking.

"Forty-four."

"Trainee Forty-four, Young Jin Chun."

"It's okay. You don't have to do that here."

"Yes, sir."

He asks me a few, simple yes-or-no questions and I respond with a Yes, sir or No, sir. He asks if I know what his rank is and I respond No, sir, and so we go over the different ranks and what to call them. He writes them in his notebook and I write the English equivalent. I had brushed up on military ranks in English the month before I was inducted, back when I still thought the US Army was still a way out.

"*Sowi*," he says, pointing at the silver diamond on his chest. Second lieutenant.

"I understand, sir."

"Forty-four, listen," he says, closing the notebook. His tone has gotten more serious. "You know that we can't send international mail here, right? This is a small unit and the post office here can't send mail to America." He's talking slowly and with simple words so I'll understand.

"I understand, sir."

"Do you have anyone to write to?"

"No, sir."

"Then let's work on your personal information sheet."

"Yes, sir."

I see what he's doing. He's keeping me occupied while everyone else writes their letters, like giving a child a coloring book and crayons while Mom and Dad take care of business.

"What does your father do?"

"I don't have a father, sir."

"You don't have a father? Did he *doragashyeosseo*?"

"I didn't hear you clearly, sir." This is one of the expressions that has become an integral part of my linguistic repertoire, an expression used to mean "What?"

"*Doragashyeosseo*. Die."

"No, sir. My dad… my dad and my mom … uh…." Damn. I don't know how to say divorce. I don't know how to explain that my father left us when I was in middle school, that he ran away with another woman and has a new family now. Okay, technically I still have a father.

"I have a father, sir."

"So you have a father or you don't?"

"I have a father, sir."

"Are you sure?"

"Yes, sir."

"What does he do?"

"I don't know, sir."

"You don't know?"

"No, sir. I… don't know Korean, sir."

He laughs. "Does he work in an office?"

"Yes, sir."

"What kind of office?"

"I don't know, sir."

He sighs.

"He's an engineer, sir."

"What?"

"He's an engineer, sir."

He sits for a second and then a flash of comprehension. "Oh, *en-ji-ni-eo.*"

"Yes, sir."

"What kind of engineer?"

"I don't know, sir."

"Well, what kind of things does he work with?"

"I don't know, sir."

"You don't know in Korean?"

"No, sir. I don't know."

"You don't know what kind of engineer your father is?"

"No, sir."

The look he gives me, you'd think I dug up Confucius from his grave, put sunglasses on him, and took him out for a weekend on the beach.

"Okay, just write down engineer."

I sit and look at the paper, pen in hand. I just sit there.

"What's wrong?"

"Write... I don't know, sir."

He tells me the spelling phonetically and I try to write exactly what he says in the blank.

"What does your mom do?"

Is this how I'm going to spend the next forty minutes? I curse the fact that my parents couldn't have worked jobs that are easier to explain until I realize that I don't even know the word for housewife. If only she worked in a barbecue restaurant ("meat house") or supermarket ("super"), I could handle that.

"I don't know, sir."

He laughs again. "Does she work in an office?"

"No, sir. She works in a store, sir."

"What kind of store?"

"I don't know, sir."

"What does she sell?"

Formal wear? Bridesmaids dresses? Tuxedos? I don't know the words for any of these so I settle for the words I think could possibly be the same in Korean.

"Wedding dresses, sir."

"What?"

"Wedding dresses, sir."

"Oh, *we-ding deu-re-seu*." He's getting better at this, which is good because I'm not.

"Yes, sir."

"You can write *we-ding shyap*."

I sit and look at the paper, again, and he steps in before the awkward silence sets in again.

"You spell it like this…"

Thinking about Mom is depressing me. As I write down the characters for wedding shop, I imagine her sitting in her store, six-thousand miles away. Is she crying in front of the sewing machine, her face buried in her hands? I talked to my brother Jason shortly before I was inducted and he told me she had cried for days when she found out what happened.

It was hard to imagine when he told me, mostly because I've almost never seen my mother cry. It's painful to imagine now in this office because the cause of her tears is me.

When I was a child, my mother told me this folktale about a troublemaking, disobedient green frog. The green frog lived with his single mother and, being mischievous and unfilial, never listened to his mother. In fact, he would do the exact opposite of his mother's instruction. If she told him to play in the hills, he would play near the river and vice versa. If she told him to *"ge-gul"*[24] like a frog, he would cry *"gul-ge!"*

One day, sensing she would not live much longer, the mother frog called the green frog to her side. "Son, I'm not long for this world. When I die, don't bury me in hills. Bury me on the riverbank." She instructed him this way because she knew he always did the exact opposite of what she told him.

A few days later, she passed away. The green frog cried and cried, racked with guilt. "It's my fault that my mother passed away," he thought. "All this time, I did the opposite of what she told me to do. This time I'll do as she said."

The green frog took his mother's body to the riverbank and buried her there. Although he knew it wasn't a good idea, he was happy that he was able to obey his mother this one time.

---

[24] *Gegul*: Korean onomatopoeia for the sound frogs make; ribbit.

It was not long before a heavy rain came and the river began to rise up the banks. Worried his mother's body would be swept away by the river, the green frog couldn't sleep. He ran down to the river and spent the night watching over his mother's grave in the pouring rain. That is why every time it rains, you can find the green frog crying "*ge-gul*" by the riverbanks.

That's the traditional end of the story. In the version of the story my mother told me, the mother frog's body gets washed away by the river.

As I fill in the blanks for my brothers, small wet circles appear on the sheet. Great. I'm crying. I wipe the tears from the paper and put my face down close to the paper to hide my shame.

"What's wrong?" Lieutenant So asks.

"Nothing, sir."

I wipe the paper again because the tears are falling quicker, gathering at my chin, wetting my cheeks.

"Forty-four."

"Yes, sir."

"Look at me."

"Yes, sir."

I wipe my face with my sleeve as I raise my head but the tears keep coming. I'm sniffling now. Why the hell can't I fight them back? My embarrassment and my powerlessness are making things worse. The tears are streaming from my eyes and now snot is running from my nostrils.

According to Korean tradition, a man is only allowed to cry three times in his lifetime: once when he is born, once when his parents die, and once when his country comes to ruin. I can't remember the last time I cried. I couldn't cry when the divorce was finalized and I no longer had a father or when my best friend in middle school died in a high-speed car accident. I had thought I was unable to cry, that I cried my allotted three times prematurely during my stubborn childhood and Confucius had dried out my tear ducts in punishment.

I'm now choking on my tears and snot and I look around and everyone in the office is staring at me, most of them horrified. One of them is smirking, the little shit is smirking at me, and I want to kick his ass but I'm rooted in my seat, no strength in my legs.

My mother hasn't had an easy life. When things got bad with my father, she packed up our things and took us boys to Seattle to live in the basement of an acquaintance while she worked long hours keeping the books at a fish processing plant, running a small laundry drop shop, and finally, finally opening her own formal-wear shop. She never complained and never cried in front of us.

I didn't realize how old she had become until I saw her hands one day shortly before I left for Korea. They were wrinkled and worn, criss-crossed with obese, blue, protruding tributaries of veins. The fleshy areas around her arthritic joints were constantly in a state of swelling and the geometry of her skin was marred by dull, white scars where knives cut and needles pierced her hands. My mother takes meticulous care of her skin, and people always comment on her youthful appearance, but while the white-collar face may be deceptive, the blue-collar hands never lie.

And now, because of my stupidity and dumb luck, she's probably crying into those same hands.

But that's not why I'm crying. It's not the whole reason. I can't write to her and if I can't write to her, she can't write to me. I can't go home during the few furloughs I'll get; I can't see her for two years. It's not the unfairness of the situation, the inability to do something every other conscript gets to do on furlough, to go home and see his parents, that's causing these tears. It's because I imagine on, imagine that sometime in the two years, she gets sick, sicker, that her condition gets worse and she succumbs to illness in a hospital bed six thousand miles away. A lot can happen in two years. I would be cheated out of her last moments, out of the chance to be the filial son I had never been, to say sorry, to even bury her.

It's not an unfounded worry. She has always kept her health secret but there was a day I found the results of some medical test with her white blood cell count highlighted and dangerously low. The years of hardship and unappreciative and troublemaking sons had taken their toll on her five-two frame and she was sick.

Ancestors, forgive me, but I'm going to cry this one more time.

D-719 (08FEB04): A Noble Truth and a Blessing

It's Sunday, and the magnanimous bastards are allowing us to attend religious services. There's a Protestant service, a Catholic service, and a Buddhist service. Squad Leader Lee mentions some other religions—shamanism?—and how they're out of luck. He's grinning. If you're not one of the three or not one at all, you can stay behind in the barracks but no one stays behind because everyone knows that the squad leaders won't let you be, won't let you rest your weary bones. You'll just end up staring at your locker in silence for an hour or so, primping your bedding.

I was raised Catholic and then Protestant, and I choose to attend the Protestant service. We have some Catholics and Buddhists in the squad but most are Protestant or pretend to be. The churchgoers walk in a long procession, four by forty or fifty, and file into the church pews, ten to a pew. The squad leaders growl at us to take off our battle caps and be respectful before they file out of the sanctuary. Hallelujah!

We sing songs that I sang when I was in Sunday School—I've Got Peace Like a River, Jesus Loves Me, This I Know—and the chaplain's assistant encourages us to let go and have fun, hoot and holler and throw our hats in the air. It takes a few uncertain seconds and uneasy sweeps around the sanctuary for traces of the squad leaders, but a nervous whoop sounds out and soon it's pandemonium, close to two hundred recruits letting out the stress and frustration of the past ten days out in a cacophony of hoots and hollers and shrieks and cries of joy. It's a miracle. The mute have regained their voices. The soldier band winds us down with a slow number for the last song and then everyone settles into the wooden pews.

The reverend comes out and he's not wearing a uniform. He has a wrinkled face and salt and pepper hair, more salt than pepper. He steps up to the pulpit and delivers a sermon in words I can't really hear or understand but his raspy voice has a kind tone.

It's comfortable here, mentally and spiritually and physically despite being crammed tight and sitting on cold, wooden pews. The tension, all of it, is oozing from my body. I'm loose and it feels good.

After the service, the reverend asks, "Was it anyone's birthday this week?"

A couple of hands go up, recruits stating their trainee numbers.

"Come to the front."

The couple of recruits that raised their hands scoot out of their pews and walk to the front. The reverend asks them their names and they speak their names into the microphone. He then hands each of them a box of Chocopies. A whole box! Good God!

The rest of us stare at them with green eyes from our seats in the congregation. It's another unfamiliar feeling, envy. In the numbness that I've grown accustomed to this past week, the closest feeling I've felt is its exact opposite, the feeling of relief that the one getting disciplined was not me.

The reverend leads us in the Lord's Prayer and then we file out of the church onto the dirt path outside where the *jogyo* have us again line up in rows of four.

"Sit."

We crouch down close to the earth.

Soldiers walk down the line and hand each of us one Chocopie.

I tear open the red plastic wrapper and look at that little chocolate covered snack cake in my hands. I want to eat it slowly and savor it for as long as I can but my body moves of its own accord, my hand shoving the treat into my mouth and I ravenously devour it, chocolate and cake and marshmallow making a brief pit stop at the taste buds before the short trip to my stomach. I shake the crumbs from the wrapper into my mouth and lick my lips.

God is good.

My cousin Jay went to the Army an atheist and came out a Christian.

"What happened?" I asked.

"Chocopie," he said.

There's a strange connection between the Army and Chocopie. I don't know how the whole thing started and I wonder if anyone really knows but the relationship between the Korean military and Orion Confectionary is a long one.

Jay went on to explain to me about how he started going to church on Sundays just to get his weekly snack cake and somewhere along the way, he found God. All the crazies on the subway lines with their portable loud speakers and signs reading "Believe or you're going to hell" and all it takes is a chocolate-covered treat.

The Chocopie was heaven after a week and a half of God-awful, tasteless chow, but it wasn't until much later that it brought me salvation.

We arrive at the company and the recruits who went to the Catholic service have already returned. As I unlace my boots, a few of them approach the others and strike up a hushed conversation.

"What'd they give you?"

"They gave us Chocopies."

"Yeah? We got Margarets."

As my squad mates are discussing the flavors of Chocopies and Margarets in detail, the Buddhists return. They're still unlacing their boots when the questions come.

"What'd you guys get? We got Chocopies and they got Margarets."

"They gave us Oh Yes! and Margarets and yogurt drinks."

Damn.

God is good, to Protestants and Catholics alike, but Buddha's better.

The air in the auditorium is charged with an unfamiliar feeling. Excitement. We're sitting on the cold floor in neat lines by squad, but it's not for mental education, which is held in a different auditorium with pew seating, or physical training, which is held outside on the parade ground. We're in the auditorium which doubled as our processing room, this time for a Buddhist service.

It's not exactly a cause for excitement but they're showing a movie after the service. There was no mention of which movie will be shown, but we don't care because it's the first time we've been allowed some form of entertainment. It's also time away from the *jogyo*, time away from Squad Leader Lee. I guess the devil is repulsed by any holy place, be it Christian or Buddhist.

The Buddhist chaplain's assistant is a small kid with a shorn head; it almost sparkles under the fluorescence of the auditorium lighting. His thick, horn-rimmed glasses obscure the tiny black beads of his eyes.

He walks down the front line and hands out stacks of paper to be passed back through the lines. I take the stack from the recruit in front of me, take one, and pass the rest back. The paper is a block of Korean characters in groups of four. There is no grammar here. Just seemingly unrelated four-character groups with no grammatical structure or apparent meaning.

The chaplain's assistant starts tapping on a wooden gourd with a stick and leads us in chanting. I can't read beyond the speed of a first-grader, so I just move my lips to the monotonous rhythm while I skim through the paper and look for anything of which I can make sense. I recognize only one set of characters I had seen on movie posters and make a mental note to ask Johnny about it later.

I let my mind wander and I'm reminded of a time in high school in

Seattle when my mother had a Buddhist monk pay us a couple of house calls. It was odd; my mother was born Catholic and a practicing atheist. Perhaps she assumed a middle-aged, bald Korean man dressed in drab gray pajamas would suffice in filling the void created after my father left us. Maybe if he had had a combover.

Those were frustrating times. I couldn't speak Korean and he couldn't speak English so his visits were more or less meaningless, but perhaps therein lay the *koan*: if a Korean monk visits you and there is nobody there to translate, does he still lead you to enlightenment?

After the chanting is finished, we hand back the papers and the chaplain's assistant hands out yogurt drinks and Chocopies and turns on the movie. It's a low-key production, an illegally downloaded movie played on a laptop and screened through a beam projector.

The movie is a Steven Seagal flick, one I've never seen or heard of before. It's dark and some sleep, but most stay awake. Those who sleep are missing the sporadic and gratuitous scenes of flesh of some young, blonde actress. I say flesh, but it's nothing more than cleavage and thighs. To a guy who hasn't even seen a picture of a female in more than a week, cleavage and thighs are almost as good as tits and ass. There's no mistaking the movie for fine cinema, but I find myself strangely getting into it, comforted by the sound of spoken English, even if it's the constipated rasp of Seagal, and distracted by the visual input of the explosions. The blonde is making another appearance on screen when it suddenly goes black and the lights turn on. The auditorium doors fling open and the drill sergeants file in and surround us. One of them walks up to the front.

"Get up. File out of the auditorium starting from the right."

Walking back on the path, I'm feeling fine. The crunching of the gravel beneath my feet and the quiet of the night is calming. It's dark and there is little to light our path. Having had something to eat with flavor, having seen cleavage, and walking down the path in the darkness, I'm feeling a relative peace I haven't felt for a while, a peace I feel until the tiny hairs on the back of my neck stand on end. A dark aura is coming, causing havoc as it travels down the line.

It's just ahead of me and I hear a familiar voice mocking a recruit from my squad. The aura and voice belong to Squad Leader Lee. When he's finished tormenting the recruit, I pray that he passes over me. He doesn't, matching my pace and sticking his head closer to mine to figure out who his next victim is in the darkness.

"Who're you?"

"Tr-Trainee... F-forty-four...."

"Oh, it's you. Never mind. You wouldn't understand me anyway."

He snickers and skips off down the line. He seems happiest when he's causing others pain. I'm only thankful he decided against preying on me for once.

Now that Lee is gone down the line, I turn to Johnny beside me and ask him about the chanting.

"What does *sekjeuksigong* mean? Is it the same as that movie that came out a while ago?"

"Yeah. *Sek* means sex, *jeuksi* means right away, and *gong* means... nothing."

"Nothing?"

"It's hard to explain. Basically, it means nothing."

I begin to think about it. The four character group after *sekjeuksigong* was *gongjeuksisek*. Sex right away nothing, nothing right away sex? Sex is immediately emptiness, emptiness is immediately sex? I can't grasp the meaning of the lines, but my one thought as we return to company is that I wish I could clear my mind and have sex.

Just after lights out, our squad members are in a contemplative mood. Whether it was the movie or the chanting or the sugary treats, something left more of us thinking.

"I could go for *samgyeopsal* right now."

"Yeah, *samgyeopsal* and *soju*."[25]

"Let's go when we get out on our 100th-day furlough." It's still more than ninety days away, but it's all we have to look forward to at this point.

"Me? I'm going to the 588."

The 588 to which he is referring is a huge red-light district in northeastern Seoul which primarily services horny Korean conscripts and lonely salarymen. I had walked down the seedy alleyways once after my friend Simon's birthday party. The ladies were tantalizing, standing in their alcoves lit red, their surgical perfection and augmentations drawing me in even though they threw ice at us because there were females in our party, because females in

---

[25] *Samgyeopsal*: Thick, fatty slices of pork belly, usually grilled at the table. *Soju*: Korean liquor made from ethanol, somewhat similar to vodka but much weaker in its commercial form.

our party made it clear that we were only curious tourists and not paying customers. It was only months ago, but it feels like it's been years. The past week has felt like years.

I lie there quietly and listen in the darkness, listen to the spoken and unabashed desires of my squad mates. The things they would eat, the brothels they would visit, the expressions of filial piety they would show their parents. Even though what we all want is essentially the same, freedom to satisfy our desires, I envy the simplicity and attainability of their wishes. I'm surrounded by aspiring gluttons, drunkards, nymphos, and filial sons, and I find myself jealous. Although I also anxiously long for my first furlough, still months away, I realize that I don't have much to look forward to once I step outside those gates.

Desire is the cause of all suffering. This second Noble Truth is damning. By showing me what it is to desire every little thing that could be taken for granted, every right that I thought I was entitled to as a human, boot camp is teaching me the true meaning of suffering.

"2nd Company, get up." "Salute." "Salute." "Salute." "Recruits have ten minutes to report for morning call on the parade ground. Today's dress code is ACUs, earmuffs, gloves."

"Three minutes left, you sons of bitches!"

"Move, dammit!"

"1st Platoon, report to the parade ground."

"Is everyone accounted for?"

"Yes, sir!"

"One, two, three, four! Swing those arms to ninety degrees!"

"Straighten out the lines! Attention!"

Morning call is no longer so foreign to me. I've become almost mechanical in my movements and although I have no idea what the words mean, I can almost recite the entire Service Creed. Even slurring through the words, I inevitably fall behind but pick up again at the next line.

It's still painful—I don't think I'll ever get used to waking up before the sun—but I've come to terms with the pain as part of life. It's saddening but it's also necessary for my survival.

I'm standing in my place at the rear of the formation, fifteen by twenty, the night an engulfing black save the fluorescent lights shining down on the podium, temperature at ten below zero, surrounded by three hundred recruits and bloodthirsty squad leaders behind me, snarling and barking like attack dogs waiting to be unleashed. My nose and ears and mind are numb and my breath comes out in small, thick, white clouds of smoke. Staring straight ahead at the back of the recruit ahead of me, I see a small, white flake fall onto his shoulder and slowly melt into a little bead of moisture. It's snowing.

I look up into the sky and the black of night is mottled with white spots as the flakes begin to get thicker and fall in greater numbers. I feel time slowing to a crawl. I stand there, mesmerized, and the world begins to fade away. The commander on his podium, the drill sergeants scrutinizing and threatening us from behind, the other recruits in neat, lined rows, the awareness of myself, they all dissipate into nothingness as I watch the snow pass under the fluorescence of the lampposts. All that exists is the snow falling from the sky, thick, white flakes birthed from the black night sky. White dots in a field of black. The dark night of yin with the promise of the bright morning of yang. A white peace to blanket the waves of turmoil within me, the confusion and uncertainty and weariness. A smile, the first smile since entering the training battalion, cracks across the cold, stoic visage I have learned to assume at all times.

"Look forward, *ssibalsaekki*, before I come over there and make you." I'm brought back to cruel reality by the growled threat of a squad leader.

I'm alone in my affinity for the snow. When I look at the mass of recruits before me, everyone is at attention. The call for the national anthem comes out muffled over the speakers and the others begin singing the particular verse for the day. I move my jaw along to the melody.

My gaze is lower but I continue to watch the snow fall, a powdered confectionary applied lightly over an otherwise depressing situation. Are the others unfazed by this small blessing? Are they enjoying it but are disciplined or smart enough not to show it? Or am I the only one in the valley, the only one low enough to see the worth of the little things?

"Take off your field jackets and combat uniform tops."

Three hundred recruits undress in the chill winter air, folding our jackets and uniform shirts as we've been taught. The morning run is always done in our undershirts.

"Ready."

We bring our fists to our chests and hunch over.

"Run."

We double-time out of the parade ground by platoon, the snow dusting the uniforms lined up neatly in formation.

D-718 (9FEB04): Numb and Confused

After breakfast, we report to the parade ground, but not for education or training. The morning's light flurry has turned into a near-blizzard. While I was washing up, cleaning, and choking down the morning's rice and kimchi, the snow had come down thick and white and blankety over the frozen earth, three or four inches deep. It needs to be cleared before we can train.

1st and 2nd Platoons have been assigned a long stretch of road at the far end of the parade ground. Some recruits get plastic snow shovels; others get makeshift plywood shovels that could double as crude signposts, long 2x2s with a rectangle of plywood nailed to one end. I get paired with a kid from 2nd Platoon and we're given an even cruder stretcher, a big burlap bag used to deliver rice for the base wrapped around two long 2x2s. The recruits with the shovels dig and scoop and pile snow onto the stretchers, and the kid and I lift and carry and move the snow to a designated area in the bushes.

"Korean men hate the snow," my cousin Jay told me before my induction. Why, I asked. He replied, "You'll find out soon enough."

I'm finding out now. Carrying around heaps of snow on the stretcher, back and forth, I'm learning just how heavy snow can be. How it can collapse the metal skeletons of greenhouses across the countryside, causing their thick plastic skins to sag and burst. I'm learning it with my body, in my aching back and straining limbs and neck and chest damp with sweat.

I'm neither a team player nor a follower. Being the butt end of the stretcher, carrying what feels like two hundred pounds of snow at a time across the parade ground to the drop-off point, I direct my ire not at the snow—I could never hate my Taoist blessing—but at the kid I was paired with, a kid who has no coordination and arms made of rubber. The next time we load up, I'm turning this ship around and taking the lead.

A whistle blows.

"1st Platoon, grab a shovel and report to the parade ground."

I shove the stretcher into the kid's hands and double-time to the shed to pick up a shovel. My platoon is already crowded around the shed and I wait on the outskirts. The numbers thin as the others run to Squad Leader Lee with plastic snow shovels in hand. The stock of plastic shovels must have been replenished as other platoons were re-assigned to other clearing duties. I'm one of the last ones, and all the plastic shovels are taken, so I pick up a signpost.

"You, standard. Everyone line up to his right."

We line up in a single, long line, shovels at our sides where our rifles should be.

"Put your shovels down, overlap them, and move the snow to the edge of the parade ground." He grabs the two recruits in front of him and demonstrates the procedure.

The line—we stretch across a third of the parade ground's width—obeys and we overlap our shovels and move the snow together like a human snowplow. The snow accumulates quickly in front of our shovels, the ground behind us scraped as clean as possible, random white blotches spread across the brown earth where the snow has been packed down by booted feet. The going gets tougher as we push forward, and we push until we can push no more, push until even Squad Leader Lee's insults and threats are futile, and another platoon comes in with the stretchers and clears it away. Move, stop, clear, move, stop, clear.

We're waiting for the stretcher-bearers to do their work when the recruit next to me breaks the monotony of heavy breathing and coughing.

"Hey, you're from the States, right?"

I look to my left and there's a recruit from 2nd squad resting on his shovel. He's a bit older than everyone else, close-cut hairline receding, black-rimmed glasses, sharp eyes, a little on the big side. He looks like the Last Emperor but much stockier, as if he had too much sweet and sour pork. And he's speaking in English. With a Southern drawl.

"Yeah."

"My name's Gil. I'm twenty-seven, too."

"Really?" Now that I think about it, there were two others who had numbers in the seventies on that first day during processing. "Where're you from?"

The call comes from behind to go at it again and we link our shovels and push. As we push, Gil tells me he had been studying engineering in Alabama, his words coming out in small clouds of white.

"2nd Company, get up."

My internal clock is telling me it's not six-thirty. It can't be. I'm perpetually tired, tired from the moment I wake up, but this is end-of-the-day tired.

I hit the Indiglo button on my Timex sports watch. Five-thirty. What's happening?

I sit up groggily and hear the booted steps and steel myself for the lights.

"2nd company, report to the parade ground. PT uniforms, field jackets, ear muffs, gloves."

We pack up our bedding, throw on our cold-weather issue, and rush outside into the pitch black of the early winter morning, the freshly fallen snow crunching, squeaking underneath our sneakers. The answer to the question.

"Get a shovel and fall back into formation."

After breakfast and cleaning the inside of Auditorium No. 2, the *jogyo* hands out shovels and pickaxes. There's black ice all around the auditorium from the snow that fell yesterday, melted in the day's sun, and froze again, harder and slicker, and he wants us to get rid of it.

There aren't too many pickaxes. There aren't many shovels either, but there are fewer pickaxes. Of course I get a shovel, a metal shovel this time because the plastic or makeshift wood ones can't break ice. I work hard because these mindless tasks are exactly that. Mindless. I don't have to think. I don't have to think about where I am and what I'm doing here and how long I have left. I only have to think about the ice and feel satisfaction when a chunk of it breaks away.

The distraction and satisfaction of breaking ice with my shovel wears off quickly. Lots of effort, very little return. I look at a recruit with a pick-ax. He doesn't know how to use it. There's no power in his swings, the arc that the tool makes as it swings through the winter air is compact and ineffective. It's like he's digging a tunnel with a spoon but without the desperation. It's painful to watch.

"Hey, you want to switch?" I ask, holding out my shovel.

"Uh, sure."

I hand him my shovel and take the pick-ax. The weight feels good in my hands. I could do some damage with this.

I swing the pick-ax over my shoulder and around to my back, my hands in position, and bring it in a wide arc over my head, letting momentum and the tightening of the muscles in my shoulders and arms bring it hard down into the thick puddle of ice in front of me. The response sends stinging reverberations up and down my arms. Ice chips fly everywhere. The recruits around me grunt in protest, icy shrapnel peppering them.

60

I work in a frenzy, the pick-ax going around and up and over and down and around and up and over and down. My arms turn to rubber. My back burns from the strain. Sweat all over. "Take it easy," I hear someone say, but it's not a squad leader so I ignore the voice. I swing the pick-ax and embrace the jolt of electricity that rides up the pick-ax into my body when it makes contact. I continue until I can't use my arms anymore because they've become completely limp.

I know I'll pay for it the rest of the day, crawling on my belly, barely able to grasp the rifle in my hands, or sitting through mental education, the Sandman at the podium putting us to sleep and the squad leaders growling to keep us awake. I know it, but if only for this moment, I need to feel numb.

After clearing snow and ice all morning and lunch, we're on the nearly cleared parade ground for education. The *gyogam* is out there with his oversized pad of paper on its easel and three of the *jogyo* are standing next to him, one to flip the pages as he lectures, waving his baton around at the meaningless words. As far as I can tell, he's lecturing on guard procedures, which is good because our lecture with Squad Leader Lee had been cut short.

As usual, there's very little I can understand, and I hear the *gyogam* mention that there are situations where you can shoot a civilian and even earn an award furlough for doing so, but I don't hear what those situations are. I can only pray that nothing happens when I have to stand guard in my two years.

When there are no more pages to flip through, he calls the three *jogyo* to demonstrate. One of them is the stone-faced squad leader in charge of my squad for auditorium cleaning. One I've never seen before, and the one with the impish face I think is a squad leader of 4th Platoon.

"This is what you do if a drunk approaches the guard post," the *gyogam* announces.

The stone-faced *jogyo* and the one I've never seen before are standing in front of us, assuming a guard posture, feet shoulder-width apart and the butts of their rifles resting on their hips. The impish one approaches from the side, staggering from side to side, his head lolling on his shoulders. He's slurring and pointing at the guard. The guards shift their rifles into both hands and raise the rifles to their shoulders.

"Put your hands up. Stop or I'll shoot," Stone-face says firmly.

The drunk continues his staggering approach.

"Put your hands up. Stop or I'll shoot," he repeats, more forcefully.

61

The drunk continues on and so Stone-face takes him down and pins him to the ground while the other watches with his rifle still pointed at the drunk.

The three of them run through several more scenarios with the *gyogam* providing commentary. It's supposed to be a learning experience but the *jogyo* who played the drunk is having fun with his roles and it's spreading to the recruits. There are some who are even smiling.

The *gyogam* orders us to clap for the *jogyo* after the demonstration and the parade ground erupts in enthusiastic applause. I sense something dark and ominous to the right and Squad Leader Lee is glaring at us, seemingly unhappy at the applause we're giving to another *jogyo*.

"First Platoon!" he shouts. "Come on, bitches. It's time to practice."

I still spend nights asking the same question but sleep comes a little easier because of the fatigue. I wear uniform fatigues during the day and physical and emotional fatigue at night. They woke us up thirty minutes early today, but they didn't put us to bed any earlier than usual.

"I hope it doesn't fucking snow again," someone from the other side of the room gripes.

"Fucking snow."

I don't talk to Johnny after lights out much these days. I tried a couple of times out of pity. I'd listen for a while and he'd complain about his lot in life or his trick shoulder or his bad back, a slipped disc, I think. I'd listen as much as I could, which doesn't amount to much. These days, he doesn't talk to me much. Forty-two is a much better listener. The downside is that Johnny's less eager to be my interpreter during the day. I don't hold it against him.

I've only been asleep for a few hours and someone's shaking the sleep out of me. It doesn't take much; I'm not a deep sleeper. When I open my eyes, there's a dark figure towering above my head.

"Hey, get up."

I sit up and squint at him questioningly.

"It's your turn. *Bulchimbeon*."[26]

Damn. It's a nighttime guard duty and it's been rotating through the platoon. The dark figure is Johnny.

---

[26] *Bulchimbeon:* Night watch. The literal translation of the word is no-sleep-rotating duty.

I throw on my field jacket and battle cap and follow him out into the hallway.

They have me stand at the end of the hallway, the first platoon end. There are chains wrapped around the door handles and a rusty padlock hangs down between them. There's a little slack in the chains but not enough to open the doors with enough space to slip through.

I have one of the lighted batons that the *jogyo* use in the mornings to guide us to the parade ground and I'm supposed to wave it every ten minutes, back and forth in the dark hallway. I stand there in the darkness, doing nothing except waving my baton and occasionally taking a recruit to the bathroom, one at a time. There's a faint glow of orange from the bathrooms and faint green near the middle of the corridor where the fluorescent lights from outside shine in through the window above the center staircase and short lines of orange from the four other *bulchimbeon* spaced evenly down the hallway.

There's a clipboard hanging around my neck. After waving the baton, I enter the squad rooms and count the sleeping recruits and make sure the rifles are chained up. Inside the squad rooms, 1st Platoon is sleeping soundly, snoring and grinding their teeth. When I walk past the empty spot where I should be sleeping, I'm tempted to lie down. I think about sitting down for a few seconds, but I don't trust myself not to fall asleep. I finish my count, mark down on the clipboard that everyone's accounted for, and wave my baton.

D-717 (10FEB04): P-P-P-Put Your H-H-H-Hands Up

It's after breakfast, but the morning is still a pale blue. The thick, fluffy cloud cover is straining the sun's rays, dyeing everything a shade of blue, the way everything is a shade of blue when it's raining outside and you sit by the window and watch the rivulets of rain stream down the glass panes. A Seattle blue.

43.

43.

43.

We're marching single-file up a secluded mountain path out behind one of the base's rear gates. I keep my eyes on the recruit in front of me, Johnny. Falling behind means getting disciplined, so I match his pace and watch the drops of sweat fall from under his helmet and bead on his field jacket, or I watch the mess kit dangling from his cartridge belt swing from side to side, his trainee number spray painted white. 43.

I allow myself brief moments to marvel at the winterscape of the mountain. It's like walking in a Bob Ross painting, but the trees aren't happy. They surround us, looming over us, dark trunks and branches and leaves with white crests. Even the line of soldiers walking single-file on a narrow path along the slope of the mountain feels like part of the painting, only the small white numbers standing out against the dark silhouettes blending into one black, snakish line three hundred men long. Got to catch up. 43. 43.

It's not only on threat of punishment that we don't speak. There's a solemnity in the woods. The only sounds that can be heard are the occasional bumping of our rifles against the back of our helmets, the jangling of the mess kits hanging from our cartridge belts, and the crunching of snow beneath our feet.

The march continues up and over and around several mountain ridges until the path opens up into a wide clearing with concrete walls and bunkers littered here and there, spray-painted black and yellow, to practice guard procedures. The *suha*[27] practice ground.

I'm stiff and tense. Stiff from the cold and tense because I can't do this. When Squad Leader Lee went over the steps, I couldn't write everything down. I only got down what I could understand, the first two commands, and I can't even say them without stuttering. "P-p-p-put your h-h-h-hands up!" "I-I-I'll... I'll shoot if y-y-y-you move!" Not exactly the intimidating scene you expect for an armed guard.

The morning is spent going over the various stances and how to salute while holding your rifle on guard duty. When lunch time comes, we sit on the concrete steps of a covered pavilion and wait for the mess truck. We take off our cartridge belts and fold them neatly and place our helmets on top when it's our turn to get in line with our mess kits in hand. The mess kits are not the ergonomically designed, stainless-steel kits they issue in the Boy Scouts of America. They are little copper boxes with smoothed corners and a wire

---

[27] *Suha*: The guard procedure of issuing a challenge and verifying a password response in order to distinguish whether someone approaching a guard post is friend or foe. Similar to "flash" and "thunder" used on D-Day in Europe. Literally, "who and why."

handle, brush painted forest green. The cooks scoop rice into the box, scanty portions of deep-fried meat on top of the rice, and soup into a little tray that rests just under the lid. We return to the pavilion and eat, huddled and shivering. A cold wind blows through the pavilion because there are no walls and the cold seeps up through the concrete steps.

After lunch, we are to go through an evaluation of our guard skill. We stand in long single-file lines by platoon and approach the makeshift bunkers in groups of two. Naturally, Squad Leader Lee is evaluating 1st Platoon. The line is moving slowly. As I don't know what comes after "I'll shoot if you move," it's a marginal blessing, a slow line to a verbal and physical thrashing. Two by two, the recruits go and the line crawls slowly forward. I'm feeling uncomfortable in my uniform again. A sweat despite the cold makes my undershirt stick to my chest and upper back.

When the line has shortened to the point that there are perhaps only ten other nervous recruits ahead of me, I can finally see what the evaluation entails. There are two separate, solitary walls about waist-high with a trodden path between. One recruit stands in front of one wall, his rifle resting on his hip, and the other stands behind the other wall, his rifle resting in his hands, ready to fire. Squad Leader Lee approaches the bunkers and the recruits have to go through the procedures. The thing is, he's changing it up every time, sometimes he ignores the challenge and password, sometimes he pretends to be an officer, sometimes he pretends to be a spy pretending to be an officer, and so on. He finds some way to find fault and abuses one recruit, then the other. This is why our lines are moving more slowly than the other platoons.

Seeing what is coming does nothing to put me at ease. Instead, it puts me on edge because the haunting fear and imagination now has a real form and it's close and getting closer. It's a familiar feeling, a feeling from a different life but not so long ago. It's the feeling I had standing in the line at Osan Air Base two days before my induction.

I had always been wary of Army recruiters, scampering away at the first sight of them in Factoria Mall or the Safeway parking lot when I was in high school. My parents didn't censor what we watched as children, and I remember watching a fair number of movies and television dramas about Vietnam, having grown up in the post-Vietnam War era. I wasn't scared of monsters under the bed or in the closet; the gory images of soldiers' bodies being torn apart by guerillas' bullets and landmines haunted my dreams just as much as the fear of alien invasion. I realized how desperate I was when I found myself sitting in the recruiter's office at the Yongsan Garrison in the heart of Seoul.

"You sure I'll be able to get on the plane?" I asked my recruiter, a Sergeant First Class Choi.

"Yeah, we're gun' do everythin' we can to make sure you make it t' South Carolina," he assured me in his odd Southern drawl with its slight Korean edge.

"What about immigration? I'm barred from leaving the country."

"Don' worry. You won' need your passport. You're gun' fly outta Osan with your military ID and orders."

It seemed feasible. I figured the last place the Korean government would stop me was a US Air Force Base. I was sworn in as a light-wheel mechanic, given my military ID and orders, and sent to Osan Air Base to catch a flight to Fort Jackson.

Waiting in the boarding line, I was antsy. The line was moving too slowly. Although I had received assurances, I could only breathe freely once I was on the plane and it took off.

I tried to look ahead to see what was holding up the line. The curve of the line obstructed my view.

As the line inched forward, the panic began to build deep inside of me. What could be holding up the line? There's no way the Korean government would come all this way just to find me, is there?

When I could finally make out the hold-up, the panic graduated to a sick feeling, a heaviness and nausea in the pit of my stomach. The line was passing by a counter manned by three Korean immigration officers. Who knew that there would be Korean immigration at Osan?

I've heard that cows know that they're going to die as they walk up the ramp to the slaughterhouse and tears fall from their great, bovine eyes. I inched forward with the line, knowing that it was over.

The cry of the whistle shatters the blue winter sky.

"All recruits get in formation!"

I take my place in formation with a dumb look frozen on my face. Could I be this lucky? We're returning to the division. Thank God. Squad Leader Lee had taken his sweet time punishing the first two-thirds of the platoon and the last one-third of us are returning to the division cold and weary but safe and sound. For today. It's the little things.

D-716 (11FEB04): The Best Way to Get Rid of a Cold

I wake up and there is fire raging in my skull, blood boiling in my veins. The flames lick at the backs of my eyes, and pressure cracks spread across the surface of my skull. My forehead is a stovetop, hot to the touch. In a delirium, I stand at attention and give my three salutes and crumble where I stand.

"*Ssibalsaekki*, what do you think you're doing?"

I lift my head from the cradle of my hands to see Squad Leader Lee, jaw clenched, standing above me.

"I'm sorry, sir."

I scoot off the mattress and start folding my bedding as fast as my body will allow, mattress, wool blanket, sleeping back, pillow. Cold chills like needles shoot through the nerves in my neck and lower back. I feel the presence of evil moving down the line as I start pulling out my uniform and stripping down to my long underwear.

"Aaaah… I feel good," Forty-five says next to me. I sluggishly turn my head to my right and see him in a full-body stretch, a self-satisfied grin on his cheeky face.

"Fuck you," I mutter under my breath as I put on my uniform pants. "Fuck you."

The bug has been making its rounds of the company. It was only a matter of time before it got to me. Forty-five had it pretty bad yesterday. He had it pretty bad until this morning. He managed to get over his flu in just one night. I'd ask him how he did it, but I already know.

Sleep on your backs, we were instructed on the first day. We do so not only because we were told to do so but because it wouldn't work any other way. At two recruits past the room's capacity, we sleep shoulder to shoulder. There just isn't enough space to sleep on our sides. We sleep on our backs because it would be a twenty-two man spoon-fest otherwise. The exception is Forty-five, my neighbor. He has been taking to sleeping on his side, facing me. It's made me uncomfortable on many a night to wake up in the middle of the night and see his face so close to mine. It was infuriating last night.

I woke up several times and felt infected air and spittle on my right cheek. He was coughing in his sleep, coughing in my face. I put my sleeping bag over my head and tried to go back to sleep but woke up repeatedly, the sleeping bag tangled around my feet because of the damn heat, turned up because of the number of sick recruits in the company.

I heard once that the best way to get rid of a cold is to give it away. It seems there was some truth in it. This is the next lesson: if you don't want something, give it away.

The training of the day is a blur of pain. The cold is only making my head and body overheat even worse. Bayonet combat training without bayonets in the morning. Holding each step of each attack until Squad Leader Lee's satisfied and his satisfaction doesn't come easy. The ten pounds of my Vietnam War-era M16A1 feel like fifty as I hold it frozen in a thrust with outstretched arms or cocked backward and above my shoulder or parallel to my body to block. What little strength I have is not going to my arms and thighs but to feeding the fever.

Pre-firing practice in the afternoon. Frozen in three different firing stances: prostrate on the ground, crouched, or standing with the dead weight of the rifle always damnably resting in my hands. Prostrate, crouching, standing, prostrate, crouching, standing. The whole time the rifle, my "second life," weighs me down, sucking the strength from my already drained body. Balancing a white or black *baduk* stone[28] on the barrel and pulling the trigger. I can barely keep my hands steady. The stone keeps falling off before I can even try to pull the trigger. Two lines of recruits at fifty paces, a small wooden sawhorse with a paper target on it to practice aiming. Again prostrate on the ground, trying to line up the center of the target through the sights with bleary eyes.

Mental education after dinner. The pain keeps me awake but limp. I don't pretend to pay attention. I fight only to keep my burning head up and my dried-out yet somehow teary eyes open. After the nightly cleaning, I bow my head and pretend to write in my journal. I tilt my body slightly away from the door and balance the pen in my limp hand. Lights out and the reserve of strength from God knows where that was pulling the strings of this worthless body has run dry.

---

[28] *Baduk*: Also known as *go* in Japan. A strategy board game in which players place stones on a grid in order to occupy the greater amount of territory through capturing the opponent's stones and reading ahead. The stones are double-convex, like small white or black UFOs.

I wake up around midnight. The heater is on full blast to make sure nobody else gets sick and the heat emanating from my body is on full blast because I'm sick.

I can't take it. I'm hot, I'm cold, I'm hot. I can't sleep. I pull up my sleeping bag, cover my head, and when I finally drift off to sleep, I wake up again, the covers at my feet. I'm cold but my body says I'm hot. I can't tell anymore.

I can't fall asleep. My head is burning from the inside out. My brain is on the verge of popping, the pressure is building. I want to sleep. I need to sleep, but I'm in that vulnerable stage on the line between waking and sleeping, and the fever has me bound to the waking side. I'm in pain and beyond exhausted and there's nothing I can do.

The door opens and the *bulchimbeon* walks in.

"Hey," I gasp softly.

"What? You should be sleeping."

"I have to go to the hospital."

"What?" He's crouching down above me.

"I hurt a lot. I have to go to the hospital."

"Fuck. Wait here."

He leaves and I return to my suffering. A few minutes later, he returns with a *jogyo* in tow.

"What's wrong, Forty-four?"

"I'm... in pain, sir."

He puts his hand to my forehead. "Shit. Get up."

I get up, trying to be prompt but the clutches of the fever are pulling me down.

"Come with me."

"Yes, sir."

I follow him out in the hall, past the second platoon *bulchimbeon*, and to the administration office

The squad leader talks to the other soldiers on night duty. They lead me down the center stairwell, the only one that's not chained and locked, and out into the cold, dark night where a jeep is waiting. I get into the back and the *jogyo* sits up front.

I huddle in the back as we drive to the base infirmary where a medic is on call. He looks as if he's been sleeping. He's not happy.

"What's his problem?"

"The flu. It's been going around the company."

69

"Bring him here."

He takes my temperature, curses, gives me some painkillers, and sends me on my way.

D-715 (12FEB04): A Lump of Coal

The next day of training and education is a blur; the fever has subsided to a level of incoherence acceptable for training and education and the result is a numbness that envelops body and mind and a cough that gets better and gets worse several times during the day. By the end of the day, I'm used to the fever and cough as I'm used to waking up in the morning and shoveling snow and used to getting punished by Squad Leader Lee for no reason. I'm adapting.

I got my first letter today. Every night during pre-roll call cleaning, a recruit from 3rd Platoon makes his rounds with a stack of letters. Mail call is the best time of the day for most recruits, maybe the only bright part of the day, and for them, this guy is Santa Claus. When we start cleaning, it's Christmas Eve. Nobody says anything but there's an anxious energy in the air and it's a positive energy.

I find myself excited every night but I have no reason to be. I don't get mail. The only time Santa talked to me, he was asking who Fifty-two was. Nobody really knows who Fifty-two is. He's one of the guys volunteered for kitchen duty by Squad Leader Lee.

I don't know why I join the rest of my squad in their childlike anticipation at night. I don't know why I bother peeking into the mailbox near the administration office when I pass by. It's like peeking at presents at a friend's house because there are none waiting for me at home. There's really no reason for me to get any mail, but I can't help it. It must be this group mentality setting in.

Everyone else in the squad has gotten at least two or three letters by now. By far, the most blessed of the squad are Forty-nine and Forty-two, with roughly twenty letters each. They have girlfriends and caring families. Because we have no other worldly possessions other than general issue, letters are like social currency. They aren't used in a barter system because we have nothing to trade, but they delineate the difference between the rich and the poor, a difference that's getting worse by the day, a difference I don't understand. On the surface, it doesn't seem like either of them has the looks to inspire such devotion: not Forty-nine, with his droopy eyes and comically bulbous lips, nor Forty-two, with his dark, pock-marked skin and doughy physique. But they're good kids; I'm just bitter.

I'm lining up the uniforms hanging in the lockers when Santa walks in. I note his entrance and have long turned back to the uniforms when I get poked in the back. I turn around and Santa tosses a thin envelope at me. A moment later, Squad Leader Lee walks in, and Santa hurriedly finishes handing out letters and scurries down the hall.

"What's taking you bitches so long?" he asks. "Hurry up and sit down."

I throw the letter into my locker drawer and sit down. The squad members assigned other cleaning duties outside the squad room scuffle in and take their places in front of their lockers.

"Is anybody sick?"

A number of hands go up, mine included.

"*Ssibal.* Put your hand down if it's just the cold."

Most of the hands go down. Johnny's is still up.

"What's wrong with you?" he asks Johnny.

"It's my back, sir," Johnny answers meekly. "I have a slipped disc. My shoulder keeps popping out, too, sir."

Squad Leader Lee gives Johnny a piercing stare for a while and I can feel Johnny shrinking beside me. Lee breaks off his stare and decides to write it down.

Forty has his hand up, too, and Lee asks what his problem is. "*Chijil,*" Forty says, and Lee bursts out in laughter and writes that down, too.

"Okay. Now which of you bitches still has *byeonbi?*"

A few hands go up reluctantly, arms slightly bent and heads bowed down.

"Put your fucking hands straight up," he yells and the arms straighten up. I don't raise my hand; I don't know what he's talking about and can't ask while he's here. Lee writes down their numbers on his clipboard and leaves the room.

Night call proceeds as usual and lights out. The whispers ensue. Most of the squad is in conversation. Relationships have begun to form and we've learned that Lee doesn't bother to stop by the squad after lights out.

"Why didn't you raise your hand?" I hear across the room.

"There's no way in hell I'm going to raise my hand," comes the reply. "You know what happens if you can't take a shit?"

71

"No. What?"

"They stick something in your asshole and shoot water up there."

Byeonbi. Constipation. I'm suddenly glad my ignorance kept my hand at bay. Being constantly bloated and irregular is uncomfortable and a little frightening but I'm not planning on having my anus violated during my two years.

"Hey, Johnny," I say, thinking about earlier in the night.

"What?" He's not as genial as he was last week but he's still a nice enough kid to answer my questions.

"What's *chiji?*"

"Hemorrhoids."

I sit up and open my drawer. The letter is sitting on top of my notebooks. I tear open the envelope and take out the letter and lie down, pulling the sleeping bag over my head. I unfold the letter in the darkness and position it in front of my head in my left hand. I reach over with my right and press the Indiglo button on my watch and awkwardly try to read the letter.

There are no handwritten letters on the page, only computer-printed words I can't understand. I can understand the red teardrop symbol at the top of the page like the blood drops on the mess hall posters. It's a letter from the blood donation center from giving blood during processing.

Damn. I sit back up and jam the letter back into the drawer and try to find solace in sleep.

D-714 (13FEB04): Numbers

I'm sitting in a small waiting room, my ears ringing. There are seven other recruits waiting in the battalion infirmary, and they all look as miserable as I imagine I look, a dull, dumb, slightly disgruntled expression on heads bowed slightly downward, eyes focused on nothing at all or focused somehow inward.

I'm not here for the ringing in my ears, and I don't suppose any of them are here for it, either. The ringing is a result of the morning's training. After breakfast, we marched about an hour out the rear gate to the zero-point firing range. The targets were pieces of graph paper with x and y axes, and we were given three bullets to fire at a distance of 25 meters. The purpose was to make sure that the sights on our M16s were calibrated. The crack of the rifle

72

with each shot resounded in the winter sky, bouncing off the rocks and the trees and the cliff faces and returning and bouncing in my ear canal and wreaking havoc on my eardrums. The high-pitched whine came almost immediately, and it's still there as I sit and have my temperature taken.

The medic takes the thermometer from me and looks at the red line. "Forty degrees." Still unfamiliar with Celsius, I try to convert it to familiar Fahrenheit in my fever-stricken head. Celsius times nine divided by five or times five divided by nine, no, times nine divided by five and plus thirty-two. 104 degrees Fahrenheit. Five recruits had their temperature taken before me and their temperatures were: 40 degrees, 40 degrees, 40 degrees, 40 degrees, 40 degrees. We all have the exact same temperature but it's no coincidence. The medic shakes the germs off the thermometer and hands it to the next recruit. It's the same cold and the same thermometer so even if it isn't the same cold, it soon will be.

One by one, the other recruits with 40-degree temperatures enter the doctor's office, and every five minutes one comes out and another goes in.

About twenty-five minutes later, I enter the doctor's office which, aside from a few posters with medical diagrams, is indistinguishable from any other office in the battalion. It's bare and sterile in feeling only; behind a steel desk which has seen some years sits an officer. He looks to be in his thirties, a bit on the husky side; he's got the build of a rugby player, and yet he has a look of conceited intelligence which is apparent behind his wire-rimmed glasses.

"Sit," he says. He doesn't look at me. He's looking over my personal information intently. After a short while, he looks up at me, adjusting his glasses.

"You're from America?"

"Yes, sir."

"You know, I studied in America."

"Really, sir?"

I feign interest as he goes on about his American experience. *I went to such-and-such university and studied medicine.* Oh, really, sir? Yeah. *Then I came back to do my military service.* I understand, sir. *Where did you study?* Mmm… Washington University, sir. *Washington University?* He looks impressed. Not that Washington University, sir. Uh… the university in Washington state. Washington State University, sir. There's no way to say University of Washington in Korean but it doesn't really matter. *Oh, I see. You're not too good at Korean, are you?* No, sir.

He scrutinizes me for a second and then comments, "You're Forty-four."

"Trainee Forty-four, Young Jin Chun. Yes, sir."

"There was a recruit in the group before you, Jaime. He said he couldn't speak Korean. He was Forty-four."

"I see, sir."

"He came into boot camp speaking in English."

"I understand, sir."

"Everybody thought he was pretending."

"I understand, sir."

"His English wasn't very good. Everybody thought he was pretending."

"Yes, sir."

"Your Korean isn't so good."

"Yes, sir."

"Okay, well, take the medicine they give you outside and take it easy."

"Yes, sir."

"Okay, you can leave." He doesn't look at me, his disinterest ushering me to the door.

"Yes, sir."

I salute and close the door quietly behind me. The medic nods at the seventh of eight with 40-degree temperatures, and number seven goes in for his five minutes. The medic gives me two small pills, painkillers, and sends me on my way. "Report back to your squad room."

"Yes, sir."

When I return to the squad room, the others are putting away their notebooks and pens. They just had some sort of education in the squad room. I don't bother asking Johnny what it was about because I don't really care. They start putting on their boots and, because I already have my boots on, I sit down on the edge of the raised floor and wait. Shortly after, Squad Leader Lee takes us up to Auditorium No. 2 for education.

I'm taking notes of more nationalist propaganda in my notebook when my neighbor's face, bent down, is encroaching on my personal space.

"Hey, what's that?" he asks, pointing at my notebook. It's Two, a tall, goofy kid from 1st Squad. He's awkwardly hunched over, due to his height, and he's looking at me with his vacant eyes and protruding bottom lip.

I ignore him and try to look like I'm paying attention to Captain Bullshit. I don't want to get in trouble because of this kid.

"Can I see?" he asks, his left hand already pinching the right edge of my notebook.

I hand him the notebook. I don't want to cause a commotion. The *jogyo* are lolling in the back and it's better not to draw their attention.

Two leafs through my notebook and makes comments to his neighbor. I imagine that he's making fun of the nonsense that I have scribbled inside. It bothers me. I've actually grown accustomed to the constant ridicule but the reason it bothers me is because of who Two is. While there are others in my squad who are more prone to error than me, in terms of the platoon, Two is our village idiot. I feel retarded but I think he's actually borderline mentally handicapped. It's not such a great feeling to have the local idiot laugh at me. I hope that the fact that he's laughing me is not indicative of my status in the platoon.

When he hands me back my notebook, he murmurs a "Thanks." I take the notebook without looking at him, open it up to the page I was taking notes on, and pick up where I left off.

The education ends early and there's more education with Squad Leader Lee scheduled in the squad room. Before the other squads join us in our room, Lee announces that he's looking for "volunteers" for kitchen duty. He volunteers me and Forty-five. I guess he figures that it's pointless for me to be in education anyway.

At the mess hall, a soldier in a dark-blue rubber apron and galoshes meets us and leads us through the doors to the back kitchen. He opens a closet where cardboard boxes stamped with the Army logo and expiration dates are stacked high. There are more dark-blue rubber aprons and galoshes against the wall.

"Put on a 'front-skirt' and rubber boots. Come out when you're done."

"Yes, sir."

My left rubber boot has a hole in it and the layer of water covering the floor is seeping into my wool sock. The first soldier has me peel radishes the size of footballs and run them through a stainless steel monster of a food processer, the radish shavings flowing out the bottom and into a large plastic basin on the floor. Kitchen duty's not so bad, I think to myself. It's tedious work, but the mess soldiers leave me to the radishes, and the only sounds in the kitchen are the whirring of the machine, the clanking of pots and pans, and the occasional *psst* of steam from the cookers. I've worked in kitchens throughout high school and college, and I've always found such work to be calming, preferable to dealing with people, much preferable to sitting through education with Squad Leader Lee.

When the last radish has been peeled and run through the machine and the shavings pile up high in the basin, another soldier hands me a hose and a handbroom and has me sweep up the kitchen. Once that's finished, yet another soldier has me lug the food waste barrels outside. "When you finish here, you're done," the soldier tells me.

When I finish, I join Forty-five in the kitchen and the same soldier that met us takes us to the closet to change back into our boots. My left sock is soaked up to past my ankle. Having nowhere to wrench the water out, I put my moist left foot into my boot and lace up.

"Ready to go?" the soldier asks.

"Yes, sir."

He sticks his hand into a box and hastily shoves small plastic bags into our hands.

"You did a good job. Put these in your hardtack pockets. Don't get caught eating them."

"Yes, sir."

The pack is hardtack.

After lights out, Forty-five tries to open his bag quietly, secretly, but the tell-tale squeaking of a bag of snack being opened is something we haven't heard for weeks and so everyone in the room hears it. Having been caught, he opens the bag up and the whole squad rushes over to him and feasts on the little, hard pieces of baked bread. It's gone before I can take any and I'm lying next to him. I open up my locker and offer my bag up to the squad as well, making sure to save two pieces for myself. There's a smaller packet inside with small, colored candies, "star candies." I open that up, too, and take one for myself. It's gone almost as soon as I open the bag and the packet. I put the hardtack and star candy in my pocket and fold the plastic bag carefully into a small square and stick it in my uniform pocket.

Everybody is lying down and nobody is talking. I can hear the muffled crunching of hardtack in everyone's mouths. I take one of the pieces of hardtack and stick it in my mouth. It's rock hard and I can barely make enough saliva to make it into a paste in my mouth, but it's so sweet I want to cry. It's gone too quickly. I run my tongue along my teeth and the roof of my mouth and get every last bit and sigh with contentment. The second one, I chew it like gum, chew it until it's a grainy liquid, and swallow it down. It's quiet now, some of the others snoring and dreaming after our small feast. I take out the star candy—it's the size of a dried-out pea—and let it melt in my mouth. I let it melt and then I melt into sweet sleep.

D-713 (14FEB04): PRI

Meol-ga-jung-meol-ga-jung-meol-ga-jung-ga. Far-near-middle-far-near-middle-far-near-middle-near. The far targets are 250 meters, the near are 100 meters, and the middle are 200 meters. With the near targets, I can make out a human-like figure, head and shoulders and torso. I can barely make out the 200 meter targets, a tiny head and shoulders poking out of the dirt, and the 250 meter targets are specks of olive green in the brownish distance.

I'm in a chest-deep pit. My rifle has been chained so I can't turn it on the *jogyo* crouched next to the pit with ten-round cartridges in hand.

Meol. I aim at what I think is the target, slightly below so that it can ricochet off the dirt if my aim is off, exhale slowly, and gently pull back the trigger. The spent casing flies from the chamber, the 5.56-millimeter round on its way toward what I hope is the target. The cracking report has left me partially deaf, barely able to hear the *jogyo's* instructions over the ringing in my ears.

"Aim a little higher and to the left," I think he says.

Ga. Another deep breath and the bullet flies from my rifle and the force of the impact knocks the flimsy target over.

Jung. A cloud of dust flies up in front of the target obscuring it. I can't tell if the target has been knocked over and only hope the round got the target on the rebound.

After my ten shots, I eject the cartridge and pick up the spent casings in the pit. The *jogyo* confirms that I have ten, dropping them one by one in a tin coffee can, and I file down the line and down the hill.

Two shots through my second run-through, my rifle jams and the *jogyo* takes my rifle and fumbles with the bolt, cursing and grunting until the jammed casing pops from the chamber. "Hurry and catch up," he says. The time he spent unjamming my rifle is time I was to use in aiming and firing. I fire off my next shot as quickly as possible as accurately as possible before the target goes down and use an extra shot on the remaining *meol* targets. I've given up on trying to get a perfect score but don't want to dip below twelve.

There's hearsay that a perfect score will get you a phone call home. After seeing how small the targets look at 200 and 250 meters, it seems unlikely that I'll hit all twenty. Besides, I'm sure they'll tell me that an international call is out of the question. Twelve is the minimum to pass the evaluation and I don't want to do PRI.

As I walk down the line, the scores boom out over the PA. Audio in the Army is hardly clear, and with nothing to bounce the sound waves back but a wide open valley and my ears ringing badly, I can't make out my score. I ask Johnny and Forty-five but they've had a hard enough time hearing their own scores.

"Any recruit who failed to hit 12 out of 20 must report for PRI training," the *jogyo* at the bottom of the hill announces. The rest get to rest in the make-shift auditorium off to the side.

I report for PRI because I'm not sure and would rather err on the side of caution. There are a lot more recruits than I expected gathered around the short, fat column which marks the PRI training ground. The *jogyo* in charge jumps atop the column and tells us to spread out in a broad circle around the column. We jog in place and he calls out a distance—100, 200, or 250—and we stop and assume the appropriate firing stance, standing, crouching, or prostrate in the dirt. We hold the stance until he's satisfied and then we start up again. Whenever he calls out a distance, I hope he's calling for the prostrate stance. At least then I can rest my arms and the weight of the rifle on the ground. There's panting and grunting and hacking and coughing all around me.

"We can do this all day, motherfuckers," the *jogyo* bellows atop the column, dissatisfied with our endurance. I'm pretty sure I can't do this all day. I'm barely hanging onto my rifle and the cold weather and the strenuous work is confusing my feverish body even more.

"200."

After another twenty minutes, he calls for a ten minute break. We collapse in our places and sit, drenched in sweat. A cold breeze wafts through the circle of recruits. I lift up my head and observe the recruit sitting to my right. He's playing with something in the dirt. The something is his spit.

The *jogyo* returns after the ten minutes are up and we continue PRI for another thirty minutes to an hour, I'm so tired and feverish I have no concept of time. When he's satisfied, the *jogyo* jumps down from off the column, lines us up, and sends us back up the hill to try our marksmanship again.

When it's my turn, the *jogyo* at the top of the hill asks, "What are you doing here?"

I don't know how to respond.

"You hit 16 out of 20. Go to the auditorium and wait."

"Yes, sir."

I turn around and walk back down the hill to the auditorium. Damn. It's times like this I wish I could at least hear Korean straight.

The auditorium is an aluminum skeleton covered in plastic sheeting. Inside, the recruits who passed the evaluation and weren't stupid enough to go to PRI anyway are sitting on concrete steps. I find the few members of my squad and join them.

"Where have you been?" Fifty-six asks.

"I thought I didn't pass."

Fifty-six chuckles and I chuckle, too. What else can I do?

"Hey, what does PRI mean?" I ask.

"PRI stands for '*pi heulligo al begigo i ganeun hullyeon*.'" He says it slowly and clearly so I can understand.

Pi means blood, I know that much. "What does '*al begigo*' mean?"

"*Al*," Fifty-six says, pointing to his bicep. "'*Begida*' is the feeling you get after you work out."

"What about '*i ganeun*?'"

"This," he says, grinding his teeth.

PRI. Blood-spilling, muscle-straining, teeth-grinding training. It's an apt description. There wasn't any blood spilled, but that's how it felt.

The plastic sheeting in the corner has split and a cold wind is blowing through it. We sit, huddled, whispering to each other. Every so often, the flimsy door, also plastic sheeting over a wooden frame, flings open and it gets quiet, but it's usually a recruit, shoulders and face sagging. It isn't until it's dark out that our numbers fill up and the *jogyo* walk in.

When I wake up, it's close to midnight. I don't know what has woken me; it's not the fever, which has been fairly constant but bearable. There's a slight pang in my stomach but nothing more than usual. I've been thinking about my constipation constantly—Am I dying?—and decide to give it a try.

I roll up a liberal amount of toilet paper, put on my slippers, and crack open the door, trying to get the attention of *bulchimbeon*.

"What is it?"

"Bathroom."

"Hold on," he says. "There's someone in the bathroom now. You're next."

I sit down next to the door and prepare myself psychologically. You can do this. You have to do this.

The door cracks open and the *bulchimbeon* says, "Come on."

I take the first stall in the bathroom and put down a few squares of toilet paper on either side of the seat and sit down. When I sit, the pang is gone without a trace. I clench and flex, and nothing. Come on, you insubordinate bitch of a bowel.

I prop my feet against the stall door and squeeze and tighten the muscles of my stomach and rectum. Something is going to come out. It has to. Come on, damn it.

I feel a small amount of material passing and hear the plop in the basin and know that is all I'm going to get.

Tap, tap comes the knock on the door.

"Hey," comes the *bulchimbeon*'s voice. "Hurry up in there."

Damn. There are a few situations in which a man should never be rushed—when he's zipping up his fly, when he's having sex, and when he's on the can. "Okay."

"It's time for the changing of the watch."

I give a final, futile push, hear a few smaller plops, and hurriedly wipe with the remaining tissue in my pocket. The toilet paper comes back red, bloody. I look in the toilet bowl and there's nothing but wisps of blood trailing off in the water of the bowl. I throw the bloody toilet paper in the trash can next to the toilet and flush down the blood. I go back to bed, worried, unsuccessful, belly full of shit and bleeding from my rectum.

D-712 (15FEB04): First Shower

"Get your toiletry bag, towel, and a change of underwear, brown. You're going to take a shower. You guys stink like hell." I haven't noticed, but I'm sure we do. We haven't had a shower since we got here over two weeks ago. "Bring your towel, underwear, toiletry bag, and laundry."

Like everything else, we're going to shower as a platoon. When it's our turn to use the shower, we stand in the hall against the wall in a line sixty long.

80

As we walk down the hall toward the center staircase, I take a quick peek inside the mailbox. I don't know why.

"Take off your clothes, put your shit in a *gwanmuldae* except what you're going to wash, and line up in front of a showerhead."

The locker room is tiny and naked recruits scramble to put their PT uniforms in the cubbies along the left wall and enter the shower room through the door on the right to make space for the rest of the platoon. There aren't enough cubbies for everyone and they fill up quickly as the jumble of smelly, naked kids with their penises wagging proceeds through the room. I wait because there's a giant white ass taking up any space I have to strip down and I want to avoid incidental contact. I've stripped down and am reaching up to put my PT uniform on top of the cubbies when Squad Leader Lee calls me.

"You have a tattoo." The tattoo on my back is hard to miss.

"Yes, sir," I respond hesitantly, considering my state of undress.

"Come here."

"Yes, sir."

"You have one on your stomach, too."

"Yes, sir."

"Stand still."

"Yes, sir."

He's ordering me to stand still because I'm fidgeting. I'm fidgeting because I'm standing naked and Lee is bending down, staring at a tattoo at the bottom of my belly, inches away from my shriveled dick. I don't know what to do with my arms. Standing at attention, my arms should be at my sides but the proximity of squad leader face to my dick is triggering the instinctive urge to protect and cover my dick and balls.

"Fucking stand still," Lee says, not raising his head from stomach level.

"Yes, sir."

After he inspects it for a very long, awkward minute, he asks, "What does it mean?" They're Chinese characters but in simplified Chinese, something Koreans can't read.

"I-I don't know, sir."

He sucks in air through his teeth, a sign that he's getting angry. It's a sound you don't want to hear from Squad Leader Lee. It's a sound I don't want to hear when his face is still inches from my dick.

"Uh… 'sin-sincerity,' sir." It was a mistake from my first year in college. I wasn't drunk at the time but I wish I had been if only for the excuse.

He finally stands up and snickers at me. "Go ahead," he says, pointing to the shower room.

The shower room is spacious, but there are only about twelve shower-heads, so we line up four or five deep, toiletry bags and stinky, slightly soiled underwear and socks cradled in our arms. I'm not used to communal shower culture and uncomfortable standing in a naked line so I stand at the end of a line at the far end of the shower room.

"You have twenty minutes. One person gets wet, then go to the back of the line and lather up. When it's your turn again, wash off. Do your laundry while you're waiting."

The first recruit turns on the water and starts rinsing off two weeks of filth and sweat from his body. The rest of us in the line put toothpaste on our toothbrushes and start brushing our teeth.

"Hurry up."

The line moves slowly forward and after I rinse, I return to the end of the line and start lathering up. The others in front of me have dropped down and are doing their laundry so I also drop my long underwear, underwear and socks and start rinsing them in the scummy gray run-off from the showers. I run the green bar of laundry soap over them, fold them, and start scrubbing them against the floor.

"Five minutes left," Squad Leader Lee shouts from the entrance of the shower room. "The last two recruits out have to wipe down the locker room."

I wash off the lather in haste and return to my laundry. The quicker of the platoon are already heading back to the locker room with laundry in their arms. Having never washed my clothes by hand before, I'm taking far too long.

"One minute left."

My laundry is still a little soapy, but I start wringing it dry. The wool socks soak up a lot of water, and even with my forearms burning from all the wringing, they're not getting dry.

"Everyone out."

I pick up my laundry and head toward the locker room. I'm the last one in the locker room and the last one dressed. Johnny is the second to last.

Squad Leader Lee sends the rest of the platoon up and stays behind with me and Johnny. He points to a cubby with foul, crusty rags. We take rags, and stretching them out in our hands, hunch over, and run back and forth through the locker room, sopping up the dark gray water and black pubic hair along the way. When the floor is dry, we put the rags back in the cubby and follow Lee back to the squad room. He doesn't give us a chance to wash our hands.

Back at the squad room, the other recruits are hanging up their laundry on a clothesline that stretches above the lockers. I drape my underwear and socks over the clothesline and spread out the long underwear on top of the locker, placing my helmet and gas mask on top. Water is dripping from my underwear, falling onto my sleeping bag. I look around and nobody else has the same problem.

During the nightly cleaning, Alabama walks in on an errand and stops to talk to me and Johnny. Instinctively, we all look toward the door to make sure Lee's not there.

"Hey, I heard there's still a chance for us to be KATUSAs."

I look at him suspiciously. A KATUSA[29] is a Korean soldier stationed at an American Army base. It's a coveted position because things are more lax as a KATUSA. The one KATUSA I met before the Army came out on pass every weekend. I didn't even know he was a soldier until months later. While it would have been ideal for me, I didn't apply because the process takes a year and in the end, it's decided by a lottery. With my luck, I figured it wasn't worth wasting another year of my life.

"How?" asks Johnny.

"There are special KATUSA units that are sent on patrols. They choose these from recruits in basic."

"Really?" Johnny looks excited. I'm excited, too, but I don't trust my chances.

"Yeah. Maybe we'll all end up there," Alabama says and bids us farewell, running out the room.

After cleaning has finished, I check my laundry and it's still dripping. God, I hope I don't get caught during evening call. The *pit, pit, pit* of the water dripping on my sleeping bag tells me that I'm screwed when evening call begins.

The Australian comes in for evening call. It's the first time he's entered our squad room. He tells us to stand at attention. He walks up and down the line with his hands behind his back. When he nears me, I can't conceal a slight grin at seeing a familiar face.

"What the fuck are you smiling at?" he asks sternly.

The grin is gone, wiped from my face. My mistake.

---

[29] KATUSA: Korean Augmentation to the US Army.

"Is that how you stand at attention? Heels together, feet open at forty-five degrees."

"Yes, sir."

"Seul-gi," he calls and Squad Leader Lee rushes up to him. "Is this how you're training these kids?"

"I'm sorry, sir."

The Australian doesn't acknowledge Lee's words. He walks away and starts tinkering with the stand at the far end of the room.

"There's no water in this kettle. Whose responsibility is this?"

Forty-seven and Forty-eight raise their hands and state their trainee numbers.

The Australian picks up the kettle and throws it across the room. "No water for third squad tonight. Just see what happens if I catch any of you drinking water tonight."

He walks toward the door and pauses. "Lee."

"Yes, sir."

"Train these kids right," he says through gritted teeth and walks out the room.

Damn.

Lee tells the first *bulchimbeon* to get ready for duty and the rest of us to get down on our hands and feet.

D-709 (18FEB04): Cans of Tuna

We're doing PRI again in the morning, rifles clutched in spent arms, our bodies prostrate on the ground or crouched with right knee on the ground or standing with two feet on the ground, left foot in front of right. Always grounded, and the ground keeps us perpetually cold. Holding the rifle always level in front of us keeps us perpetually tired. Hunger? It goes without saying.

One. Two. Three. One. Two. Three. One....

Another squad leader has walked over and is talking to Squad Leader Lee. Lee's attention being directed elsewhere means we get a momentary rest, grips on rifles slightly slackening, a little less tension in the limbs. We tense up immediately once Lee turns back to the platoon.

"1st Platoon, stand at attention."

I get up off the ground and stand at attention, holding the muzzle of

84

the rifle and letting the butt rest on the ground next to my right foot.

"You, standard. Fall in around the standard."

We close ranks, and Squad Leader Lee leads us back to the company, to our squad rooms. "Lock up your rifles and assemble in Squad Room 3."

We're sitting on the linoleum in rows of three, knee to knee, fifty-eight pairs of boots tucked neatly under the edges of the raised floors. Squad Leader Lee stands over us, his face rigid.

"There was an accident at the grenade practice range today. A drill instructor and a recruit are dead." He speaks flatly, with no trace of pity. "The recruit was a pussy and his hands were shaking. He couldn't hold down the lever. The drill instructor tried to take it from the recruit's hand and it fell in the recruit's sleeve."

He pauses and an evil grin spreads across his face.

"Do you know what someone blown up by a grenade looks like?"

There's silence, the usual silence that follows a question posed by Squad Leader Lee. Of course, no one has ever seen someone blown up by a grenade so a simple "No, sir" would suffice, but we've become complete idiots, unable to answer a simple question. If someone threw a grenade in the middle of the room, we'd probably just sit still and let ourselves get blown up. There are no heroes in our platoon because heroism requires action.

"Canned tuna," Squad Leader Lee says, breaking the silence himself. "It looks like canned tuna, like someone took a can of tuna and emptied it all across the ground." He's waving his arms up and down and left and right as if he's upending a can of tuna across the floor, the creepy smile on his face all the while.

He gives us a moment to picture it, cans of tuna emptied on the dirt and patches of grass. Cans of tuna that used to be a recruit like us. Cans of tuna that will never go home to his parents. They'd have to have a closed casket at the funeral. Would they even have a casket? Or would they scoop up the shredded, charred bits of flesh and put it in a coffee can? Poor bastard. Lee's message is clear: those cans of tuna can be you. Tomorrow is grenade day.

"If anyone is feeling unfit to throw grenades, raise your hand."

A kid from 2nd Squad feebly raises his hand and Lee glares at him. He puts it down. Lee doesn't say anything, he just waits. Everyone in the platoon knows why. We are all looking in the same direction. We are looking at Two. If there's anybody who's going to get anyone killed tomorrow, it's him. He's tall and uncoordinated like he just had his last growth spurt and hasn't gained full control of his limbs.

He's sitting there with the same goofy grin on his face, oblivious to fifty-eight pairs of eyes telling him to raise his hand. It's an awkward silence that goes on and on.

Lee gives up.

"We're going to practice the motions of throwing grenades this afternoon. If, at any time, you think you can't do it, inform your squad leader." He throws Two another look, which is wasted.

For once in my life, I thank God that I'm short. Two and Forty-four. Forty one recruits separate us. I feel bad for One and Three. They have to be shitting their pants right now.

The march to the grenade practice ground the next morning is tense. It's tense as we practice going through the motions. One, put your fists together, grenade in your dominant hand and the pin in the first finger of the other. Two, bring your elbows together, snapping the pin out. Three, bring the grenade hand back behind your head and the other hand out in the direction of the target. Four, throw, bringing your grenade hand in an arc to rest on top of the pointing hand. It's tense and we're watching Two and Lee is watching Two. One, two, three, four. It's tense as we watch the squad leaders set off a claymore, the ground shaking and the crack of the explosion ringing in our ears.

They show us the bunkers where we'll be throwing the grenades, eight depressions with chest-high concrete walls in front overlooking a valley. At the bottom of the valley is a spray-painted circle, our target. The bunker walls have a little hole at the bottom.

"Throw the grenade into the circle. If you drop the grenade, kick it through the hole."

Now that we've practiced the throwing form and taken a good look at the bunker and the target, it's time for the throwing of the grenades.

"You're going to get two grenades. They're practice grenades because of yesterday's accident." Thank God. More than one recruit lets out an audible sigh of relief.

We cycle through the platoon and I throw my first grenade without problem. The grenade is heavier than I thought; it has a good weight, like a fistful of quarters or a fist-sized rock. I watch it as it arcs through the air and bounces into the circle, popping in a burst of smoke.

"Not bad," the *jogyo* says.

I get back in line and about five minutes has passed when I hear a commotion toward the bunkers. I can see smoke from where I stand at the far end of the practice ground. The few squad leaders patrolling the grounds run past to the front of the line.

"I bet it's Two," I hear somebody say in front of me. That'd be my bet, too.

The second throw goes like the first, and I can't help but feel sad that they're just practice grenades. I'm here and there's no changing that; the least they could do is let me satisfy my need for destruction by giving me a real grenade. When it's all over, I won't be able to say I've thrown a real grenade. I'm sure the squad leaders don't share my sentiment.

After 1st Platoon is done, they sit us in neat rows off to the side near the latrines. It's cold, a soggy cold where you can't tell if your ass is soaked from the ice in the ground melted by body heat or if it just feels that way from contact. It's not long before a squad leader stops by asking for volunteers for manual labor.

"Who here is handy with a shovel?"

I raise my hand. I don't know why. Maybe because I'm cold or maybe because I'm bored or maybe because I know that there's more work to be done and I might as well get a real shovel for once. Nevertheless, I'm surprised by my own raised hand.

"All right, Forty-four. And Thirty-nine."

I'm right. He gives us shovels and chooses six more for stretcher duty. He traces a large circle in the dirt with the heel of his boot. "Dig up the ground in this circle and pile it on the stretchers."

Once we've loaded the stretchers, the stretcher bearers have to carry the brown earth up the mountain behind us, lugging the dirt up a narrow, winding path to the bunkers to be re-fortified.

The frozen earth doesn't give way at first, the shovels bouncing back with a loud clang, but soon small chunks of dirt start to break off. I break a sweat but it feels good. The squad leader has gone up the mountain to direct the unloading and re-fortifying and it almost feels as if I'm tilling my own small, circular plot of land.

I wipe my brow with the sleeve of my field jacket and look over at the rest of the platoon shivering near the restrooms. I'm sure they're looking back at me, glad that they didn't volunteer, but I look back at them and think how sad and imprisoned they look.

D-707 (20FEB04): Disappointments

In the morning, we're called out to the parade ground with helmets, cartridge belts, gas masks, and rifles. I have a bad feeling. This is the first time we've been told to take down our gas masks from their perches on top of our lockers, and the only times they've had us wear our helmets, cartridge belts, and rifles were for marches to other training grounds. We just practiced grenades yesterday and they haven't instructed us in anything since.

"We're doing two laps around the base," the *jogyo* at the podium announces. "Do not fall behind."

Damn. I can shoot and shovel and clean, but one thing I've never been able to do is run more than half a lap without getting winded and cramped. Acute asthma. Just like my acute scoliosis—bad enough to suffer, not bad enough to sit one out.

Squad Leader Lee gives the call for 1st Platoon to run, and we head the procession out the parade ground.

A quarter of a lap in, and I'm already having trouble. Throat and lungs coated with phlegm from weeks of the flu. I gasp for breath between hacking coughs. A sharp pain in my side. I can barely lift my legs. My groin and thighs burn. The long underwear and uniform pants and combat boots pull me down, make me feel as if I'm running through quicksand. I can't keep up. Beside me, Fifty-seven and Fifty-eight try to spur me on. You can do it. Come on.

I keep up with the platoon for another quarter of a lap on sheer willpower, but my pace is slowing, slowing, slowing, and the platoon leaves me behind. I'm weak. I can't do this. I move off to the side to let the other platoons pass by but I keep jogging at a pace that barely qualifies as a jog.

I'm jogging by myself. I'm in such agony I only look up once in a while to make sure I don't jog off the path. I pass my first straggler, the fat white-looking kid from the first squad. Another half lap and I pass a few more fatties from the other platoons. They're walking, their heads tilted back, and they're holding their rifles by their arm straps. I pass by Two. He's given up completely and is taking a leisurely stroll. As I jog past, my head down, on the verge of complete collapse, Two asks, "Hey, can you hold my gun for a second?" I barely turn my head to look at him and pick up the pace.

When I return to the parade ground, all the recruits who kept up with the pace have returned to the barracks and about thirty recruits are on their hands and feet.

"Forty-four, get down on your hands and feet."

I drop down onto my hands and feet, resting my rifle on top of my hands. It's time for punishment along with the rest of the fatties and weak-willed.

"You let down your squad. You let down your platoon. You let down your comrades. 'I will' on one, 'do my best' on two. One."

"I will!"

"Two."

"Do my best!"

"One."

In the lull before dinner, a soldier escorts me to a small room next to the bathrooms I've never noticed before. He knocks and a voice from inside the room gives permission for entry. The soldier opens the door and motions for me to enter.

"Come in," Lieutenant So says from behind a desk. He has an office. It would've been nice if our previous encounter had been here so I could've cried my tears in private. "Sit."

"Yes, sir."

"Who told you that you might be a KATUSA?"

I give him a dumb look. How the hell does he know? I haven't told anyone—I can't—and I was the one who heard it. The only place I mentioned it was in my journal. Damn, that's it. I've written everything in English but I forgot about the Australian.

"I want to make this clear. You can't be a KATUSA. Whoever told you was wrong. Do you understand?"

"Yes, sir."

He sighs.

"I'm going to try to get you a position as an *eohakbyeong*.[30] Do you have a Korean-English dictionary?"

"No, sir."

---

[30] *Eohakbyeong*: Linguist.

"Do you have anyone in Korea to send you a dictionary?"

"Yes, sir. I have relatives here, sir."

"Call them and ask…," he stops in mid-sentence. "Never mind, I'll call for you. Go back to your squad room."

"Yes, sir."

D-706 (21FEB04): A Glorious Day

"You're going to get to use the PX today," Squad Leader Lee says. He'd seem magnanimous if he didn't have such a sour expression on his face. It's clear it's not his choice and he's not happy about it. "We're giving you an advance on your first paycheck. Choose two representatives to go for the squad."

"You have to eat everything you buy. Don't even think of hiding any of it for later. I know where recruits hide their shit and if I find a Chocopie in a boot or behind a locker, I'm going to kick the shit out of you."

The rotten smile has returned to his face.

"There was a recruit once who ate hardtack after everyone fell asleep. He lay in his sleeping bag and ate them until one of them got stuck in his throat and he choked to death. Nobody knew he was dead until the morning.

"Choose your representatives and report to the administration office."

With those parting remarks, Lee leaves the room, the smile still on his face.

We hold in our excitement until Thirty-seven confirms that Lee has moved on and then quietly break out in giddy excitement. Having no clue about Korean snack offerings, I let the others go at it, choosing representatives and telling them their snack orders. Whatever they choose is fine by me. Just give me something with sugar, something with actual flavor. Give me a lot of it.

After the two have left, the rest of us take out the foldable tables from our lockers and start writing letters. I write in my journal, careful not to write anything incriminating even though I'm writing in English. Every time someone passes by the squad room, everyone stops writing and looks toward the door. I look around and it seems like nobody's really writing. They're holding the pens over their pads of paper, but who could concentrate when snacks are on their way?

After about twenty minutes, the two representatives return to quiet fanfare, their arms laden with huge cardboard boxes overflowing with sugary delights. Twenty dollars, standard monthly pay for a private, might not be much in the real world but in terms of cookies and candy, it can go a long way.

They distribute the snacks fairly, one by one, first a can of soda, next imitation M&Ms, then Oh Yes snack cakes, Vic pies, Swing potato chips, another can of soda, Chocopie....

Most of us don't start right away. We want to see the extent of our wealth stacked high in front of us before we sacrifice it to the gods of our bellies. When the boxes of treasure are emptied, there are piles of sweets in front of each recruit. We share childlike grins; the sound of the first person tearing open a plastic wrapper is like the crack of the starting gun, and we unceremoniously shove the treats in our gullets in a binge food orgy frenzy.

The others whisper to their neighbors or write letters but the flow of sugary snacks goes uninterrupted. I give up the pretense of writing and sit quietly, facing my locker, savoring every sweet, sugary, chocolaty, salty bite. I'm indulging in a state of processed-food nirvana when I feel a tap on my shoulder. It's Forty-nine, the Michelin man from processing and our platoon guide.

"*Hyeong*, here," he says, handing me a small, folded piece of cardboard. It's the top of an Oh Yes box. I take it, and he scurries back across the divide. I unfold the cardboard flap and it's a letter.

Hi! Young Jin-*hyeong*, it's me, Yong-hyeon. I'm writing you a letter.... Writing on the top of a snack box, ain't it cool? It's already been almost 4 weeks since we got here, and meeting here is fate and so I hope this fate can continue on... ok? Even though we will be separated when we go to our permanent stations, take care of yourself and let's work hard in the time we have left in basic training!
Fighting!
2004.2.21
From Yong-Hyeon
Ha Ha Ha!

The sentimental lunk. I'm choked up and I have to take a break from stuffing snacks into my mouth. How did he know? I don't remember mentioning that I never got mail to anybody. I haven't really had a conversation with anyone except Johnny. So this is camaraderie.

I tear off the back of a Chocopie box and attempt to write the first letter I've ever written in Korean.

Yong-hyun,
Thank you for writing me a letter.

I don't know what else to say and there's not much I really can say. I decide the best course of action is to echo some of the sentiments from his letter. I wrap it up with a "Fighting!" of my own and I cross the divide to hand it to him. He gives me a toothy grin and returns to his letter-writing and snack-eating.

As I head back over to my side of the room, I hear a "Hey" from down the line. Fifty-six is beckoning me over. "Come here."

He invites me to sit, and I squeeze in between him and Fifty-seven. We face the lockers because we're not supposed to be fraternizing. It's our way of covering our asses. Fifty-five through Fifty-eight make a little space and Johnny and Forty-five scoot closer together so at a glance, it doesn't look like anyone is out of place.

Fifty-six's name is Jeong, and after some small talk with him and Fifty-seven, Seok-bae, he gets to the point.

"Could you do me a favor?"

"A favor? What is it?"

"There's this girl I've been writing to," he says sheepishly as he hands me the letter he was writing. "Could you write something in English at the bottom?"

"Does she speak English?"

"A little. She works at Incheon International Airport."

I see. He wants to impress her.

As I'm writing, Seok-bae speaks up, "*Hyeong,* do you have anyone to write to?"

"No." I guess it's not much of a secret. This is the bond between brothers in arms and suffering. While I was spending my free time creasing my pillow and blanket, my squad mates were worrying about me.

"I have this friend, you want to write to her?"

"Huh?"

"She's my sister's friend actually. She's cute. I tried to get with her before, but to her, I'm only her friend's younger brother." He digs in his locker and takes out a picture. She is cute. "She's cool. Write her a letter. Her name is Ye-jin."

"Okay. Thanks."

He gives me her address and I go back over to my place in the line, just in time. Squad Leader Lee walks back into the room.

"You have twenty minutes left. Remember, you have to eat everything."

Our eyes were too big for our stomachs. Looking at the small mound of snack cakes in front of me, I see there's no way I'm going to be able to finish all that junk food in the time remaining. I'm already feeling sick, but I try to choke down another Chocopie, not willing to throw any of it away. I can't throw any of it away, not something this precious.

Some of the more gluttonous of the platoon have returned from the head, wiping the sweet vomit from their lips. I can't do it. To eat anymore would be punishment in itself.

Despite Squad Leader Lee's express warning, some of my squad mates have begun searching for places to stash their treasure where moth and rust and Squad Leader Lee cannot find them. Inside their extra pair of boots, their sleeping bags, their mattresses, it all seems too easy to find. I'm too paranoid for such risky, commonplace hiding spots.

I see my pillow. I take it in my hands and squeeze. There's room to spare. The opening is Velcro, but it's been stitched closed. I take out my Monami pen and pop open the stitches.

Inside are hard plastic tubes like dry macaroni. I cram a pack of imitation M&Ms inside, close the Velcro and check the consistency of the pillow and whether it makes any suspicious wrapper noise. It doesn't so I stick what I think I can't manage to finish inside.

Relatively confident that my stash is safe, I take out my letter paper to write to Seok-bae's sister's friend. "Dear Ye-jin," I start when I feel a pang in my stomach that I haven't felt in such a long time. Is this happening? I wait, and it hits again. It is happening.

I roll up a liberal amount of TP and jam it into my pocket, scoot toward the edge of the linoleum, put on my slippers, and parade march to the head.

In the confines of the stall, I have the most mind-blowing bowel movement of my life. As far as I am concerned, nobody in the history of man has ever had such a glorious shit. The floodgates have opened and little cherubs with trumpets herald an encompassing and jubilant release. It's more than physical; it's mental as well, the release of all the pain and suffering of the past weeks. It's practically spiritual. It hurts like hell—there's no way weeks of festering chow being flushed through my poor sphincter wouldn't be—but it's a joyous pain. I'll never know the joy and pain of childbirth but I'd like to argue that I've taken a step closer than any other man. Hallelujah.

I had other snack cakes and potato chips and candy and soda, but I attribute my "success" to Chocopie. Thank you, oh mighty Chocopie. I have been saved.

I walk out of the stall a new man and return to the squad room with the air of a conquering hero returning home to fanfare.

"You had a success?" Thirty-nine asks.

Yes, I did. Yes, I did.

D-705 (22FEB04): These Boots Were Made for Rabbit-Walking, the Bootstrings...

After religious services in the morning and a sincere prayer of thanks for yesterday, we've been given another time for writing letters after lunch. It's strange that they're allowing us such a restful Sunday. I would have expected some manual labor or mental education at the least. As I didn't have time to write to Seok-bae's friend yesterday on account of the shit of all shits, I take out the unfinished letter and start wondering what I should write to this girl I've never met before.

"The following recruits report to the administration office." What's this? "One. Two." Sucker. "Eighteen. Thirty-one. Forty-four...." Damn.

I put on my slippers and line up behind the other recruits in front of the office. When all the recruits have arrived, there are about thirty of us.

"Put on your boots and report to the parade ground. You have five minutes. Go."

The thirty of us scatter to our respective squad rooms and put on our boots.

"Where are you going?" Seok-bae asks.

"I don't know."

When I get to the parade ground, I take note of the other recruits called out. It's a gathering of the rejects, the fat and uncoordinated and weak-willed.

"You're going to be punished for not finishing the run with your platoons. You, right standard. Rows of four."

We hurry to close ranks in rows of four. I'm sandwiched between two behemoths of recruits, in terms of height and girth. To my left is a baby-faced monster of a kid; I think it's One from the first squad. He looks like a younger, Korean Jonathan Winters. To my left is a recruit I've never seen before and I wonder how I could've missed someone so big.

"Put your arms around each other's necks."

The behemoths put their arms around my neck and each arm feels like they're a good fifty pounds. I strain to reach my arms around their necks but my disadvantage in height is further hampered by the weight of their arms.

"Sit." "Stand." "Sit." "Stand." "Sit." "You failed your comrades. Stand." "Sit." "Stand." "Sit." My ass and legs are burning. My neck and shoulders are sore from the weight of my neighbors' arms. Damn Korean Jonathan Winters. It feels like he's leaning on me, making me help him stand. My hands are slick because my neighbor's necks are slick with sweat. "Rabbit-walk around the parade ground." "Don't drop your arms from each others' necks."

I learn rabbit-walking is basically walking while crouching; it looks like we're hopping the way we bounce up and down with each step. There's too much weight on my shoulders. I can't keep my head up. I can barely feel my ass and legs and neck and shoulders anymore. They're not numb. My body is a single ball of intense pain.

"We're going to sing a battle hymn. '*Meoshitneun Sanai.*' One, two, three, four."

This might be the sorriest rendition of a song titled "A Cool Man" that ever was heard.

"Cool (cool!) / men (men!) / Although there are many
That's exactly what I am / A man / A cool man
Undefeated in battle
Passionate in love / Passionate in love
That's exactly what I am, a man"

Every "man" is either grunted or shouted in agony or lunacy. The rest of the words are a confused slur mixed with coughing and spitting and whimpers. The pitch is like a roller coaster, the highs prompted by challenges from the *jogyo*—"Is this the best you can do? Louder."—which degenerates into pained grunting for the lows.

When we've completed a lap of the parade ground, they order us to stand.

"Are you going to let down your comrades?"

"No, sir!"

"Louder."

"No, sir!"

"Sit." "Stand." "Sit." "Stand." "Next time, nobody drops out, got it?" There's going to be a next time?

"Report back to your squad rooms."

Johnny's not in the squad room when I return from the punishment, my knees wobbling and my uniform damp with sweat. My sweat and sweat from Korean Jonathan Winters with the logs for arms. I unlace my boots and scoot back to my place in front of my locker.

"Where's Johnny?" I ask Forty-two.

"I don't know," he answers. "Where did you go?"

"Getting punished for not finishing the run two days ago."

"That sucks."

"Yeah."

I try to get to writing the letter for the third time but am interrupted again by Squad Leader Lee walking into the room.

"Put on your boots. Time for mental education."

After dinner, the platoon is led to a squad room past the administration office. Instead of sitting through more mental education, we're going to watch an instructional video. The video is on how to detect the warning signs of a comrade contemplating suicide, that much I can understand.

I look around for Johnny. He's still not back from wherever he went before dinner. I worry about him. These days when I talk to him, he always has something depressing to say. He's been complaining about his shoulder and back more and more lately and he's always slow to get ready. Squad Leader Lee has caught on to that and has been picking on him with greater zeal. I wonder how long he's going to last and what will happen when he breaks.

On the screen, the camera pans up the body of a dead recruit on the coroner's table and stops at the grayish corpse's face and neck. The corpse has an average kid's face; I could probably mistake the guy for sixty percent of the company. None of us really have much color in our faces, either. The striking thing is the thin, dark purplish line around his neck. The kid had hanged himself with his bootstrings.

I cringe reflexively. If I had to, I'd choose a nice, thick rope over bootstrings any day. Every time I lace up my boots, the strings dig into my fingers and leave behind purplish-pink indentations. As an instrument for hanging, it might only win out over guitar strings. What a painful way to go. I guess there's not much available to a soldier. Unlike the civilized parts of Korea, the buildings on base are mostly one-story structures. At three stories, our barracks is the tallest building I've seen and the windows in our rooms are barred to prevent a jump. We don't have access to knives, and I doubt a spork could break skin even if you jabbed it in into your wrist.

When the video ends, Squad Leader Lee turns on the lights and orders us back to our squad rooms for nightly cleaning.

Johnny's waiting for us in the squad room when we return. When he turns to greet us, he's grinning. It's maybe the first time I've seen anything resembling a smile on his face. He usually has this lost, deer-in-the-headlights look, as if the Army caught him unawares. The look I probably have, now that I think about it.

"Where have you been?" I ask as I put away my notebook and get ready to clean.

He just gives me a smile and a shrug and runs off to wash rags. There's a spring in his step as he leaves the squad room. This unexpected cheer continues through cleaning and evening call. When Squad Leader Lee takes account of the injured or sick, Johnny doesn't raise his hand.

"Nothing from you today?" he asks Johnny, an eyebrow raised.

"No, sir," Johnny replies with the crispness that's very becoming of a soldier.

After the whispers have died out and everybody has fallen asleep, the question I can't shake is: What happened to Johnny?

D-703 (24FEB04): Individual Battles with Some Help from My Friends

The training ground for today's individual combat evaluation looks like hell, probably the closest thing to what I've imagined a battlefield might look like. The training ground is not a "ground" but a mountain. It has to be at least a forty percent grade. From what I can gather, today's training is essentially the "soldier singlehandedly storming the hill and taking it alone" scenario. Strewn across the face of the mountain are natural and man-made obstacles, a generous spattering of worn tires and barbed wire, and the tears and suffering of thousands and thousands of recruits who had the misfortune of training at the 37th Division.

They've given us old Korean War-era uniforms, worn, drab olive green uniforms to wear because the severity of the training is going to ruin the uniforms we've been issued, which have to last us the two years. The training is going to ruin our bodies but our status right now is slightly below uniforms.

The first fifty meters are an uphill crawl over cold, rocky earth. On my belly, I extend my arms with rifle in hands, raise my right leg to make a ninety degree angle, push with my elbows and right foot, and repeat at a furious pace. My elbows are being rubbed raw, shocks running up to my shoulders as bone is repeatedly brought down hard on the sharp rocks scattered here and there. It feels like my dick is being scraped off my groin as I drag my body across the unforgiving terrain.

When we were to practice crawling on the parade ground the day before, Squad Leader Lee drew a long line in the dirt with his boot and announced that the last recruits across the line would get punished. I crawled as if my life depended on it and when I made it across the line, I realized I had made it first out of the twenty-two in my squad.

"Forty-four. Come here."

I stood up, gave my trainee number, and ran up to him.

"Good job," he said, giving me the only compliment I've ever heard him give anyone. "Maybe there's some use for you after all."

I was proud of myself and could feel the envy and spite of the rest of the squad, especially those who finished last. My pride was short-lived.

"Give me your rifle," Lee ordered, and I handed him my rifle, stating my trainee number and rifle serial number. He took a quick once over and the flung the rifle at my feet.

"Get on your hands and feet."

In my haste, I hadn't been mindful of the muzzle of the rifle and there was a small amount of dirt in the tip of the barrel. I finished first for the first time throughout training and I still ended up doing pushups with the stragglers, my usual group. This is the next lesson: don't stick out. If I had finished in the middle of the pack, Lee wouldn't have checked my rifle and I wouldn't have been punished.

By the end of the fifty meters, my body feels like it's been run through a meat grinder, my elbows raw and bloody. I get up and take cover behind a large outcropping of rocks for the next session of the training.

The next fifty meters is not much easier on the body, but at least I'm upright the entire time. There is a series of obstacles and at each call from the *jogyo*, we run to take cover behind the next position and assume a firing position. The rest behind each obstacle, some boulders or a short wall or a bunker, is short but welcome. At the end of the fifty meters is a tire on a post, and I swing at it with the butt of my rifle before moving on to the next section.

Ahead of me is the typical barbed-wire field, and thankfully the mud beneath the barbed wire has frozen over. This time, instead of crawling on our bellies for the fifty meters, I wriggle on my back, my left hand holding on to the tips of my rifle and helmet and my right hand making sure I don't get caught on the barbs. It's slow going, the only propulsion coming from my feet and the slight right-left-right-left wriggling of my shoulders. The front of my body has received adequate punishment from the first fifty meters; it's now time for my back and ass.

When I emerge from the other side of the barbed wire field, my whole body has received a thorough beating. I pretend to throw a grenade and charge the last fifty meters up the mountain, rifle at the ready, yelling at the top of my lungs. As I charge, I hope that war never breaks during my two years and decide that if it ever does, I'll never charge foolishly into the fray to be cut down while out of breath and trying to yell at the top of my lungs. Retarded as I am, even two years of brainwashing wouldn't be enough to make me act so foolhardy.

At the top of the mountain, I'm now fighting for breath between coughs that rack my whole body. A long string of thick, tensile spit hangs from my lips practically to the ground, the result of the combination of dehydration, dry weather, and the persistent flu.

"You," the *jogyo* at the top of the hill yells out, pointing at me. "Jog back down to the bottom."

"Yes, sir," I choke out, the spit dangling back and forth with each syllable. I cut the fishing-wire phlegm at my lips with my hand and jog back down the hill to wait in line for a second run-through.

The next morning, the company has assembled on the parade ground with helmets, cartridge belts, gas masks, and rifles for a second go at the base run. I'm in no better condition than at the end of last week. Any stored energy I might have had from the weekend's sugar binge has been depleted by yesterday's evaluation, which has also left me sore, bloody, and bruised. My flu is still at a level similar to last week. The only difference is that I know how long and brutal the run is and what awaits me if I don't finish with my platoon.

"1st Platoon, run," Squad Leader Lee commands, and we lead the procession out of the parade ground.

At the same point as in the previous run, the pangs hit, a shiv just under my right lung, puncturing my right lung, deflating it and me. I can't do this. The imagined hands reaching from the ground and pulling on my legs. I can't do this.

"Come on," Seok-bae urges me from my left, just like last time. This time I know who he is and a small sense of camaraderie pushes me on, pushes me past the mark I gave up last time. The breaths come short and sharp as I come down with each step and every fourth step I take a deep, gasping breath that lasts for two steps, then three steps, four steps. I can't breathe. I'm choking on the hardening and layering phlegm in my throat. I'm gasping and wheezing and making all sorts of sounds unbefitting a soldier, or any human being with a shred of dignity, for that matter.

The tightness in the small of my back is unbearable. My body is failing on all fronts. My willpower is running on empty. I can't do this.

In that moment, for some reason, I think about Mom. I imagine that same picture—her sitting in front of the sewing machine in her office, her glasses on the table, her head cradled in her hands. I'm a piece of shit with a piece of shit body and this is not how she raised me. This is not the son she worked long hours at menial jobs for, the son she's grieved over so many times. There's no possible way she'll know, but I'm going to finish this run for her.

The rest of the first lap is a battle but I make small goals. Hang on until the end of the first lap. Hang on for another quarter lap. Hang on for another quarter lap.

When the last half lap is remaining, the road stretching out in front of me, I feel a lightness in my body and soul. I can do this. I'm doing this. I look up into the bleak, winter sky, and I must be hallucinating due to a lack of oxygen, but I can almost see Mom smiling.

After mental education, I'm called back to Lieutenant So's office. I'm to translate something to see whether I'll be eligible for the test to be a linguist. He hands me the dictionary that my uncle sent and a sheet of paper on which two fairly lengthy blocks of Korean words have been typed.

"You'll have an hour," the lieutenant tells me with the worried look he seems to have whenever he talks to me. "Go back to the squad room and work and bring it back to me when you are finished."

"Yes, sir."

I turn to leave and when I'm at the door, he calls me.

"Yes, sir?"

"You have to do it by yourself, got it? No help from your squad mates."

"I understand, sir."

Back in the squad room, the others are getting ready for cleaning. I tell them sorry, I have to translate something and sit down in front of my locker. I inspect the dictionary first, one of my first truly personal possessions. It's a standard Korean-English only dictionary, blue pleather with a plastic dust cover, the sections marked on the side by character. It's a nice size; at about 3.5" by 6", it's a good fit for most of my pockets. The others want to see and I let them because, unlike mail call, I got something and they didn't.

From what I can gather, the sheet of paper is a personal statement for a Lieutenant Choi. I'm actually surprised at how much I can gather although it's just the general sense of the document and not the specifics. The first paragraph is an introduction, talking about his parents and his studies and duties as an officer. This guy is our *Jeonghun* Officer. Troop Information and Education Officer, the dictionary says. He's one of the *gyogwan* that gives long-winded speeches for mental education. The second paragraph is about his motives for applying to become an Airport Officer? Aviation Officer?

I get the feeling that I'm being used for free translation but I don't mind because it's going to be shitty anyway. I have a dictionary but some things just don't make sense. His family was harmonious? His mother had sentiment? Some things I just can't find in the dictionary. *Daejeokgwanhwaknip* and *Gukgag-wanbangongjeong*.[31] There's a lot of talk about being diligent and "doing his duties" and "making efforts" and "doing his best."

---

[31] I still don't know exactly what these terms mean.

After endlessly flipping through the dictionary and jotting down translations of the many, too many, words I don't know, I set about putting them together into coherent sentences. For the most part, I skip the sections where I don't understand the word or expression and put in my own interpretation when it doesn't seem so important. It doesn't seem like this lieutenant knows how to write anyway.

It's nearing the end of the hour and I've left a couple of sentences untranslated, mostly because I have no idea what they mean. The other members of the squad are returning from or finishing up their cleaning duties and preparing for evening call.

Thirty-nine is behind me, lining up the uniforms in my locker.

"Hey, Se-hee," I say. "Could you help me for a second?"

"Sure, *hyeong.*"

"What do these things mean?" I ask, pointing at the few things that I don't understand.

He kneels down to pretend to straighten up the bedding and looks at it with me.

"It's hard to explain," he says and grabs Fifty and eventually a small group convenes near my locker to help me with the translation. From the jumble of whispers, I get that the long strings of characters have something to do with a soldier's mentality regarding enemies and "Reds," Communists.

I thank them and they scatter quickly as I finish filling in the blanks. As I return to the squad room after turning in my translation to Lieutenant So, I realize that although I have to get through this experience, I'm not alone.

D-701 (26FEB04): Comprehensive Training

Today's the big day. Comprehensive training. Two days, one night, two forty-kilometer hikes with full packs, and the gas chamber. I'm coherent when I wake in the morning. Just my luck. Yesterday, I experienced a flare-up of my fever and after a visit to the infirmary, I was sent to a squad room reserved for sick recruits to recuperate. I only got an hour or two of sleep before I was kicked awake by a *jogyo* to get ready for pictures. In all the pictures of the company, platoon, and squad, I'm sure I had a look of a man in pain, furrowed brows over squinted eyes, the ends of my mouth curled downward. That's the story of my life, never sick enough to be excluded but always sick enough to look stupid. Forty has hemorrhoids. He'll be riding in the mess 10-ton to the training ground. Some guys get all the luck.

We spend the morning packing. Spare uniform, PT uniform, long underwear, underwear, and toiletry bag in the pack, two pairs of socks in the front pocket, mess kit secured above it, field shovel to the side, nylon blanket folded and secured beneath, wool blanket rolled up tightly like a Tootsie Roll and secured around the frame. The wool blanket is the difficult part. It involves measurements using our Monami pens, which double as a ruler, and teamwork in rolling it tight and folding it into itself. The straps on the bags are falling apart and on closer inspection have been sewed over and over again. One strap seems like it'll give out on the way, so I take out my sewing kit and try to sew a few more stitches into the tough fabric, which has hardened through the years. The needle meets stiff resistance. I wonder which will give way first, the fabric of the strap or the cracked and bleeding skin of my fingers.

Squad Leader Lee has stopped by a few times but has mostly left us to pack in peace and quiet. Checking the door first, I open up my pillow with my back to the door, dig through the plastic macaroni and find the last of my stash: a pack of imitation M&Ms and an Atlas candy bar. I stick them in my gas-mask pouch and inspect the bag to make sure it's not conspicuously lumpy.

After lunch, we put on our full gear and packs, helmets on our heads and gas masks slung around our bodies. They unlock the gun-lockers, and we get our rifles and sit on the linoleum and wait until they call us out onto the parade ground.

The march is going to be long. A forty-kilometer march with a twenty-kilogram pack on my back. The squad leaders say that we're going to get blisters on our feet and our shoulders are going to be rubbed raw. The best way to prevent blisters is to wear women's stockings under your socks, they say. There's no way to get women's stockings, so some recruits double up on socks. I save my extra pair of socks for my shoulders.

The first leg of our journey starts out through the local alleyways. We walk in two long lines on either side of the road. Messages for converging or diverging our ranks come from the front, and messages to watch out for passing cars and to slow down when the rear ranks are lagging are passed up and down the lines with a tap on the shoulder.

We soon pass the few country homes in the vicinity of our base and walk along the side of a country road. An old woman waits at a bus stop. There hasn't been a single trace of a bus for the past forty minutes. No cars, either.

The pack of the recruit in front of me is coming apart. It's Two. With all the converging and diverging, he has somehow ended up in front of me. First, his mess kit falls to the ground with a clank. It's followed by his field shovel and nylon blanket. He's slowing down the line. A *jogyo* runs up.

"You," he says, pointing at me. "Pick up his things."

Damn it.

Two and I pick up his shit and cradle it in our arms with our rifles and continue on with the march.

After another half an hour, they allow us to take a bathroom break at a small open area at an intersection next to a stream.

"You have ten minutes. Check your equipment. If you need to piss, piss over the ledge over there." The *jogyo* points over at the drop off next to the stream.

I toss Two his equipment, drop my pack on the curb, and go to piss. It's just like processing, a long line of recruits pissing side by side into the stream. I piss, button up, stretch my neck and shoulders, curse, check the knots and straps on my pack, stretch some more.

When the ten minutes are up, the *jogyo* call us back into formation.

The second leg is a winding mountain road. The grade is steep. My legs burn, lactic acid burning in my calves. The mountain is endless. Around every curve and bend, the mountains climb ever higher. I'm learning the topography of Korea with my body. Seventy percent mountain. "A sea in a heavy gale" and the crest of the wave is nowhere in sight.

Somehow we are marching on level ground again. All around us are flat fields of amber. Where have the mountains gone? We stop. A ten-minute break is called again, and we lower our packs to the roadside and sit in the ditches on either side of the road. I straddle my pack and rest my rifle across my lap. The slight breeze chills my chest, wet with sweat. I shiver.

I watch Squad Leader Lee pass and slip my hand into my gas-mask pouch. I tear open the pack of M&Ms, scoop out a small handful and slip them into my mouth. I let them melt there. I don't dare chew. The squad leaders have eyes like hawks.

I stare out into the fields and let the chocolate-laden saliva wash down my throat. I don't know if it's the sugar or the rest but I feel some of my strength returning. I stretch and rotate my shoulders and give them a good rub. I look up and down the line again and then slip another small handful of the forbidden chocolate into my mouth.

We arrive at the comprehensive-training ground and are at once set to the task of setting up camp. The field is a broad, elevated stretch of land with a deep ditch around its periphery. The earth is frozen solid, the ice giving the ochre terrain a silvery sheen. They assign us a plot, two to a plot, and we get to work.

Forty-five and I stretch out the two olive-green tent sheets and start buttoning the sections together. Like everything else, the canvas sheets are Korean-war era and half of the buttons don't clasp together. We use our shovels to hammer the pegs into the frozen earth.

As we set up our tent, the sun sets and darkness falls over the camp.

We are called over to the adjacent grounds where the mess two-ton has set up preparations for dinner. We eat quietly, soup in the small mess-kit tray and fried rice in the main tin. After eating and washing out our mess kits, we again get into formation. It's pitch black out.

We're going to do night-firing practice. They take us in groups of ten to a ridge at the far end of the camp. They say there are targets at the other end of the field, but they aren't visible in the dark. At the order to fire, we fire at random, emptying our magazines in the darkness.

At night, the cold is unbearable. A chill draft surges into our tent. I take off my uniform and put on my PT uniform and then put my uniform on top. I drift in and out of restless sleep.

The flap opens and a flashlight shines at the entrance of the tent.

"Wake up," the *bulchimbeon* says. "It's your turn."

"I'm awake."

I put on my boots at the entrance of the tent. The black leather is freezing to the touch. I lace them on and step out into the cold. I follow the previous *bulchimbeon*, Johnny, to the command post and we report the shift change.

The temperature is at least fifteen below zero and the camp is silent. The frost on the ground has accumulated, and the ground sparkles from the white of the floodlights near the command post. It crunches softly beneath my feet as I stroll between the tents.

After my hour is up, I walk back to my tent and wake Forty-five up. I have no qualms in waking him from sleep. When we report the shift change, I notice a boiling pot of water. I fill up my canteen to the brim and then walk back to my tent in the darkness, Forty-five lighting my way with the flashlight.

Back in the tent, I lift the canteen to my lips and scald my lips and the inside of my mouth. I curse and then lie down, exhausted. I pull the sleeping bag over my head and clutch the canteen to my chest. It's giving off enough heat for me to drift off into restless sleep.

The next day is the one we've been dreading the most. The last course of the comprehensive evaluation is a trip to the gas chamber. Squad Leader Lee lectured on the gas chamber a couple of days prior, and the one thing that stuck in my head was that he said that CS gas was prohibited by almost every country in the world.

1st and 2nd Platoons are called off to the side and sit. 3rd through 5th Platoons are standing in formation in the middle of the field. We watch them from what we consider a distance. A *jogyo* walks over, appoints a standard, and orders them to gather in tight around the standard.

A *jogyo* in a gas mask walks into the center of the group and moments later, I see a small cloud of white smoke rise from the center of the group. Watching the group, I see the cloud of smoke trail off in one direction and then the other. The *jogyo* is circling the group. The cacophony of retching and coughing echoes across the field and a few *jogyo* stand on the outskirts of the crowd and stop recruits who are attempting to flee. We watch, happy that it's not us, but not for long. A strong wind blows down from the mountains and my eyes are burning and I'm retching, too. The gas has lost a lot of its potency as it traveled across the field on the wind, but it's still enough to be painful.

Squad Leader Lee approaches.

"You think you're lucky, don't you? You're not. We don't have enough gas pellets so only 1st and 2nd Platoons are going into the gas chamber. Those guys? They're done."

"When you're there, listen to the squad leader's instructions carefully. Don't try to run. The door is bolted from the outside. If you try to run, you will have to go through it again."

"After we let you out, don't rub your eyes. If you rub your eyes, it'll only get worse. Stick out your arms like an airplane and run. If your eyes still burn, wash them out with water from your canteens. But run first."

They call us up in groups of ten. We walk up a path behind the gas chamber and wait. I'm scared.

"You're up."

We walk single-file into a small, dark room. There is no light in the room.

Two *jogyo* in gas masks stand in the front of the room.

"Listen to us carefully or you'll have to do it again," one of them orders with a megaphone so we can hear clearly.

"Yes, sir!"

"Put your gas masks on."

One of the *jogyo* is huddled over a small contraption in the front. He lights something. There's a phosphorescent flare and then long, thick tendrils of white smoke snake out from the center of the room.

"It's fine with your gas masks, isn't it?" It is. Everyone has put on their gas masks correctly and is fine.

"Take them off." Damn. I reach up hesitantly. The room is full of white smoke. "Take them off, sons of bitches."

I pull the gas mask off and am immediately assaulted by the effects of the gas. In an instant, my eyes, nose, and throat are burning, are on fire, and filling with tears and snot and phlegm. I'm coughing so violently, I can't breathe. I'm going to die. One of the *jogyo* walks over to one of the other recruits who has refused to take off his gas mask and grabs him by the front of the uniform. Take it off, son of a bitch, I think as I'm doubled over, thick, salty liquid streaming from every orifice.

"Everyone get up. Put your arms around each other's necks." At this point, one recruit has broken from the group and is rushing toward the door. "Stop. Nobody can leave until we finish."

They make us sit, stand, sit, stand, sit, do some calisthenics, and finish with a battle hymn. "Louder, you sons of bitches. We're going to keep singing until I'm satisfied."

I'm going to die. I'm going to die. I can't breathe. I'm losing consciousness. The words of the song come out as a death rattle.

"Stand up." I will myself up. The *jogyo* knocks on the door and the door opens, blessed sunlight streaming into the room. We hurriedly march single-file into the light.

Even outside, the contaminants are still spread throughout our respiratory systems.

"Don't touch your eyes," the *jogyo* at the door orders. "Run."

We run with our arms outstretched like airplane wings, run the length of the field and curve around to the left. The wind brushes some of the contaminants from our eyes, and breathing the clean air has helped a little with the gas in our throats and lungs, but at the end of the track, I'm still in pain. I collapse onto my hands and knees and try to empty my lungs, coughing and spitting copious amounts of contaminated mucus in long, sticky strands.

"Here," a squad mate says, holding out a canteen. I rinse out my eyes, and when the pain in my eyes is bearable, I gargle with the water and spit it up across the ground.

After everyone has gone through the gas chamber, we break camp and start on our march back to base. It's already getting dark. The few street lights along the mountain roads flicker on, and the rows of soldiers pass beneath in silence. In the mountains, there are no lights, and we proceed, following the lights of the batons the *jogyo* wave intermittently. We travel over the mountains and through the valleys and finally return to a familiar path, the one leading to the rear gate of the base. We circle around the parade ground and return to our squad rooms, completely spent and abused.

"Put away your equipment and change into your PT uniforms," Squad Leader Lee orders and leaves us to tend to our wounds.

After the equipment is put away and we've changed into our PT uniforms, many take off their socks and inspect their blisters. I pop with my sewing needle and drain the fluid from a couple of large blisters on the balls of my feet. The blistered skin peels off easily until it's just one large blister about the size of three quarters. My feet are disgusting, like a tub of cottage cheese in which part has hardened into a cracked crust, and the rest is raw and smooth. I look at the others, some of whom are sewing thread into their blisters, leaving a black X of thread inside.

Squad Leader Lee returns and sends us to the mess hall. We sit on long tables like picnic benches on the other side of the mess hall, the side that has been blocked off from us. A few recruits are chosen to hand out bowls of cup ramen, and we go by table to fill up with hot water from large urns on tables against the wall.

There's nothing different about the ramen but it's the best ramen I've ever had in my life. My nose runs from the spicy MSG broth, and my taste buds are overloaded with the salty, spicy flavor.

D-695 (03MAR04): The End of Boot Camp and a New Beginning

With the comprehensive training behind us, there is nothing of substance to learn for the remainder of boot camp. March 1st is a national holiday in Korea, and while we are not allowed to kick our feet up, they've given us menial tasks like giving the mess hall trays a wiping down. The atmosphere is much more hospitable and even Squad Leader Lee's visits are infrequent.

The next day, we turn in our uniform tops to get our actual name tags and private insignia sewed on. When I get my uniform top back, I marvel at a name tag that actually reads my given name instead of the white tag that read 2-44.

The day before graduation, they have us gathered in the auditorium again. At the front, a screen and projector have been set up, and a middle-aged woman, the first woman I've seen in five weeks besides the old lady at the bus station, is working on the computer. On the screen is a spreadsheet with the ID numbers of all the recruits in our training unit. She presses a button and seemingly random numbers pop up in the column on the right of the screen. She presses it again and the numbers change. We're being given our occupational specialties by a random number generator. It's a lottery.

It's here that we are being assigned our stations in the next stage of our existence as privates. The lucky will be *unjeonbyeong*, truck drivers and officers' chauffeurs, at a unit close to their hometowns, and the unlucky will be lugging 20-kilogram artillery shells or manning a lonely guard post overlooking the East Sea.

The woman announces that these results are our final results and starts reading down the numbers and occupational specialties. Stifled groans and muted squeals of joy can be heard throughout the auditorium. Seok-bae is going to be an *unjeonbyeong*. Good for him, I think. He deserves it after all the shit that Squad Leader Lee has given him. When my name is called, I don't know how to respond. 100th Replenishment Unit.

"You're going to Daejeon," Alabama whispers when he stops by the squad room later in the day.

"You sure?"

"Yeah, I have it on a reliable source." Everything Alabama tells me is "on a reliable source," but everything he has told me has also been complete bullshit.

The last full day of basic training is spent in preparing for and partici-
pating in the closing ceremony. We spend the morning marking out our positions on the parade ground so that the formation is perfect when seen from
the podium, where later in the day the commander of the 37th Division gives
us a long-winded speech and his congratulations. Basic training is over. We've
graduated. It's only the first stage, and there is still a long road ahead, but I
admit I feel pretty damn good.

Even Lee's occasional barbs have little effect on us.

"You're looking forward to going to your permanent stations, aren't you?"

"Yes, sir!" we respond in unison.

"It's better you don't. You have *donggi*[32] here. At your permanent stations,
there's nothing but devils," he says, smirking as he walks out the room.

The last day at boot camp, they hand out duffel bags and give us time to
pack all our belongings after breakfast. Everybody is headed to different units
across the countryside, and there's much asking about where each person is
going. Most have a general idea where they are going. The 31st Division is in
Gwangju, the 39th is in Changweon, the 50th is in Daegu, and the 53rd is in
Busan. Most are in the far southern areas. Johnny and I are both going to the
100th Replenishment Unit but nobody has heard of it before.

"I think it's in Seoul," one of my squad mates a couple of lockers down
shares as we pack. "Lucky bastards."

Once we're finished packing, we're called out of the squad room to
crouch in long lines that stretch down the length of the hallway on either side,
waiting for the bus that will be taking us to Cheongju railway station.

"Where're you going, Chun?" It's the *jogyo* who played the drunk in the
guard-procedures lecture. He's the most approachable *jogyo*, probably chosen
to be a drill instructor solely on account of his height and build.

"100th Replenishment Unit, sir."

"Hmm… I'm not sure where that is. I think it's in Busan." The south-
eastern-most tip of the peninsula.

Everybody seems to have their own answer for a question I didn't ask
and couldn't give a damn about. It doesn't really matter where I'm going; I
don't really have anyone to come visit me on an occasional weekend or spend
time with on my occasional furloughs. Seoul would be preferable to the countryside, but only because I know Seoul. Busan has beaches. I don't know anything about Daejeon.

---

[32] *Donggi*: People who started at the same time and are therefore one's peers

At Cheongju Station, my group gets on the slow train for a short trip to the hub at Jochiweon Station, where we head out in our own respective directions, head onward to our permanent stations.

Jochiweon Station is chaos, an Ellis Island reserved for the transport of recruits in transition. It's a sea of dull green; nervous young men in fatigues balancing themselves against the weight of their duffel bags, either marching or standing in orderly formations. The members of my company who have transfers at Jochiweon and I are crouched at one end of the platform, where a squad leader is calling out names and directing us where to go. We can barely hear his shouts over the steady sound of boots against the concrete and the trains running in and out of the station, taking another batch of fresh fish with them. Johnny and I are sent to join another group of soldiers on yet another platform to wait for our train.

All the seats in our train car are occupied by soldiers. Johnny is ordered to take an empty seat near the rear of the car and I'm directed to take an aisle seat toward the middle of the car. Following orders, I lower my duffel bag between my legs and hang my hat on a peg that protrudes from the wall of the car. The soldier sitting beside me is rigid and silent, practically comatose, and I follow his lead. Twenty minutes later, when the call for the next stop comes over the speaker, he wordlessly gets up, puts on his hat, slings his duffel bag over his shoulder and marches down the aisle and out the door. As soon as the car door closes behind him, I promptly scoot over to the window seat so I can watch the countryside pass by and to see if I can make out the direction the train is headed.

After a few minutes of waiting for passengers to board, the car door opens again and a young woman enters the train car. She is out of place for so many reasons. The only civilians who have boarded the train since Jochiweon were a handful of elderly countryfolk, their backs hunched and their skin wrinkled and darkened by the sun like overripe squash on the vine. By contrast, she is young and vibrant, fair-skinned and dressed smartly in a black skirt and ruffled linen blouse underneath a wool suit jacket. The first attractive woman I've seen in five weeks. The eyes of three dozen sexually frustrated soldiers fixate on her as she strides down the aisle, upright in the way *Homo erectus* first walked and made the other, lesser hominids watch with envy.

She sits down in the empty seat beside mine. Before she even settles in her seat, my palms are moist in the prisons of my tightly clenched fists, and my heart begins to race, beating furiously against my dog tags. The next ten

111

minutes are agonizing as I struggle over whether to break protocol and speak to her. I would surely be heard in the unnatural quiet of the car and subsequently and promptly chastised by the noncoms that patrol the aisles. But surely fate had brought her to the seat beside mine, a golden opportunity to soothe my hungry soul. Fortune had made a mistake and, for once, favored me, but would I be so bold as to capitalize on its error? Should I? Should I not? I don't know. I can feel the stares of the noncoms as they pass by, greedily taking in the presence of the young woman before menacingly glaring at me with unspoken warning.

The train comes to a halt at the next station, and the war being waged in my head is interrupted when, to my dismay, she stands up, straightens the pleats in her skirt, and exits the train. A feeling of loss overcomes me. Not the feeling that if only I had the courage to defiantly laugh in the face of punishment and speak to her, something spontaneous and beautiful, albeit short-lived, would have sparked between us—a torrid love affair with the promise of perfume-scented correspondence and hopefully at least one night of awkward passion at a small love hotel in the countryside during my 100th-day furlough. It is the sorrow of a lowly private fresh out of boot camp who has lost his only chance of having a charitable stranger act as his proxy in buying a Chocopie from the lady that periodically passes through our car with her snack cart full of forbidden fruit.

With more than a pound of regret, I unhook the clasp of the duffel bag which rests between my legs and take out the MRE[33] that we were issued before leaving the training division. The contents are printed in small black letters on the face of the tan cardboard box. Fried rice. I tear open the hard plastic packet of fried rice and the thin, clear plastic which holds the utensils and stick my fork into the rice. The fork meets with resistance, and when I pull the fork out of the packet, it's missing two tines. The rice has congealed into an impermeable solid block during its shelf life, impervious to my four-pronged attack. I try again and succeed only in breaking off the remaining two plastic tines. There are no other utensils in the box, so I break up and scoop a small chunk of rice out of the packet with my hand and unceremoniously shove it into my mouth. I pick up the box; I have to check if it has been dehydrated, it is so dry and tasteless. Even in my hunger, and despite the fact that my taste buds have been desensitized throughout basic, I cannot

---

[33] *Jeontu shiknyang*. Combat rations. Korean equivalent of an MRE (Meal Ready to Eat).

stomach any more beyond what I have in my mouth, so I force the last, hard grains of rice down my throat, pack the contents back into the box and put the MRE back into my duffel bag.

The rest of the trip is uneventful, so I spend the time sneaking glances out the window from time to time, trying to figure out at least which direction I'm headed. Recruits from other training centers come and go, and the concessions-cart lady continues to tease me as she makes her rounds after every stop. After several hours, the noncoms direct a number of us to get ready to leave. We are herded out of the train, through the station and outside into the plaza to stand in formation, four wide and six deep. While we are rushing to stand in formation, I glance up at the large sign that graces the front of the station; four characters in broad, blue, steel lettering. *Dong-dae-gu-yeok*. East Daegu Station.

Permanent Station
Daegu Metropolitan City, Korea
Second ROK Army (SROKA) HQ
6 March 2004 - 19 July 2004

D-689 (09MAR04): The Linguist Test

"Only one of you is going to stay here at Second Army Headquarters," the corporal from the 100th Replenishment Unit tells us as he leads us across the street. "The other is going to get sent to a division somewhere. You don't want to go to a division."

He leads us into an empty office and sits us at desks on opposite sides of the room.

"Wait here," he says and takes his leave.

There are no words of encouragement, his curt responses typical of the members of the Replenishment Unit. Johnny and I are unwelcome guests in their company, like strangers that sit around in your extra bedroom all day, there when you leave for work and there when you get back. They don't like us because we do nothing all day but sit in the spare squad room and stare at the wall. I don't like being there because all day I have to sit in the room and stare at the wall. That he even spoke to us at all must be borne of the relief that we'll be gone soon with the results of the test.

When he returns, he has the test sheets in hand.

"You have thirty minutes."

On the sheet in front of me are two questions, one in Korean and one in English. The one in Korean is four lines long, a paragraph, and the one in English is a single sentence.

I skim the first question for words I know.

"2005 September *gaechwoedweon 4cha 6jahwoedam-eseo ne gaji cheukmyeon-eseo euieui-reul gajinda*. First, *6jahwoedam-eui* goal *jaehwakinhayeo* North Korea *bi-haekhwa* problem *geomjeong* possible peaceful way *dalseonghagiro haetgo*; second, North Korea and the U.S. relationship *jeongsanghwa-e habeuihaetda*. Third, North *haek* throw away *ihaeng-eui daetga-ro* energy support *hagiro haetgo*; fourth, Korean peninsula peace *cheje hyeopsang-eul chujinhagiro habeuihaetda.*"[34]

I take a look at the second question, the question to be translated into

---

[34] "The fourth round of six-party talks initiated in September 2005 held significance in four aspects. First, it was agreed to resolve the problem of the denuclearization of North Korea in a peaceful manner, re-assessing the goals of the six-party talks. Second, it was agreed to normalize diplomatic relations between North Korea and the US. Third, it was agreed to provide energy support to North Korea as recompense for the abandonment of the North Korean nuclear program. Fourth, it was agreed to pursue negotiations toward the establishment of a peace system for the Korean peninsula."

Korean.

"President Bush stated last week that he would consider an exchange of energy and food aid in return for a renewed commitment to end its nuclear-weapons program."

I stare blankly at my paper for ten minutes, sigh, laugh, and descend into despair.

By the time the thirty minutes are up, I've managed to finish the test, which only means I have something written down for both questions. Unfortunately, the former consists primarily of bullshit, filling in monstrous gaps with guesses and ambiguous language, and the latter is written with the flourish of a pre-schooler—I'm fairly certain it's gibberish.

The written test is followed by an interview during which I prove my inability goes beyond the written word. After lights out, Johnny wants to talk about the test but I'm not in the mood to talk.

It's not that I'm disappointed. It's only natural that Johnny, who was acted as my interpreter during boot camp, is going to do better than me, who needed one. I'm not even sure I want to be a linguist. Put me in a job where I don't have to talk at all—that would make the most sense. My unwillingness to talk after lights out is because today was just another reminder of my inability and inadequacy, even after six weeks of hearing nothing but Korean. It was another reminder of why I shouldn't be here.

Johnny is smoking outside with another standby, a sergeant from a new recruit-training unit—a *jogyo*. He's a nice enough guy, but when he told us earlier about how often *jogyo* get to leave on award furloughs, it irked me that the Army is rewarding pricks like Squad Leader Lee.

When the door opens, I expect Johnny coming back from his smoke, but it's the corporal from the administration office.

"Change into your uniform and pack your duffel bag. You're going to your permanent station now." I must be going to a division, leaving early for the long trip ahead.

"Yes, sir."

"Hurry up," he says as he leaves the room.

While I'm packing, Johnny and the sergeant return.

"What're you doing?" Johnny asks.

"They told me pack. I guess I'm leaving."

Johnny helps me pack while I change. I've just got my boots laced when the corporal returns and tells me to follow him. I pick up my duffel bag and sling it over my shoulder, mouth a silent goodbye and good luck to Johnny and follow the corporal out the room. I'm glad that Johnny's going to be staying here. I never got around to asking what happened to him on the day his attitude changed and, even though he's been doing much better, I still worry if he'll be able to stick out the two years.

There's no jeep waiting out front. Instead, we cross the street and into a room in the same building the linguist test was held. Personnel Office, the door reads.

D-688 (10MAR04): Fresh Fish

After processing at the first personnel office for the base, I'm sent to a second one for the company. I'm greeted by three conscripts, all corporals, two of them smiling broadly. "I'm your father," one of them announces. I tell him I understand, sir, but I have no idea what he means.

I'm trying to wrap my head around how I ended up here. Johnny should be here and I should be on a train to Gwangju or some small unit in the countryside which needs a linguist who can't translate or interpret.

"There are forty linguists in the company," the sergeant at the first personnel office told me during processing. "The longest we've had is around ten years, but most are less than four years." He was talking about time spent overseas, which was in response to my response that I lived in America twenty-two years.[35]

While on standby in a squad room next to the company administration office—yet more sitting at attention and staring at the wall—I get plenty of visitors because I lived in America for twenty-two years.

Most of my visitors stop by only briefly, long enough to laugh at my pronunciation or my inability to answer their questions. It happens each time although I've gone through it thirty or forty times today. As it nears dinner and my self-esteem is at a new all-time low, the door flings open again and two nasty-looking sergeants burst into the room with broad, ear-to-ear smiles on their faces.

"You're the American, right?" asks the shorter, older-looking one with

---

[35] I was 25, but my father's business took us to Korea for two years from 1988 to 1990 and I had been in Korea for a year before the Army.

bad skin.

"Yes, sir."

"You're pretty good at English, then?"

"Uh… yes, sir."[36]

"You know any Korean songs?" the other one butts in.

"A li-little, sir."

"Sing."

I hesitate. My mouth hangs open on its hinges as I think of the words to explain that I don't know any songs well enough to sing without the lyrics on a karaoke screen.

"Now," the first one demands, the smile gone from his face.

"Y-yes, sir," I stammer and start singing but I'm nervous and stressed and I can't remember the words and because I can't remember the words I lose track of the melody. I keep going because they haven't told me to stop and my face is burning, burning a bright beet red, and I fight to continue through the numbing humiliation, coarse laughter ringing in my throbbing ears. The sergeants are rolling around on the floor, holding their sides, choking on their laughter for air.

"That's… enough…," one manages to choke out between giggles.

Once the giggles have subsided, the sergeants jump up and run out the door, leaving me to soak in my humiliation.

It's my first day and I've already realized Squad Leader Lee was right about things being worse at our permanent stations. As awful as boot camp was, at least recruits suffer together. What's worse, the others find me a curiosity, and being the object of curiosity in the Army is a hellish thing. I'm the freak show, the Elephant Man on display for the others to gawk at and poke between the bars. Admission is free for everyone to see the American and make him sing and dance.

The company commander, Captain Jin, has a grotesque appearance. When I enter his office for my enter-interview, I see what looks like a water-logged corpse in an Army uniform, bloated flesh about to burst through the seams. His face is swollen and ruddy, his eyes wide and bulbous.

"Sit," he says gruffly, pointing to a chair in front of his desk.

"Yes, sir."

---

[36] Korean modesty dictated that I say no, but I couldn't very well say no, considering English was my only language.

He looks over my personal information sheet for long moments with those bulging eyes before he addresses me again.

"What do you think about *dongseongae*?"

"I d-didn't hear you clearly, sir."

"*Dongseongae*," he repeats.

"I don't know wh-what that is, sir."

"You know, a man and a man having *seonggwangye*.[37] Gays."

"I don't know well, sir. I guess it's o-okay, sir."

"You're not gay, are you?"

"No, sir."

"You're from America. There're a lot of gays there, right?"

"Yes, sir."

"But you're not gay?"

"No, sir."

"Okay. That's it. You can go."

As I walk back down to the administration office, I'm puzzled. He doesn't give a damn that I'm an American or that I can't speak Korean. He doesn't care that I'm in the Army against my will. It seems all he cares about is whether or not I'm homosexual.

D-687 (11MAR04): Private Lessons

It's the morning, just before breakfast. I'm sitting in the squad room, Squad Room 15, at attention, my back rigid, my arms rigid, my fists balled and resting on my knees, my gaze straight forward. I'm the only one. The others are all supine, sleeping, the brims of their battle caps low over their eyes. "Beaver," "the Professor," "Udon," Jeong-hyeon, "Big Dick" In-shik. These are my squad members and this is my squad room and I've never felt more uncomfortable.

Jeong-hyeon, the "father" whose locker is next to mine, stirs and looks up at me. "Lie down. Sleep. It's okay."

"Y-Yes, sir."

When I hesitate, he repeats, "It's okay."

"Yes, sir."

I uneasily lie down. There's no way I could sleep. I'm too tense. I've

---

[37] *Dongseongae*: Homosexuality. *Seonggwangye*: Sexual relations.

121

finally built up the nerve to lie down when I hear, "Fuck. Are you crazy?"

I snap up back to attention. Beaver is still lying down but glaring at me with one squinty eye cracked open.

"Privates don't get to sleep."

"Yes, sir."

I sit alone at attention and in silence for another ten minutes, until Beaver decides it's time for breakfast.

"Let's go eat," he announces and everyone gets up on cue. I wait until everyone has left the room, grab the squad water bottle, turn off the lights, and run after my squad.

"There are six of us," Il-su says. "Your *donggi*. January '04 serial numbers."

Il-su is a round head with round eyes and round glasses. We're in an empty squad room across the hall that is being used as a storage room, mattresses and linens strewn across the raised floors. As my *donggi*, he's brought me here to teach me my responsibilities in the company. I'm grateful because no one has bothered to tell me what I'm allowed to do but everyone is quick to tell me when I do something I'm not.

"We also have fifteen 'fathers.'"

"I was wondering about that. What does that mean?"

"'Fathers' are other conscripts who started one year earlier. Our fathers are January '03 serial numbers."

"But... what does it mean?"

"They take care of you. When you go on your 100th-day furlough, they iron your uniform and polish your boots, and when they get discharged, we make *rolling paper* for them."

I don't know what *rolling paper* is but I figure I don't need to know for now.

"There are almost two hundred people in the company. Right now, except for your *donggi*, everyone is a *gocham*." I've figured out that *gocham* means a soldier with more seniority. The way they use the word, it seems to mean something closer to "god." "You have to learn all of their names and their ranks and how many months they've been at their rank."

This is going to be a problem. Korean names all sound the same to me. I can't even remember the names of my squad members. How will I ever remember this information for each of the 150 members of the company?

"Even privates that started a month earlier, December '03 serial numbers, are your *gocham*. Watch out for Private Ja-hong. He's a December '03 private, and he's a mean son of a bitch."

"Oh, okay," I say, but I've already forgotten the name.

"As a private, you have to be the first to any company meetings, and in the morning, you have to come out before everyone else and pick up cigarette butts and garbage around the company before call. There are cleanings of the company and the headquarters building twice a day, and once you get assigned an office, you'll have to clean that, too."

I nod, but it's not a sign of understanding. Since I arrived in Daegu, I've been nodding and saying I understand, sir, ceaselessly, but the truth is I don't understand anything. My head is muddled. There's too much information to process and nothing ever makes any sense. Boot camp was a shock, but to a certain extent I expected it to be. Daegu is incomprehensible.

There were things in Korean culture that I didn't understand during my year of teaching before the Army: 25-hour convenience stores or the ignorance of the concept of personal space or how the Korean teachers would coddle and cater to Andrew, our director, when he'd show up to the karaoke and sing thirty-year-old *bhongjjak*[38] songs, wailing plaintive melodies with the machine bellowing its hokey *bhong-jjak bhong-bhong-jjak* beats. Korean Army culture is Korean civilian culture on acid.

Outside the door, I hear the muffled sounds of the PA, muted vibrations bouncing off the walls of the narrow hallway. Il-su pauses and opens the door to hear better. When the vibrations have stopped, he closes the door.

"You'll also have to listen to every PA message and inform your squad members if it's something they need to know."

I nod but with a heavy heart. I've heard the PA often while in the hallway—announcements come over the PA practically every ten minutes—and have yet to understand a single one.

"I should get back. If you need anything, let me know. I'm in 13th squad."

---

[38] *Bhongjjak* (also known as "trot"): A genre of music which originated during the Japanese colonization of Korea in the first half of the 20th century, widely popular in the 1960s and still popular among the older generations.

D-686 (12MAR04): Sergeant Beaver

I never call Sergeant Yong-gil Beaver to his face. I'd probably get lynched by the entire company if I ever let it slip. I learned of the nickname from Sergeant Hyeong-jun, the linguist I'll be replacing at the Mobilization Branch. I'm washing up after the morning cleaning when Hyeong-jun walks in, looking bored. I assume he's looking for Beaver because Hyeong-jun seems to be Beaver's only friend in the company.

"Hey, Chun."

"Private Young Jin Chun. Yes, sir."

"You know *bibeo*?" he asks in broken English—his English is terrible for a linguist—pointing at a little cartoon sticker underneath the tap admonishing soldiers to conserve water.

"Yes, sir."

"That's Yong-gil. That's Yong-gil. He's *bibeo*." He breaks into self-satisfied laughter.

Sergeant Yong-gil does bear a striking resemblance to the cartoon beaver, short and plump with squinty eyes and buck teeth. I don't know if I'm allowed to join Hyeong-jun in his mockery. I decide not to because Beaver's not only my squad leader but also the administrative assistant for the Mobilization Branch. I have to spend practically my entire day with him.

There's a part of me that feels pity for Beaver but it's completely trumped by my loathing for him. He's not more than five feet tall and absorbed with StarCraft, and it's pitiful but I hate him. It's not his love for StarCraft that bothers me although it's hard to watch StarCraft constantly. As the squad *wang-go*, king *gocham*, he decides what we watch and it's always StarCraft. The matches on the television are almost invariably re-runs and he often hobbles over to the TV to give a play-by-play to ears that only pretend to listen because he's our *wang-go*.

No, what irks me is his attitude: he's always giving me these looks, chin slightly tucked and atilt, staring at me sternly from the corner of his eyes whenever I discover yet another thing I'm not allowed to do or I'm supposed to do but didn't know. The look is always followed by an order to someone else to take me outside and "educate me."[39] It's the way he knows that he'd never have any power in real society and is determined to abuse what power

---

[39] *Gyoyuk sikida*: To discipline. Depending on the person and the offense, it compasses a broad range of mental, emotional, and physical punishments.

he has while he has it.

At the nightly cleaning of headquarters, Beaver tells me to follow him while the corporals are giving out cleaning assignments. I follow him up to the fourth floor and we stop at the door for the Mobilization Branch. He fishes a key from above the doorframe—he has to jump to reach it—and unlocks the door.

He leads me through the rows of desks clustered in the center and the filing cabinets along the wall and sits at a computer at the far end of the room.

"Sit," he says, pointing to a sofa directly behind him.

He turns on the computer, and when the computer has booted, he navigates through a long string of folders to find the icon he has hidden like porn on a family computer. I feel a small sense of relief when the Blizzard splash screen pops up on the screen and he logs on to the online server he set up with the other sergeants. I watch in silence as he plays, building his structures and sending out his troops to war like the diminutive Napoleon he is.

All of a sudden, the door flings open wide. I jump, always anxious, always nervous. Through the open door, an officer with piercing, hawkish eyes barrels straight toward us.

"*Chungseong!*" I get up and salute but Beaver stays seated.

The lieutenant colonel, a pair of flower insignias on his lapels, is fuming and yelling as he charges toward me. He's staring directly at me. I don't know what he's yelling; my blood is thundering in my ears. I stare wide-eyed and frozen in his warpath.

He stops his charge a step in front of me but he hasn't stopped yelling, his sharp jaw pumping up and down like a piston. The end of his last shout twists up into a question, and his jaw is now clenched, his eyes burning holes into me.

I look to Beaver for help, for intervention, for some sort of indication of what's happening and notice he has discreetly reached down and shut off the computer.

"Well?!" the colonel demands.

"I-I-I didn't h-hear you clearly, sir."

I can see in his expression, his hard stare, and his steep frown, that I've given the wrong answer.

"This is our new recruit," Beaver finally interjects. "He's going to be working here from Monday, sir."

"Oh," the colonel says, calming down. "Clean up quickly and return to the company."

"Yes, sir."

The colonel turns around and leaves the office as abruptly as he entered.

"Let's go," Beaver says.

I'm still shaken as we walk back to the company. Shaken and feeling used. I had wondered why Beaver took me with him but I know now. I was cannon fodder.

D-682 (16MAR04): Colonel Jeong and Colonel Kang

The Mobilization Branch has five officers—two majors, two lieutenant colonels, and a full colonel as chief—and a civilian contractor. The chief has a separate office off to the side, and when I come for the nightly cleanings of the office, after I've emptied all the restroom trash cans in the building full of soiled toilet paper, I have to clean his office as well, wiping down his desk and coffee table and sweeping and mopping and lining up his ornate name plate on his desk and re-stocking the coffee and tea tray for his visitors. He's a gruff, weathered, dark man who never smiles and never leaves his office. The two majors are outranked by the colonels and mind their own business and take care of their own work. They've risen through the ranks only to become the lowest ranked in the office, and they respond to the injustice by keeping quiet and waiting for the day they sit in their own office and order other people around again.

Colonel Jeong and Colonel Kang[40] are the de facto leaders of the Mobilization Branch, and they are as different as night and day and get along in the same way, by staying out of each other's ways. Colonel Jeong is the bushy-eyebrowed lieutenant colonel from the night Beaver brought me along as cannon fodder. He is a serious man comprised almost completely of sharp angles. The skin and muscles of his face are drawn tight around his skull and his uniform pokes out at odd angles as it hangs on his jaunty body. Colonel Kang is light-hearted, given to smiling and joking as he gives me pointless

---

[40] I've adopted the US Army custom of referring to both lieutenant colonels and full-bird colonels as simply colonel. Of course, in the Korean Army, a three-flower colonel would never allow a two-flower lieutenant colonel to be addressed in the same way.

things to do. His smile stretches across his broad face and he leans his stocky body far back in his chair when he jokes in self-satisfaction.

I'm copying the text from a thick, phonebook-sized manual to familiarize myself with typing in Korean, on orders from Beaver—"Do it until you can type 400 characters per minute," he said—when Colonel Kang taps on my shoulder.

He leads me to a small cubicle in the corner and indicates for me to sit. He slides a bucket of golf balls closer to me with his foot and hands me a rag.

"These are the chief's," he says, smiling. "Get water and clean them well."

He talks to me in simple terms as if talking to a child. I'm thankful but can't help but feel a bit insulted at the same time.

"Yes, sir."

He picks up one of the balls and holds in front of my face. "Do your best to clean the grass stains."

"Yes, sir."

I fill a small Dixie cup with water from the restroom and spend the rest of the morning and most of the afternoon in the corner, meticulously scrubbing the chief's golf balls and wondering what I'm doing here. I wonder what I would be doing if Lieutenant So hadn't arranged for me to take the linguist test and I ended up in an infantry or artillery unit. Is this what I'll be doing for the next two years—typing and cleaning and tending to the chief's balls?

Not that scrubbing the chief's golf balls isn't preferable to sitting in front of a computer or answering the phones, or rather being unable to answer the phones and getting sworn at by the caller and laughed at by Beaver and Hyeong-jun, but there are a lot of balls and my fingers are getting rubbed raw by the crusty rag, its sharp bristles unfazed by the water.

"Chun! Where's Chun?"

"I'm here, sir," I respond and rush out from behind the cubicle wall.

"Come here," Colonel Jeong beckons.

I approach the colonel's desk and stand at attention.

"What have you been doing?"

"C-cleaning the chief's golf balls, sir."

Colonel Jeong looks at me curiously for a second. "I need you to pick up my dry cleaning. You know where the dry cleaner is, don't you?"

"Yes, sir." I went there with my "father" after processing on that first day to get my unit insignia stitched on my uniforms and met Ballerino for the first time.

"Good. Hurry back."

"Yes, sir."

"When you get back, you can finish cleaning the chief's golf balls."

"Yes, sir."

D-681 (17MAR04): Private Ja-hong

I'm shredding papers in the Mobilization Branch, feeding Secret and Confidential files into the jagged mechanical teeth five pages at a time. There's an endless supply of files to be shredded because it seems every document has to be handwritten and typed and edited over and over again until our paper stock is depleted and the printer is out of toner, and only then is it signed and approved and filed away in a binder and locked in the closet until it needs to be shredded to make space for the next document. Every time the stack dwindles down to the end, Colonel Kang drops off several binders' worth of paper to facilitate the unceasing flow of new documents. I don't mind shredding paper because it's a step higher than wiping down the chief's golf balls in the corner, and I find it ironic that they're handing stacks of Secret and Confidential files to the one recruit who hasn't a shred of loyalty to the bureaucracy that is forcing him to stand in an office and shred files for pennies a day.

"Hey."

The voice belongs to a broad, slightly pear-shaped face beckoning from the doorway, another private from the Headquarters Company. He's smiling as he waves his hand with palm downward in the manner that you'd beckon a dog or a small child. I look around, and the officers and conscripts aren't paying me any heed. I walk over to the doorway and out into the hall.

The moment I step out into the hall, the private's smile disappears and his features contort into an angry mess, cheeks puffed-up and little wrinkles above a furrowed brow.

"How can I help you, sir?" My eyes scan for our unit insignia and his name, something that has become automatic for me as I'm expected to know the identity of all my *gocham*. Private Ja-hong. The name is somehow familiar.

"What is this?" he asks, pointing at the water cooler next to the central stairs.

I'm confused.

"You're not going to answer?"

"It's... a...," I begin, taking a long, distended moment to remember the word for water cooler. "It's... a... *jeo-jeongsugi*, sir."

"Did you not see it overflowing?"

"No, sir."

"Did you check the reserve tank?" he asks, kicking a white jug sitting next to the water cooler with the tip of his boot. It's the first time I've noticed it.

"No, sir."

"It's your responsibility, isn't it?"

"I don't know, sir."

"If you don't know, that's the end of it?" It's a question I often heard from Squad Leader Lee. A frustrating, irrational question. The nuance is that I should know something I had no possibility of knowing.

"No, sir."

He launches into a tirade I half understand, something about how he had to go to the bathroom and fetch the mop and mop the whole damn mess by himself and how the mess stank like shit because people dump coffee with creamer in the tray and the creamer rots in the tank. He's a private, too, so he can't have that much seniority over me. While he's ripping me a new one, I notice he's got a lazy eye. He stops yelling and the right eye is directed at me intensely, piercingly, and the left is staring at something off to my right. I fight the urge to follow his left eye's gaze.

"I'm sorry, sir," I begin but he has already turned and headed down the hall.

Over the course of the following week, Private Ja-hong establishes himself as my most avid tormentor, a distinction among fierce competition. The novelty of the private who can't speak Korean hasn't worn off, and the sergeants and corporals continue to resort to mocking and humiliating me as a remedy for their ennui as needed. With well over fifty sergeants and higher-ranked corporals, it happens often and the constant jeers and snickers and insults are my lot.

It's after dinner and the lesser ranked assemble at the far end of the company for the march to Headquarters and our nightly cleaning. A handful of sergeants and corporals mill loosely around the formation when we begin our march.

"Chun!" It's the particularly disfigured corporal from 1st Squad with the large, crooked witch's nose and bulging cheeks.

"Private Young Jin Chun," I call out from my spot in formation.

"Private Young Jin Chun," he repeats in a nasal falsetto, the sergeants and corporals giggling as they run and play grab-ass around the procession like flies around a turd.

"Private Young Jin Chun," I repeat, again caught in the damning infinite loop.

"Private Young Jin Chun," he repeats, not letting it go, pleased with the amusement the sergeants are getting from the interaction.

"Private Young Jin Chun."

It isn't until we arrive in front of Headquarters, over five minutes later, that he stops. The sergeants and higher-ranked corporals have already run up into the building for their StarCraft and he joins them after assigning cleaning duties.

Il-su grabs my forearm and gives me a look of pity as we run off to the bathrooms. He takes the lower two floors, and I head up to the top two.

I open up the last stall and pull out a rusty pair of tongs and plastic trash bag and make my rounds of the bathroom stalls, using tongs to pick up the soiled toilet paper from the trash cans that sit beside every toilet because the plumbing can't handle it. The tongs never feel long enough; it's as if I'm picking up the shit-stained paper with my fingers, taking shit from people I despise, the figurative and the literal meeting every cleaning time.

I lug my sack of shit paper down the hall to the next pair of bathrooms and down the stairs to take care of the next floor. When I open the door to the officer's bathroom, I run into Ja-hong and a PFC, who are taking a break from cleaning the bathroom.

"What the fuck do you want?" Ja-hong demands.

"I-I came to empty the trash, sir."

"Don't you know to knock before entering?"

"No, sir."

"If you don't know, that's the end of it?"

"N-no, sir."

"Try harder, damn it."

"Yes, sir."

"Don't stand around like a dummy. Get on with it."

I enter the first stall and start emptying the trash, the sounds of snickering just outside the stall door.

D-675 (23MAR04): Sergeant Hyeong-jun

The base is normally an unnerving quiet, unbroken save the mornings when the various units go for their jog after morning call, but today the sounds of the wind rustling through the pine needles are drowned out by the steady rumbling of 2-ton trucks and jeeps and buses. The center of the activity is the "Bunker," a tunnel cut through the base of the mountainside, with rooms branching off on both sides for offices necessary for wartime administration. Today is the first day of RSOI.

"RSOI," Hyeong-jun explains, "stands for Reception, Staging, Onward movement, and Integration. It's a joint ROK-US exercise for moving American troops from Japan to the front."

"Yes, sir."

"Look over these well," he says, tossing a small stack of print-outs on the desk in front of me. "Because this is my last exercise." He giggles his high-pitched, chortling giggle before heading out the door.

Unlike Beaver, who is always perched in front of his computer, Hyeong-jun is rarely around. I've never actually seen him do any work and although I'm his replacement, this is the first time he's ever taught me anything related to my responsibilities at Mobilization. Not that I mind. I'd rather have Hyeong-jun's brand of indifference than Beaver's constant scrutiny and passive-aggressive comments. Hyeong-jun's approach is going to hurt in the long run when he's gone and I have no idea what I'm doing, but I figure he doesn't have much to teach me anyway.

The papers are copies of PowerPoint slides for the morning briefing, a page in Korean followed by the same page in English—Hyeong-jun's translations, I assume. The translation isn't as bad as I had expected. He's managed to sound official and incomprehensible at the same time, liberally using words such as "enhanced" and "rear area" and "logistics" and acronyms like nK and SROKA for North Korea and the Second Republic of Korea Army.

I'm looking at the translation when Colonel Kang drops a couple of thick binders in front of me.

"Here. Take the pencil," he says, placing a pencil in my hand. "Put numbers at the bottom of the page. Here."

"Yes, sir."

I spend the entire day writing numbers at the bottoms of hundreds of pages, the task taking much longer than need be because I'm constantly interrupted by Colonel Jeong calling for me to deliver print-outs. My seat is inconveniently located in front of the printer and he's working furiously to deplete our paper stores. At the end of the day, I'm close to finishing the second binder when Colonel Kang stops by to add several stacks of paper in the middle of each binder.

"You're going to have to re-number the binders. You can start over tomorrow morning."

Around dinner time, Beaver and Hyeong-jun stroll into the temporary Mobilization Branch for the shift change. Hyeong-jun promptly disappears, waddling out the door with his knees knocking together.

"Chun, return to the company," Beaver says, not looking up from his computer.

"Yes, sir."

I walk out to the entrance of the Bunker and wait with a couple of conscripts from the Signal Battalion, yellow triangles on their chests, for the shuttle bus to the enlisted mess. When the shuttle arrives, I slide into the back and take out my notebook to review vocabulary I've written down over the weeks. While I'm trying to commit the words to memory, Hyeong-jun jumps into the shuttle along with two other sergeants from Headquarters Company.

They haven't noticed me, so I maneuver myself behind the seat in front of me, obscured from their view. I cherish these rare moments I'm alone.

They're loud and rowdy, laughing and rough-housing each other. I try to ignore them and study as the shuttle reaches the bottom of the mountain and passes by Headquarters.

There are times when you can't help but eavesdrop: when you hear your name spoken nearby or when your attention is drawn by impassioned cursing. Hyeong-jun does both.

"Chun, he's such a *byeongshin*, completely retarded," he says blithely. "Private! Young Jin! Chun!" He's mimicking me in a nasal falsetto, and all three break out in cacophonous laughter.

"Private! Young Jin! Chun!" the sergeant next to him repeats, his voice also exaggeratedly nasal. I'm beginning to wonder if there's something wrong with my voice for the first time in my life.

"You know he can't even answer the phone? It's so fucking funny. *Tong-shin b-b-boan, Ibyeong Chun Y-Y-Y-Young Jinibnida.*"[41]

The mocking laughter fills the cabin of the shuttle bus, echoing in my ears. As Hyeong-jun continues to mock me, I'm steaming in the backseat, the fury building inside of me, growing, festering, poisoning. The rage forces me to watch and listen, the bonds of my low rank stay my hand, and the utter frustration causes the corners of my eyes to water.

I imagine leaping from the back seat, my meaty hands clamping around his scrawny neck with my wrestler's grip, his slightly crossed eyes rolling back into his head, his taunts replaced with a death rattle as I crush his windpipe. I look down at my hands and notice that I've dropped my notebook and my hands are balled up, my knuckles turning white.

As we near the mess hall, one of the sergeants happens to turn to look out the back and spots me. He tugs on Hyeong-jun's shoulder and we make eye contact.

"Oh, Chun, you were here," he says, flustered. "I knew that."

I don't respond. I don't volunteer my name and rank even though a *gocham* is addressing me. I can't. My jaw is clenched too tightly, the burning flames of anger threatening to escape through my mouth if I give it an opening.

Hyeong-jun turns around in his seat and slouches down. The other sergeants follow suit. I can hear muffled giggles coming from the front.

When the shuttle comes to a stop, Hyeong-jun and the other two sergeants run off, jumping and howling in laughter. I pick up my notebook and put it in my pocket and step off the shuttle. Once on solid ground, I can't move, my feet rooted where I stand. I take a deep breath and swallow the anger and frustration and feelings of injustice. As a private, this is all I can do. As soon as my breathing becomes shallow, I pick up my feet and head to the mess hall to eat by myself.

The shifts at the Bunker are long. I feel as if I'm coming down with cabin fever, sitting in the dank and dark, the low concrete ceiling and walls closing in around me; the dim, flickering glow of the overhead lights is no replacement for the natural light I see only briefly at meal times. Colonel

---

[41] The protocol for answering the phone. "Communications security (meaning the line is secure), this is Private Young Jin Chun."

Kang has added a couple of more pages, and I feel as if I've scrawled thousands of numbers, but I've lost track.

Hyeong-jun hasn't been around in the mornings to pass on what he did over the night shift. He's been avoiding me since the incident in the shuttle, which is fine by me.

I've opened up the binder again to get started when Hyeong-jun appears at the room's entrance.

"Hey, Chun. You want to go to the American PX?"

It's a peace offering. I don't really want to spend any more time with him than I have to but I really want to go to the American PX. As sublime as the day we were first allowed to use the PX in boot camp had been, there was something lacking. I realize now that it was that the Atlas candy bars and Oh! Potato and Swing potato chips were not the Snickers and Doritos of my childhood. Korean snacks are tailored to the Korean palate and they're just not the same. The only brand I can recognize is Cheetos, but they're sweet and not cheesy at all.

I've often paused to sneak a look inside the room the Americans are using for their PX as I passed by in the hallway, but privates aren't allowed access by our *gocham*. In the end, the allure of American snacks forces me to swallow my pride.

"Yes, sir."

"Let's go."

I follow Hyeong-jun and another sergeant, one of the sergeants from the shuttle, down the hall and inside the room that houses the American PX. There are a few freezers with ice cream against the wall and a table for a small assortment of snacks. I greedily take in the sight of the candy bars and chips on the table as I hover behind the two sergeants.

There's so much that I want. If I had the money, I'd clear out the entire place. But Hyeong-jun doesn't seem the generous type and I'll have to choose one item carefully. I hover behind the two sergeants, my eyes scanning the snacks on the table thoroughly.

Hyeong-jun and the other sergeant move over to the freezers and the moment they step aside and I look inside, I know what I want. It's one of those transcendent shopping moments when you walk into a store and see something and know right away that it was meant to be yours. Once the sergeants are out of the way, I reach in and put my hand around a Snickers ice cream bar.

There is no cashier in the PX. Instead, it's the honor system, a plastic jar filled with green dollars and blue 1,000 won bills sitting on the edge of the table unattended. Hyeong-jun sticks a couple bills in and turns to me, grinning.

"Chun, you know I'm not paying for you, right?"

D-672 (26MAR04): Poor English Whore

The last day of the exercise, the atmosphere is noticeably more relaxed. Everyone is looking forward to ENDEX and the end of 12-hour shifts in the dank and dark and chill of the Bunker. After the morning briefing, some of the Americans have begun breaking down their stations. Carts laden with equipment ramble past the door; the rumble and clanking echo incessantly up and down the tunnel.

Sitting in front of the printer, I look at the top page of a stack of papers nearby. It's an incident report from around the Army. A private at one of the homeland divisions hanged himself at a motel with his bootstrings during his 100th-day furlough. There isn't an explanation, but it's probably either one of two things: mental and physical abuse by his *gocham* or girl troubles. At one of the divisions on the front, a sergeant stabbed a PFC with his bayonet. The sergeant was sent to military prison. The reason for the stabbing was that the PFC forgot the challenge and password. It was a bad mistake to make, especially on the front, and the stabbing was "education."

I'm reading the report when Colonel Kang walks in with another officer.

"Chun."

I stand, turn around, and give my name and rank.

Colonel Kang says to the other officer, "This is him."

The officer introduces himself as a major from the Engineering Branch and gives me time to salute. The major has a disproportionately huge melon, the sheer size of it accentuated by squinty eyes and thinning hair.

"You lived in America for 22 years?" It's always the same, tired question.

"Yes, sir."

"Come with me."

I follow the Engineering officer to the operations center, the largest room in the heart of the Bunker, at least four times the size of the Mobilization office. There are long lines of desks in an array around the center of the room, where an American officer is speaking, a PowerPoint presentation splayed against the wall.

The major takes me to his assigned seat and tells his subordinate officer, a lieutenant, to scram so I can take his seat. Once we've settled in our seats, the major reaches over me to tap on the shoulder of the female U.S. Air Force lieutenant sitting to my right. She acknowledges his return with a polite smile.

"He is Private...," the major starts but realizes he didn't bother to remember my name. I tell him and he continues, "Private Chun. He's interpreter."

So that's what's happening. I've been pimped out by Colonel Kang as an interpreter.

"Hi," the lieutenant says, smiling.

"Hello, ma'am," I reply. The title feels strange as I speak it, not only because she's clearly younger than me but because I've never addressed a female officer in English before.

Introductions taken care of, the major starts speaking to me in Korean. "Ask her if she knows about Daegu."

"He wants to know if you know much about Daegu."

"Not really. I'm stationed at Osan," she replies. Osan Air Base is one of the major Air Force bases in Korea, located about an hour south of Seoul. It's also the place where I was caught trying to flee the country. "This is my first time in Daegu."

"She says she doesn't, sir."

"Okay. I'm going to tell her about Palgong-san."

"Uh... I don't know what Palgong-san is, sir."

"It's a mountain about 20 kilometers north of Daegu. You pay attention, too," he instructs me. "Palgong-san is the *jinsan* of Daegu. It's famous for *gwanbong seokjoyeoraejwasang*, which is *yeongheomeui sangjing*. It's a *jwabulsang* in *Daehanli* valley. Many people go there to *giwon* hope.[42] Tell her."

"Uh... he was talking about Palgong Mountain. It's 20 kilometers north of Daegu."

The lieutenant nods and smiles and the major goes on.

"It's called Palgong-san for eight *gaegukgongshin* of Goryeo *myeongching*.[43]

---

[42] "Mt. Palgong is the guardian mountain of Daegu. It is famous for the Gwanbong Seated Stone Buddha, which is a symbol of miracles. It is a seated statue of Buddha in Daehan-li Valley. Many people visit it to pray for hope."

[43] "Mt. Palgong is named for eight meritorious retainers who contributed to the

Tell her."

I don't know what to say but he's watching so I lower my voice and come clean, "I'm sorry. I didn't understand any of what he said. He was trying to explain why it's called Palgong Mountain." I use exaggerated body language so it looks like I'm explaining what he said.

"You don't understand Korean?" the lieutenant asks.

"No, ma'am. I'm American."

"How did that happen?"

I look at the major and he's growing impatient. This is his conversation, not mine. "I'm sorry, ma'am. It's a long story."

The major clears his throat and tells me to translate more boring facts about Daegu. I translate what little I can and when I can't, I bullshit and apologize to the lieutenant with my eyes.

Once ENDEX is declared, the officers leave the breaking-down of the office and moving the equipment back to Headquarters to the conscripts. Carrying the copier, shredder, computers, and printers down three flights at the beginning of the exercise was painful enough. Carrying them back up the three flights is absolutely grueling, even taking breaks at the halfway point and top of every flight. I return to the company, exhausted. I'm about to change into my PT uniform to get ready for dinner when there's a knock at the door.

"Chun, they want you at the administration office. Don't change."

I lace up my boots again, grab my battle cap, and head downstairs to the office, where a major from the Personnel Branch is waiting for me.

"You're Private Chun?"

"Yes, sir."

"Come with me."

I follow him out of the company building to where a sedan is waiting for us. The driver, another conscript from the Motor Pool, opens the front passenger door for the major, and he gets in.

"Get in the back."

We pass through the rear entrance of the base and out into the streets of Daegu. I watch as the sedan drives toward the heart of the city.

"Do you know Major Kim?" the major asks from the front.

"No, sir." In the office, there's a Major Maeng and a Major Seo, but no

_____

founding of the Goryeo dynasty."

Major Kims, which is surprising considering how overrepresented the surname is.

He turns and gives me a hard look. "Major Kim from the Engineering Branch."

"Oh. Yes, sir." I don't know what the major's name from yesterday was but I remember that he was from Engineering.

"He told me about you. That's why I'm taking you along."

"Yes, sir."

"You lived in America for 22 years?"

"Yes, sir."

"Good. We're having dinner with a U.S. Army lieutenant colonel. You're going to translate for me."

"Yes, sir." It's too late to tell him I'm worthless as an interpreter. We're already around fifteen minutes off-base.

After a long bout of silence, we drive by the imposing walls of a military installment.

"Have you ever been to Daegu?"

"No, sir."

"See that over there? That's Camp Walker."

"Yes, sir."

As we drive past, I find myself wishing that it was our destination, but I'm not sure why.

We arrive at the restaurant, and it's a traditional-style building with paper screen doors where you have to take off your shoes and sit on cushions. The major, his driver, and I take off our shoes and enter the room where the lieutenant colonel is already waiting. The American officer is an older, distinguished man with cold, calculating eyes behind his glasses. He has a reserved, stoic air about him that I find a little disconcerting.

The major orders a roast-duck platter and a couple bottles of soju. The major can speak some English and he makes small talk with the colonel while the driver and I sit quietly. The waitress enters, bringing the alcohol and four shot glasses. The major takes the bottle and pours a shot for the colonel and one for himself. As an afterthought, he pours soju into my glass as well.

I fight the urge to drain my glass. This is the first alcohol I'll have in two months and who knows when the next will be.

"In Korea, when we 'Cheers,' we say '*geonbae*,'" the major explains.

138

He holds out his glass and indicates he wants me to join as well for the sake of the colonel.

"*Geonbae.*"

I take a sip from my glass. I let it linger on my tongue for a sweet moment before I swallow it.

"Private," the major says, snapping me out of my alcoholic reverie.

"Yes, sir."

"Ask colonel*eui gaekgwanjeokin euigyeoneseo* if war breaks, American Army *wonhwalhan chuldonge daehan* Korean Army*eui* preparation*taese*, how was it?"[44]

I turn to the colonel. "Uh… he… the major wanted to know… he wanted to know what you thought of the exercise."

The colonel narrows his cold, dead eyes at me. He knows. It's as if he can see right through my pathetic charade. He responds, "I thought it was well executed, with fluid cooperation between the Korean and American counterparts."

"The lieutenant colonel said… it was good… he thinks it was good."

"What?"

"The lieutenant colonel… said… the preparation…."

"What are you talking about?" The major is not happy, a look I can only describe as utter disgust on his round face. "Can't you speak Korean?"

I bow my head in shame. "N-no, sir."

He gives me a long, hard stare.

"Just sit and be quiet." His words drip with contempt.

The major turns to the colonel and attempts to explain what he was saying in his broken English. The two officers ignore me completely. When the duck platter comes, I don't eat. It looks expensive, the thin slivers of duck meat with a glistening red edge of skin arrayed in concentric circles around a decorative garnish of greens and rice paper. I guiltily sneak small portions of my rice and the side dishes splayed across the table, bean sprouts and kimchi and tofu, and listen to the major tell the colonel about the dish and how to eat it.

Eventually the major tells me to try some duck, but it's spoken as an aside, and it certainly feels as if he only offers because of the American officer at his side. I take the first piece at his command, and the duck is sublime,

---

[44] "Ask the colonel what his objective opinion is of the Korean Army's readiness with regard to facilitating the smooth mobilization of American Army troops in the event war breaks out."

soft and fatty, almost melting on my tongue. I sneak a couple more pieces throughout the meal, always making sure the major is distracted, busy trying to explain something complicated to the colonel in his broken English. I finish the soju in my glass and let the alcohol burn on its way down. I run my tongue around the inside of my mouth and savor it, knowing there won't be any more.

The ride back to the base is dense with an awkward silence and a seething disappointment coming from the front seat directed toward the disappointment in the back seat. I watch the street lights pass by, thankful the night is over. When the driver stops in front of the company to let me off, the major grunts a reluctant and insincere "Good work."

I walk up to the administration to report my return to the company. It's almost lights out, and I'm exhausted; the reminders of my inadequacy, the judging looks, the discomfort and lack of dinner, and the deathly silent ride back at the end of a long day in the Bunker and the move back to Headquarters have drained all energy from my body. As I walk up the stairs, I feel as if what I've been through today has earned me some rest or at least a pat on the back.

"Private Young Jin Chun. I've re-returned to the company, sir."

The corporal in the office isn't happy. He's never happy; I've only seen him grin once or twice, but I can tell the difference between when he's slightly angry or pissed off. It's the latter.

"Why didn't you call and inform us that you were coming back late?"

I'm confused.

"Why didn't you call to say that you were coming back late?"

"I didn't know, sir."

"You didn't know what?"

"I didn't know I had to, sir."

"If you don't know, that's the end of it?"

The same line again. I hadn't known where I was going, that I would be leaving the base, and how long I'd be gone. Nobody had mentioned anything to me about this sort of situation. Not to mention I had no access to a phone and the office knew who I was with. Nevertheless, I know better than to argue. "No, sir."

"Next time, you better call or you're in deep shit."

"Yes, sir."

I walk back up the stairs to the third floor and enter the squad room. My squad members are pulling out their bedding to get ready for bed. Corporal Jeong-hyeon is pulling out mine as well. They glare at me as I enter. It's not over.

Jeong-hyeon tells me to follow him and again I'm taken to the empty storage room so that the *gocham* won't be kept up by the sound of "education."

D-671 (27MAR04): Conscript of Interest

I briskly walk down the hall on my way to 13th Squad to look for Il-su. I make this trip countless times a day because of the countless muffled announcements of the PA that echo off the walls and peter out just in front of Squad Room 15. If I'm not already out the door, Beaver will give me one of his annoyed glares out of the corner of his eye until I am.

Il-su's the only one on the third floor I can ask about the messages because I'm not allowed to ask questions of *gocham*. If I can't find him, I have to go down to the administration office and ask the corporal there, who also gives me a hard time every time I walk through the door. It's the corporal I see walking up the steps as I walk toward Squad Room 13.

"Don't bother," he says knowingly. "It's you. You have another phone call."

I follow him down the stairs to the office where he points to the phone, the receiver lying on the desktop. I'm strangely expectant although I can't think of a single person who would call, who even has the phone number. I don't even know the number.

"The line is secure. This is Private Young Jin Chun."

"This is ————— from the Ministry of National Defense." I don't hear the name but he gives me plenty of time to pay my respects.

"*Chungseong!*" I salute, my free arm involuntarily rising with the call.

"How are you adapting to Army life?"

"Yes, sir."

There is an uncomfortable pause on the other end, awkward as my answer had been. "Uh… I see. Keep working hard."

"Yes, sir. *Chung….*"

Click.

"… *seong*," I finish to myself and the dial tone.

"Two times already," the corporal remarks. "Why'd they call this time?"

"I don't know, sir."

"It must be because you're a conscript of interest."

What's that supposed to mean?

I don't know much, I don't have time to think about much, but I know that I won't be getting another call. The official had shown even less interest than last time and I realize nothing is going to come of it. I'm sure he just needed a "Yes, sir" so he could report to his superiors that I'm adapting and leading a fulfilling life as a private in Daegu.

Adapting, everyone asks how I'm adapting but no one really gives a damn. Sure, I'm adapting. I'm adapting like a man adapts to being strapped to a wooden plank and having little drops of water dripped onto his forehead.

I'm adapting to the constant lectures and insults, the jeers and snickers. Not that I don't feel my face flush red each time someone mocks my pronunciation or yells at me for something I had no idea I had to do or avoid doing.

I'm adapting to running around, acting the lackey to the same tormentors, the hundred and fifty *gocham* in the company, asking these children if they slept well, sir, or if they had a good meal, sir. There's an honorific element in the Korean language that makes the "sir" less a sign of outward respect and more a sign of abject self-debasement. The language I have to use toward these kids, who were still suckling at their mothers' teats when I was trading baseball cards and flipping up girls' skirts, it's the same formal language Koreans reserve for only for the most important people, say, your boss's boss or the president.

I'm adapting to the banality of a menial life, picking up toilet paper soiled with the shit of these kids and sorting through garbage and spending work hours shredding paper and making coffee. I jump every time the phone rings because I have to be the one to answer it even though it takes me four times as long to say the line is secure and my name and rank and how can I help you and inevitably getting stuck in the catch-22 of I didn't hear you clearly, sir and insults from the other end of the line before Beaver or Hyeong-jun decide to step in. I know that they enjoy watching the pain and stress it causes me.

By adapting, I mean that I've come to terms that this is life here—a humiliating, frustrating, hostile, frantic, desperate, and solitary servitude—and have learned to avoid the worst of it when possible. I keep to myself and politely refuse any offer that resembles kindness. I'd cry myself to sleep if I wasn't so tired by lights out.

"Did you hear about Ballerino?"

I look over my shoulder but thankfully the corporal is not talking to me. A private first class turns to look at the corporal, his face a greenish-white with lather.

"No, sir. What is it?"

It's just the three of us in the face-washing room and, relieved that no one is talking to me, I return to washing not my face but a sickly yellowish-gray rag for the evening cleaning of the squad room. The two of them continue their conversation, oblivious to my presence. I'm invisible unless a *gocham* is in need of some entertainment or stress release.

"He doesn't have to go to the office anymore. Captain Jin confined him to the squad room."

"Really, sir?"

"Yeah. He even gets to take showers by himself. Captain Jin said he can't take showers with anyone else."

"That's a relief, sir."

"Yeah. Gay fucking bastard."

The first time I met Private Ballerino was on my first day in the company. After processing at the personnel branch, my "father" took me to the base drycleaners to get my unit insignia stitched on my uniforms. Ballerino was walking out the door, uniforms slung over his arm.

I saluted because I had not yet learned that I'm not supposed to salute a company member if I'm with another company member of a higher rank.

Instead of returning my salute, he reached out his hand. I shook it apprehensively, as I did and do everything, and his hand had the vigor of wet manicotti. He was slim and slightly feminine in the way that old, feeble, malnourished people become, his round, inquisitive eyes full of excitement as he shared about his studies in the States.

"It was nice to meet you," he said in parting, saluting to my "father" before heading back to the company.

"That was Ballerino," my "father" said. "He studied ballet in the States."

"You know Ballerino?" Hyeong-jun asked the day he taught me Beaver's nickname.

"Yes, sir."

"He's gay," he said, snickering.

"I understand, sir."

"No, really. He's gay."

"Yes, sir."

"He's in love with Andy in 13th Squad. He gave him a birthday present, and when he put it in his hand, he went like this," he said, grabbing my wrist with one hand and sliding the other down my palm from base to fingertips.

I take back my hand, trying to hide my annoyance with being touched, and respond, "I understand, sir."

Hyeong-jun snickered as he walked out the door of the face-washing room, having satisfied his need for amusement.

When I leave the face-washing room, the corporal and private are still talking about Ballerino.

Ballerino was the reason for the interrogation about my sexual orientation by Captain Jin during my enter interview, I realize now. It seems that Ballerino is a real black eye for Captain Jin and a major source of gossip among the *gocham*.

Walking back to the squad room with rag in hand, I'm reminded of the comment about conscripts of interest. If there's another conscript of interest in the company, it's Ballerino. I feel bad for him. Not that I'm in any position to feel bad for anyone, but I understand probably more than anyone else. I understand what it's like to be the frequent target of these puerile morons: the scrutiny and gossip and badmouthing and ridicule, being discriminated against and the object of ridicule and alienation for something over which one has no control. At least he had the option of keeping his mouth shut about it.

D-665 (2APR04): Time

I eat breakfast and dinner with the squad, but because lunch requires leave from the branch officers, I usually go to lunch with Beaver and Hyeong-jun. We only march to the mess hall together; they usually ditch me once we're through the door, leaving me to eat by myself. When I was young, my family moved around every couple of years, and always being the new kid at this school or that, I hated being ditched, which inevitably happened. It made me feel lonely, or maybe it just made me realize how lonely a child I was. Here,

144

I don't mind being ditched because loneliness is preferable to any other option.

After I finish my rice and kimchi, I quickly wash my tray and spork in the troughs off to the side and hurry back to the squad room to get some studying in before the afternoon at the office.

As I cross the street, I spot a handful of *gocham* lounging under the single basketball hoop beside the barracks. I salute crisply and hold it until I pass because no one acknowledges the salute. When I reach the foot of the stairs, I hear someone call my name.

"Hey, Chun!"

Here we go again.

"Private Young Jin Chun!" I shout as I turn and report for another round of abuse.

The sergeant from 12th Squad who hailed me is grinning as he beckons me closer.

"Do you know who this is?" he asks, jabbing his thumb toward a tall conscript with dark, pock-marked skin and bright, round eyes. He's wearing an apron and the rubber galoshes that indicate he works in the mess, another facility manned by members of the company. I've never seen him before, but mess hall conscripts wake up early, sleep late, and mostly keep to themselves. That doesn't mean that I don't have to know who they are.

"No, sir. I-I'm s-sorry, sir."

"This is Ho-ju. He's your father."

"I understand, sir."

"He just got back from Arabic-language training. See, he's fucking dark, just like an Arab."

"I understand, sir." I don't laugh at his crude attempt at humor.

"All right. Get lost."

"Yes, sir."

That makes sixteen fathers, one more father who couldn't give a damn about me. Aside from Jeong-hyeon in my squad, it seems like the other fathers harbor an apathy to me that they don't feel toward the other sons. I've seen them coddle Il-su and the others while completely ignoring me. It's funny how Army life imitates real life. At least they refrain from picking on me.

When I get to the squad room, U-don is reclining against his locker. Nobody bothered to explain why they call Corporal Yun-seok U-don, but I assume it's because his curly hair somewhat resembles a tangle of Japanese noodles. He sits up when the door opens; as the sixth of eight in our squad hierarchy, he's not allowed to recline in front of the others.

"Oh, it's just you," he says, leaning back against his locker. He's holding a calendar in his hand.

"Did you have lunch, sir?"

"Yeah," U-don replies, his gaze fixed on the calendar.

I take out my study materials—my Korean-English dictionary, my notebooks, and the easiest reading from our small library—and am studying Korean when he interrupts me.

"Hey, guess how many days I have left."

"I'm sorry, sir. I don't know, sir." I should know the month every *gocham* started their service but I'm still struggling with remembering their names.

"Three hundred," he says blithely. "I only have three hundred days left. How many do you have left?"

I do the math in my head—roughly six hundred and sixty—and I realize how a number could have such crushing weight.

"Never mind. Privates shouldn't think about it."

It's more a command than advice. It's an unspoken company rule that privates can't say how many days they have left. The reasoning is that if privates have time to calculate the number of days they have left, they aren't working hard enough.

U-don lies down on the raised floor with a smile on his pimple-ridden face, dreaming of the days to come, I assume. I don't think he meant to be cruel—he's more of the lighthearted, self-deprecating type, the only one in our squad—but the damage has been done. I return to my studying with a heavy heart, weighed down by the thought of six hundred and sixty more days of damnation.

D-663 (4APR04): AWOL

It's Sunday morning, and the company has been assembled on the lawn in front of the barracks. The privates and PFCs stand in line by squad, the frosted grass crushed beneath our sneakers while the corporals with seniority and the sergeants frolic and horse around in the brisk winter morning.

146

The assembling of the company on the weekend means that we either have some large-scale manual-labor task or company-wide punishment awaiting us. It's a common occurrence. Sundays are never days of rest, but I could be wrong. There's no concept of time in a black hole. The past few weeks have felt like one insanely long, horrid day.

The first to emerge from the company doors is the sergeant-on-duty, yellow band around his upper arm and clipboard in hand. The sergeant-on-duty gives the cue for the corporals and sergeants to stop their frolicking and join the ranks. *He* is coming.

From the relative darkness of the entryway, Captain Jin emerges and strides out to the center of the formation with lumbering steps. He clears his throat and looks out at us with those protruding frog's eyes.

"A conscript from the Signal Battalion has gone AWOL," he announces, sweeping his gaze across the fifteen squads. "He went missing in the night and didn't report for morning call. All available company members are to form small groups and conduct a sweep of the base. That's all."

Once Captain Jin has disappeared in the company, Beaver calls the squad together.

"Jeong-hyeon, take In-shik and Chun and patrol the perimeter of the base."

The sergeants and higher-ranked corporals trudge back into the barracks to return to sleep and Beaver heads off toward Headquarters, U-don in tow. They must be planning another StarCraft bout.

The three of us, low-ranked and useless at StarCraft, set out from the company, Jeong-hyeon in the lead with In-shik beside him and me in the rear. We march in step past the Security Company, take a left at the Motor Pool, and make our way to the main parade ground. It's a beautiful Sunday morning, the sky a cloudless pale blue, but it's hard to appreciate the day when it's wasted on a patrol.

We walk past the main parade ground to the rear entrance of the base.[45] Beyond the guard post, I can see the streets of Daegu, the sun shining a little brighter on the people and cars passing by.

---

[45] "Rear entrance" is a misnomer. The actual rear of the base is a vast wilderness in the mountains, blocked off with a chain-linked fence and barbed wire. There are small cans hanging from the fence at intervals to help detect if someone attempts to tamper with the fence. The "rear entrance" is a gate about 100 meters from the "front entrance" along the main civilian street in front of the base.

We take another left and head toward the main gate, paralleling the wall that separates the black hole of life on base and the bustling activity of the free world. I can't keep my eyes off the wall and all it stands for. Behind one of the buildings, I spot a small path where the grass doesn't grow and trails off and up to the wall. For some reason, the ground rises up so the wall would be around chest-height. A good distance from both the front and rear entrances, it'd be no problem to hop over the wall and catch a taxi undetected. That's where I'd cross over if I wanted to escape.

"Corporal Jeong-hyeon. The wall, sir."

He looks over but keeps walking. "Don't worry about it. The guy's probably long gone. They'll catch him at the train station probably."

I realize that the two of them haven't been looking around at all, that it's not the purpose of our walk. We've received orders for yet another futile weekend task and our walk is all we can do. At least it's not the usual landscaping.

From the main gate, we walk up the hill past the commander's residence and the officers' quarters and stop by the PX nearby. We get ice cream and cross the street to the playground and rest.

While Jeong-hyeon and In-shik talk, I wonder what would possess someone to go AWOL. Not that I don't understand the motivation. I understand more than the next guy. Rarely an hour goes by that I don't wish I were free on the other side of the wall. It's the only thing I want right now.

But with the airports closed off, there's really nowhere for me to run. I'd get caught eventually, get sent to *yeongchang*, military prison, and when I was finished with my sentence, I'd be back in the service to pick up where I left off, my discharge extended by however long my sentence was. When I was in boot camp, there were two recruits from 1st Company, the floor below us, who went AWOL. Johnny told me that they would have to start boot camp over from the beginning once they finished their time in *yeongchang*.

After our break, we loop up around the Bunker and head down past the zero-point practice range, Headquarters, and back toward the company.

When we near the company, Jeong-hyeon asks if we want to use the phones. In-shik doesn't and he returns to the company ahead of us.

There are a few payphones scattered throughout the base, but I'm not allowed to go to use them unescorted.

I'm excited because I can call home for the first time. I used a good portion of last month's paycheck to buy an international calling card at the

PX and I've been itching to use it. Maybe calling home will get my mind off pipe dreams of desertion.

Luckily, there isn't anyone at the payphones next to the base personnel branch. There are only two booths and whenever I pass by, there usually is a line of conscripts waiting to use the phone. Jeong-hyeon gets into the one on the left and I step into the remaining one. I take out my calling card, tear open the plastic wrapping, and follow the instructions on the back.

The phone rings a couple times before my mother's voice comes over the receiver. "Hello?"

It's been over two months since I've heard her voice. The last time was the morning before I left for Jeungpyeong.

"Hi, Mom."

"Young, is that you?" Her voice is cheery, a change from her normal business tone when she's making sure I'm taking care of myself or making friends. For a second, I forget that I'm on a Korean Army base, surrounded by hundreds of soldiers and officers whose only goal seems to be making my life miserable.

"Yeah, Mom. It's me."

"How are you doing?"

I want to tell her about everything that's happened, about how difficult boot camp was, how I thought of her and it got me through that full-pack run during the last week, how strange and frustrating life is at the Second Army, but I can't bring myself to do it.

"I'm okay," I lie. I've caused her enough heartache. Wary of her mother's intuition, I change the subject. I can already feel all the feelings I've locked away rushing to the surface. "How is everything back home?"

"Everything's fine. I'm healthy." Even if it's a lie, it's reassuring. "Business is slow at the store, but I'm getting by."

I find myself unable to respond. I stand with the receiver in my hand and stumble over what to say next.

"Mack is getting fatter every day," she continues. He was a puppy, just a year old, when I left for Korea. "Your brothers are fine. Nothing new. I wish they would stop by more often."

Again, I have no response. I don't know why. Maybe it's homesickness. The past couple of months have kept me so busy and tired and dazed that I haven't had much energy to think of home and how much I miss it. When I was living in Seattle, I hated how slowly life seemed to play itself out and wanted nothing more than to escape, but now I'm finding solace in the static permanence of life back home.

"By the way," she adds. "A reporter from the Seattle P-I wants to interview you. Give him a call when you have a chance. Do you have a pen and paper?"

"Hold on."

I take out my pen and notepad and take down the number.

"Make sure to call, okay?"

"I will," I say. "I'll call again when I get a chance." I don't know why I'm cutting our phone call short. I want to talk, but I can't.

"Oh, okay."

"Bye, Mom."

"Bye, son. I love you."

"I love you, too, Mom."

I don't want to hang up but know I have to before I lose my resolve to be strong.

After I hang up the receiver, I look through the glass at Jeong-hyeon, who is still busy talking on the phone. I can only take as long as he takes, but it seems like he's going to be a while, and I can't go back by myself. My first urge is to call her back, but I can't. I look down at my notepad and figure I might as well call the reporter.

"Hello?"

"Hi, my name is Young Chun. My mother told me to give you a call. I'm calling from the Korean Army."

"Oh, Mr. Chun. Hi, my name is John Iwasaki, and I'm a reporter for the Seattle Post-Intelligencer. How are you?"

"I'm doing okay."

"Do you mind if I ask you a couple of questions?"

"I don't mind," I reply, shocked at the civility of his question and the cordial tone of his voice and eager to have a conversation in English that isn't being forced by an officer or *gocham*.

The reporter asks me the same questions I've struggled with since that first night in boot camp, and I answer frankly and openly. It's almost as if I'm talking to myself, trying to work everything out. I vent all of the frustrations I couldn't bring myself to share with my mother, how I can't understand anyone, how I'm tired of the unwanted and negative attention. I say some uncharacteristically positive comments, almost as if saying them will make them true.

There's a knock on the glass of the booth, and Jeong-hyeon gives me the signal to wrap it up. I nod as respectfully as possible with the receiver in hand, and I snap out of my contemplative trance.

"I'm sorry. I have to go."

"Thank you for your time, Mr. Chun."

"Thank you," I say and hang up the phone.

The rest of the day goes by uneventfully. I manage to fit some studying in before having to do manual labor in the afternoon.

At evening call, the sergeant on duty announces to our squad that the soldier has been caught. The MPs picked him up in front of his girlfriend's house, and he went with them without a hassle. He was having girl problems—one of the leading motivations for suicide among conscripts, according to a session of mental education—and I feel bad for the kid, but I have a wealth of problems of my own to worry about, none of which are female-related.

When the lights go off, I have trouble falling asleep. It's strange because I'm usually so tired I've been falling asleep promptly at lights out, but there's an ominous feeling tumbling around in the back of my head. Did I forget to do something? Did I make another mistake today? I run through the events of the day, but it's hard to remember.

The realization hits me like a cinder block. I talked to a reporter. I gave an interview. I can't reason why it's bothering me to this extent but it just feels like I've made a grave mistake. I try to remember what I said to the reporter, but I can't remember. It was as if I was on autopilot, the words more for myself than for the reporter. I can barely remember if the reporter said anything at all. I don't think I said anything that could get me in trouble but I can't shake this nagging feeling.

I'll call the reporter the next chance I get and ask him to give me some time to think before he writes anything. That's right. I have to remember to call.

D-655 (12APR04): The Shit Storm

I've been called to the company commander's office again. I don't know the reason, but the way the conscripts in the administration office are giving me pitying looks as I stand and wait worries me. One of the corporals takes me up to the commander's office and knocks apprehensively on the large wooden door.

"Enter." There's a harsh tone to the command instead of the usual disinterested tone.

The corporal cracks open the door for me and runs off down the hall. I enter the room and salute.

Captain Jin is steaming, his face an even brighter red than his normal sanguine complexion. His jaw clenched and his eyes popping halfway out of their sockets, he looks as if he's about to explode. Through gritted teeth, he orders me to approach and stand at attention.

He doesn't talk for a long moment. He just stares at me with those bulging eyes, trembling in anger. He opens his mouth as if to speak but stops himself. He takes another long moment.

When he finally regains a modicum of composure, he manages to spit out, "You did a *myeonjeop*, didn't you?"

I don't know the word. "I didn't hear you clearly, sir," I say, knowing that it will only make him madder.

"Shit. *Myeonjeop*. You don't know *myeonjeop*?"

"No, sir."

"*Myeonjeop. Inteobyu.*" Interview. Oh shit, I've been so busy the past couple of days, I completely forgot to call back the reporter from the Post-Intelligencer. "You did, didn't you?"

I can't reply. I've been tripped up by my stupidity again.

"You son of a bitch," he begins his tirade, spittle spraying from his lips and a purplish vein throbbing in his temple. Caught up in the flames of intense anger and pure hostility, he spits his invective in a flare of machine-gun fire, accentuated by a continuous stream of expletives. "—you damn moron—fucking idiotic bastard—" The curses I understand completely although as he builds momentum, he joins them in combinations I've never heard in Korean before. "—you retarded fucking son of a bitch dick bastard—" I can only pick up bits and pieces of the words that aren't curses because of the speed and intensity of his attack. "—my superiors—call from Headquarters—without permission, you fucking idiot—" The tempo of his rant has reached a climax; his face has turned a marvelous red, and I'm now able see that purple vein writhing. When it looks like he's about to have a heart attack, he pauses for air.

"Act up one more time, do any little fucking thing, if it reaches my ears, I swear the next thing you know you'll be in a jeep on the way to *yeongchang*. Got it?"

"Yes, sir," I say in the most disciplined and respectful yet meek tone I can muster.

Whether it's my response or his simply having gotten it out of his system, he seems to calm, the vein I had fixated on slowly disappearing underneath the skin of his temple.

"Get lost."

"Yes, sir."

I salute at the door but a twitch in his scowl tells me he's clenching his teeth and I quickly make an exit before he decides to resume his yelling. I leave his office and head to the mess for lunch, woozy from the abuse and hoping that I can manage to stay out of trouble for at least the rest of the day.

D-630 (8MAY04): 4.5 Seconds

The past two weeks have been hellish, more than the norm, and not because of Captain Jin. I've managed to stay under the radar, looking both ways before leaving the squad room or crossing the street.

Last week was spent at the reserve training center, organizing mobilization training for Army reserves, ex-conscripts in their second through fifth years after finishing their military service. Army reserves are a lazy bunch and spend most of the day sleeping or frequenting the temporary PX while not in mental education or training. There is little morale or discipline because they've done their time and aren't getting paid for the training beyond bus fare. They don't even have the motivation to aim while shitting in the squat toilets and I spend the last afternoon cleaning shit with a handbroom and bucket.

This past week, there was a streak of chickenshit sergeants on duty and we did *mishing* three times over the course of two days. *Mishing* is a thorough, Army-style cleaning with the smallest, most inefficient tools possible. First came the *mishing* of Headquarters where I was given the duty of scrubbing the toilet-paper wastebaskets with a sponge. I returned to the company that night covered in shit water only to do *mishing* of the company bathrooms, scrubbing the urinals with toothpaste and a rag. The next day was *mishing* of the mess hall, sweeping and scrubbing the floors with detergent and toothbrushes.

It's been a tough two weeks, but nothing can put a damper on my mood. Today, I'm going on my 100th-day furlough.

After breakfast, I wash up quickly and return to the squad room to put on my "grade-A" uniform and boots.[46] Last weekend, one of my fathers "grabbed lines" on it, meaning that he ironed creases down the fronts and backs of my uniform top and field jacket. Another polished my grade-A boots to a mirror shine, using shoe polish heated with a lighter. Ho-ju, my linguist father, bought me a new battle cap from the drycleaners to replace the floppy, "shapeless" hat I was issued in boot camp. To the untrained eye, I look the same as any other day, but I get a few comments on my sharp appearance as I walk down the hall.

There have been few moments in my life that can compare to the feeling in my chest as I walk down the long road past the Motor Pool and main parade ground. When I see the free world outside the guard post, my heart leaps. The outside is in sight and I'm leaving with permission. I haven't planned anything for the furlough at all. All my thoughts are completely trained on walking through those gates.

I hand the guards my leave papers as if those papers carry proof of all the shit I've waded through to make it here. I walk out to the street and pause. I take a deep breath and exhale it slowly, my mouth wide open and smiling.

It's only been 100 days but time runs differently on the inside. 100 of the longest days in my life. Although I'm still in my uniform, those 100 days are already in the past.

I catch a cab with some of the others out on leave, and the taxi zips through the Daegu traffic on its way to the station. I buy my ticket with most of what's left of my paychecks for the past three months and stop by a convenience store to buy a box of Margarets for the trip to Seoul. On one of my last days in boot camp, I stopped by 1st Squad to deliver a message, and one of them slipped a Margaret into my hand. I've longed to have one ever since, but they don't sell them in individual packets, and I couldn't splurge on a whole box with my meager salary. I take a seat on the train in as empty a

---

[46] Only officers and *unjeonbyeong* get dress uniforms. As a result, conscripts set aside one set of their everyday uniforms and their extra pair of boots for special occasions.

section as possible, take off my battle cap, and eat my Margarets in peace.

Seoul Station is almost sensory overload—the colors, the noises, the people. Young people dressed for weekend trips, old people with packages bundled in brightly colored cloth, families with young children running around at play. As I wait to use a pay phone, I watch a little girl and her sister playing hide and seek. I take out my last two packets of Margarets and offer them to the older of the two. She looks at me apprehensively and then to her mother, who is standing nearby.

"Go ahead," her mother says, and she reaches out to take them, giving one to her little sister.

"Say thank you to the soldier uncle," her mother adds, and the little girl bows at the waist and says thank you. She runs off to resume her game with her sister, and I take my turn at the phone to call my aunt and tell her I'm on my way.

"Young, *sugohaetda*," my aunt says as I walk through the door. My dictionary tells me it means "You've toiled," but the way I've had to say it to my *gocham* at the end of every task, it's something akin to "Good job."

"Thanks," I respond in earnest. I've heard the words a few times in Daegu, but they've always come across as insincere and dismissive. I only wish it could've been from Mom and in my own house.

"You can use your cousin's room while you're here. Go get changed and come out for dinner."

"Yes, ma'am."

The box of clothes I sent from boot camp is waiting for me in my cousin's room, and I strip off everything, even my undershirt and underwear, and put on my own clothes for the first time in 100 days.

After dinner, I retire to my cousin's room and don't leave until the next morning. I turn on the computer and try to check my e-mail, but it's been closed due to inactivity. I set it up again and send Seok-bae, Fifty-seven, a message, giving him my cousin's phone number. My cousin's also letting me use his phone while I'm out.

I spend the rest of my first night lying on the bed and watching television. It isn't much, but it's what I need. Lying on an actual bed in my own clothes, watching something that isn't StarCraft. But more than any of those things, I cherish the privacy. In Daegu, I'm constantly surrounded by people and yet have never felt so alone. Now I'm on my own, no squad mates snoring or grinding their teeth and no guard duty at night or reveille in the morning, I fall into a deep and restful sleep.

My aunt doesn't disturb me the next morning until ten, but I've been awake since six, my internal clock tuned to Army time. I'm surfing the internet when she knocks on the door and tells me to get ready for brunch. We meet some relatives by marriage at a barbecue restaurant and I'm drunk on soju by noon. Itching to make the most of my day, I lie and say I'm meeting up with friends and head out into the city.

I spend the afternoon wandering with no destination, just walking wherever feels right, breathing the free air and marveling at the lives of ordinary civilians until dark. My buzz gradually wears off, but I've been on a natural high since yesterday. I lose myself in the multitudes and allow myself to pretend that I, too, am a civilian. I walk with my hands in my pockets and listen to music with my headphones in my ears, two things I can't do when in uniform. I see beautiful young women pass by and am comforted by the fact that my first impulse is not to have them buy me a snack and comforted that my carnal impulses are intact after such prolonged inactivity. I'd stop by the red light district if I knew where it was and had more than the small amount of spending money my aunt gave me after brunch.

It's night in the city, and the street lights and neon and blaring music are an old friend welcoming me back. I'm watching the people eating and drinking inside the shops when I feel the phone ringing in my pocket.

"The line is secure," I say when I pick up the phone and hate myself immediately.

The voice on the other end of the line belongs to Seok-bae, Fifty-seven.

"What are you up to?"

"I'm just walking around."

"Come to Bupyeong," he says. "Everybody's here."

"Okay," I answer and jump in a cab.

I meet them at a night club. Jeong is there, too, and three others from our boot-camp squad, Forty and Thirty-nine and Fifty-eight. It's a "booking" club,[47] and we get a table with a bottle of whisky, and the waiters drag girls

---

[47] A booking club is a night club where the waiters will drag girls to your table to drink with you. The clubs are typically expensive and require the purchase of a bottle of whisky or a sufficient amount of alcohol. The girls are not professionals but girls that came to the club to dance and/or meet guys. The girls are free to

over to our table to drink with us. I quickly learn that Korean girls aren't interested in soldiers—with our short hair and dark and sallow skin, there's no mistaking us for civilians—and they leave almost as soon as they sit down. So we drink and shout over the repetitive thumping of the bass and the screeching electronica about our respective fates after parting ways in boot camp. Seok-bae brings up Ye-jin and I tell him that she never wrote back. He tells me he asked about it and she said she didn't know why she never wrote back. By the way the girls at the club are looking at us, I have an idea why.

When the bottle is empty, we stop by a convenience store to pick up alcohol and stumble into a karaoke, where we pass out into a drunken slumber one by one. When I wake, the owner is kicking us out and we say our sloppy, tired, daylight goodbyes out front. Seok-bae offers me his house to sleep and I agree. We jump in a cab and I have dreams of meeting his sister.

The next morning, I feel awful. I think it's the hangover, my tolerance having dropped to an all-time low because of the hundred days of nothing but a single shot of *soju*. I take the subway to my aunt's place and fall asleep as soon as my head hits the pillow. When I wake up for dinner, the hangover is gone, but the awful feeling remains. It's not a physical sensation. It's unfamiliar because it's a feeling I haven't felt since puberty. Depression. I only have two nights before I have to leave this freedom behind, two nights before I have to return to the hell that is waiting for me.

It wasn't this bad in the days leading up to my induction. It was bad—a fair number of those nights were spent hugging various toilets all over Seoul—but it wasn't this bad. I think part of it is because I was dazed and confused. I think part is because I didn't know what was waiting for me.

I spend my last night in good company, the friends who drank with me and patted my back on those many nights before my induction, but it's a bittersweet meeting because I know that this is the last time I'll see a good number of them. Most people who come here to teach English only stay for a year. It had been my plan as well. I don't know when I'll be out on furlough again, but it won't be for another three months at the earliest.

On the morning of my fifth and last day, the depression is debilitating. My heart sinks with practically every step I take on my way back. Every stop on the train down to Daegu is a dagger in my chest. When I step out of East Daegu Station and see those familiar blue letters, I can barely drag my feet

---

leave whenever they want, which was immediately in our case.

forward. Outside the rear gate of the Second Army, I sigh a long, drawn-out sigh that doesn't end until I'm back at the company. It lingers through evening call and on into the night until I finally find sleep.

During the evening cleaning of the company, Jeong-hyeon asks how my furlough was and I try to mask my sadness when I respond that it was good.

"It goes by pretty quickly, doesn't it?" he asks.

"Yes, sir."

U-don chimes in and sums it up nicely. "Four days and five nights? More like 4.5 seconds."

D-600 (8JUN04): Thoughts of Home

They say that Ballerino hadn't shown any homosexual tendencies until after his 100th-day furlough. Some of the corporals say that up to that point, he was "FM"—short for field manual—slang which means that he was a disciplined soldier who did everything by the book. They say that when he returned, he changed completely, the way he walked and talked and hit on other soldiers. There's even speculation that coming out of the closet was a clever ploy to get an early discharge.

I don't know how much of the hearsay is the truth, but if it is all part of some gambit and Ballerino is a skilled tactician and actor, I can understand why. Since I returned from my 100th-day furlough, I've been sullen and depressed, and although I try to hide it lest I earn an "education," I've noticed that the others in my squad have been giving me somewhat of a wide berth, which only means that they ignore me a little more than usual.

There'll be little sleep tonight. We've been told that there will be another "situation" tonight after midnight. It's to practice our "battle readiness," which is ridiculous because it's hard to consider us soldiers. When the announcement comes out over the PA at two in the morning, I rush down to the administration office to get the key for the gun locker and hand out the rifles for my squad. We pack our duffel bags with all essential items, put on our uniforms and gear, black our faces, and head outside where several 2-tons are waiting to take us up to the area around the Bunker, our assigned defensive position.

We stand around in the middle of the mountains, pointing our rifles at passing helicopters and not much else for four hours. When we walk back down the mountain, the day is starting to break. There is much grunting and cursing as we make our way back to the company. I lock up the rifles while the others change back into their PT uniforms and go back to sleep. I don't change because I'm on the first shift of the night watch after the situation.

They let us sleep until lunch, but we're expected to be at our offices for the afternoon. Most of the squad opts to sleep during lunch and I go to eat lunch alone. When I return from lunch, I find most of them are still sleeping but someone, I presume it's one of my *donggi*, has left a piece of mail in front of my locker. It's in a U.S. Postal Service air-mail envelope, and the address is my home address in Seattle. It's from my mother.

I tear open the envelope and inside is a pack of developed photos, glossy 4x6s like the ones I spent the year printing before coming to Korea. In one picture, our pug Mack is sniffing around the flower garden my mother planted in front of the house. In the next, from the way Jason is kneeling down next to Mack, it's clear that my mother told him to get in the picture. There are pictures of the house and the neighborhood as they take Mack for a walk. It's a beautiful spring day in Seattle, and spring days in Seattle are some of the best anywhere, the silver lining of all the rain in the fall and winter. After the walk, there are pictures in the living room, the sunlight streaming through the bay windows on my mother and younger brother playing with the dog. All the pictures were taken over the course of a few hours. I can picture my mother telling my brother to take the pictures to get developed at the Rite Aid down the street and her giving them to the postal worker in the morning at the office near her store.

On second thought, these aren't the pictures like ones I printed when I was working at the one-hour photo. I'm not in any of these pictures, either, but it almost feels as if I'm there behind the lens, there spending a beautiful Seattle spring day with my family instead of here spending my day patrolling the mountainside and now sitting in a squad room with other conscripts who couldn't care less about me unless I do something to inconvenience their lives.

There are times here when it feels as if the world outside is moving on without me, as if I've been sucked into a black hole and time is stagnant while everyone I've known and loved is going on with their lives, living and loving and changing jobs and starting families and being generally happy. At the other end of my service, when I leave the gates of the Second Army for the last time, I'll be the same person, but two years older, and with nothing to show for my time. It'll be as if I've slept like Rip Van Winkle for two years, but having dreamt horrible dreams. Will I be able to pick up where I left off? Will people have the same affection for me, or will it have diminished over time?

In those moments, I'm sometimes thankful that I'm kept busy and abused because I don't have the leisure to think those thoughts. But now, forty minutes before the afternoon's work and with all my squad mates asleep, I leaf through the pictures over and over and I'm reminded that there are still people who are thinking of me and there's a place that I can return to and belong.

It's a Thursday when Beaver goes on his final furlough and he's as good as gone. He returns from the furlough on a Saturday night for evening call, and he's gone before breakfast on Sunday. When I return from breakfast, his locker is empty. He didn't bother to say good-bye. I spent the last four months with the little creep and it's just as well that he disappeared silently.

With Beaver's discharge, our squad goes through some changes. Jeong-hyeon and U-don transfer to squads on the second floor. They haven't been getting along with the corporal who had been in the hospital my first two months with the squad but couldn't leave previously because of pressure from Beaver. Our squad of nine has been reduced to six: three sergeants, two corporals, and me, the lowly private.

The Professor, Sergeant Hyeon-seok, is the new squad leader for 15th Squad. They call him the Professor because he was studying science or engineering at Johns Hopkins when he returned to do his military service. Somewhat of a recluse, he hasn't spoken to me more than once. It's a surprise when he peeks into the squad room on a weekend afternoon when nobody else is around.

"Chun, come here," he says, beckoning me over with his hand.

I run through the events of the past couple of days to see if I've done anything wrong. Instead of heading down the hall, we step out the door to the third floor landing of the outside stairwell.

I steel myself for verbal abuse but instead the Professor shoves a crumpled brown paper bag into my hands.

"Eat it quickly," he says nonchalantly.

After a moment of hesitation, I open up the bag and peer inside. It's a Whopper Junior. I'm dumbfounded. I've been ordered to eat quickly but all I can do is look at him quizzically. I ask him a question with my confused

160

expression because I don't dare ask with words.

"I was out of the base on business and the officer took me to Burger King," he explains. "It's just leftovers. Eat it quickly."

I have no idea why he's giving it to me. While it's true that he doesn't really associate with the other members of the squad, I can think of at least a dozen other people in the company he could've given it to.

"Thank you, sir," I manage to choke out. I'm seriously choked up.

Fearing the others might come or that the Professor will change his mind, I stuff the small burger into my mouth and devour it. It's gone in seconds. I don't take the time to savor each bite, but it's maybe the best burger I've ever had in my life. I've been subsisting on mostly rice and kimchi since January, five months without tasting the food I grew up with and love, and this burger was home. I have to fight back the tears.

The good news, now that Beaver is gone, is that there are empty spots to fill with fresh fish, privates to whom I am the *gocham*. All of my *donggi* have already cast off the title of lowest in their squad hierarchies, leaving the dirtiest and most menial tasks to February, March, and soon April subordinates.

The bad news is that now I'm the one who is called to the Mobilization Branch when there is work to be done, even on the weekends, as is the case today. I was getting my cleaning assignment for the nightly cleaning when a private relayed the message from the administration office—a call for overtime from Colonel Jeong.

As I walk to Headquarters, I look up at the building and notice that the lights in the office are turned on, in stark contrast to the rest of the building, which stands dark against the moonlit sky. When I enter the office, Colonel Jeong is sitting at a desk with an extra chair and a stack of handwritten papers for me to type.

"Sit down," he orders. "We've got a lot of work to do."

While I work, he gets up and pours himself a bowl of corn flakes. I hear him the flakes crunching in his mouth as I type up his reports. *Crunch, crunch, crunch.* That should say *weonhwal*, not *weonhweol. Crunch, crunch.* Put a table in this table here and use bigger bullet points. *Crunch, crunch, crunch.*

Around midnight, Colonel Jeong suggests that we take a break.

"Do you want some cereal?"

"I'm okay, sir." I'd rather finish up as soon as possible and get at least a little sleep before my shift on guard duty at the Bunker.

161

"Have some," he says, pouring me a bowl of cereal.

"Yes, sir. Thank you, sir."

I take the bowl and try to make quick work of the corn flakes.

"Where're you from?" he asks.

"Seattle, sir."

"Did you go back to Seattle on your furlough?"

"No, sir. I can't, sir."

"Are you sure?"

"Yes, sir. I… uh… I looked it up in my journal. In the back, there's… regulations."

The last fifteen to twenty pages of the journal they handed out in boot camp has a complete list of regulations for conscripts. I spend most of my free time studying Korean, but I've also scoured the section in the back of my journal related to furloughs countless times, with dictionary in hand, trying to find some hope that I'll be able to go home for at least a visit and never finding it.

"Let me see," he says and reaches out and plucks a thick book from the books lined up on his desktop. He leafs through the pages and starts reading. "It says here that conscripts with foreign residency can go abroad once. They pay for your ticket and even give you a couple extra days for travel time."

"Uh… I don't think… I can do that, sir. I don't have foreign residency, sir. I have foreign citizenship."

"Is there a difference?"

"Yes, sir."

He raises one of his bushy eyebrows and starts flipping through the pages. "I don't see anything for foreign citizens."

"Yes, sir. I don't know if there is anyone else… like me, sir."

He chuckles. "I guess they didn't consider someone like you would be here."

"Yes, sir." I don't chuckle. There aren't any regulations to let me go home because there shouldn't be someone like me in the Army. Meanwhile, kids who only have a green card and may not even have family abroad are taken care of. I've come to terms with being stuck here, but every so often I'm given a hard reminder of the hand I've been dealt.

It's a little before lunch when the phone rings. I've always disliked using the phone, but the Army has taken this mild dislike to full-blown aversion. There's just too much to say without stumbling over my own words.

"The line is secure. M-Mo-Mobilization Branch, this is Private Young Jin Chun."

Then I have to deal with what comes after, usually mocking laughter or disdain and a question I won't be able to understand or answer. Nine times out of ten, I have to hand the phone over to Corporal Yeong-jun, our commuter soldier,[48] but it's my job to answer the phone because I'm the lowest ranked.

There is stifled laughter on the other end. "That's enough, Chun. Do you know who this is?"

"No, sir. I'm sorry, sir."

"This is the Interpretation Officer, Lieutenant Kim."

"*Chungseong.*"

"We're having a meeting on the third floor in fifteen minutes. You know where it is, right?"

"Yes, sir."

There are supposed to be around forty linguists in the company, but there's only about half that number present when the meeting begins. Lieutenant Kim hands out copies of a report to each of us.

"They're activating a new unit at the JSA.[49] As you guys may have heard, the U.S. Army is slowly pulling out and new units need to be activated in order to take their place. They need linguists to facilitate the transfer of duties from the Americans to us."

I look over the report, which is an official notice for the unit's recruitment. There is a list of conditions for potential unit members. They're only

---

[48] Commuter soldiers are conscripts who are allowed to serve at a base near their homes and commute to and from the base daily. I heard that they allow young men with health problems to be commuter soldiers, but the majority of the commuter soldiers in the company were forced to do manual labor as their primary duty. Another of the Army's ironies.

Corporal Yeong-jun was a decent guy. I wonder if it was because he was able to go home at the end of the day.

[49] JSA: Joint Security Area. The area on the Military Demarcation Line between the North and the South.

accepting PFCs and corporals. That's why all the higher-ranked linguists are absent.

"Think about it and inform your company personnel office if you're interested," Lieutenant Kim says and dismisses us for lunch.

Most of the others throw away their copies of the report on the way to the mess hall but I fold mine carefully and put it in my pocket. They discuss the meeting as we eat.

"Are you going to apply, sir?"

"You kidding? You want to be at the bottom for the rest of your service?"

"Yeah, I guess not."

"Besides," one PFC says between mouthfuls of rice and deep-fried fish, "who'd want to go to the JSA? It's comfortable here."

I listen quietly while I work on my rice and kimchi. The PFCs don't want to go because they don't want to be someone else's lackey for the rest of their service. The corporals don't want to go because they're unwilling to surrender the comfort they've built up during their time here.

I'm not going to be a PFC for another two weeks but I want to go. The last three weeks haven't been comfortable for me, not only because I'm just a private, but also because I'm just not cut out for working in an office. The best times have been the times when I've been used as manual labor, at least when it coincided with work hours. Paving the home for the mentally handicapped, even moving the office equipment to and from the bunker and pruning trees. I often wish that I'd never taken the linguist test. I don't feel like a soldier. I'd rather not be a soldier altogether but, seeing as I have no say in the matter, I might as well be an actual soldier.

On the next workday morning, I step out of the office using the bathroom as an excuse and head down to the personnel office on the first floor. When I walk through the door, Ho-ju calls out to me. I thought he was working in the mess hall, but it seems they've moved him to Headquarters Personnel.

"Chun, what are you doing here?"

"I want to apply for the JSA, sir."

He takes me to the desk of the officer in charge of the applications and explains my reason for coming.

"What's your name, soldier?"

"Private Young Jin Chun, sir."

I give him my serial number and he types it in the computer and frowns that same frown I've seen so many times.

"You can't apply. They're only taking PFCs and corporals."

"I'm becoming a private first class next month, sir."

"It doesn't matter. Besides, your health is Grade 3. They're only accepting conscripts who are Grade 1." He turns back to his computer as if to say our business is done.

"I understand, sir."

I would argue that my health ranking is only because of my tattoos and inability to speak Korean, but I know that even if I were able to express myself perfectly, it would still be futile. I should've known better. More than anyone else, I should know that technicalities aren't overlooked in the Army.

When I return to the company before dinner, I can feel a lecture in the air, the strange, unnatural quiet and the looks given back and forth. Sang-jun sighs. "I'll do it." He gets up and leaves the room, motioning for me to follow.

"When I was your rank…," he begins and even though I've heard the same lecture twice earlier today, I sit and listen quietly.

The lectures are a response to a couple of incidents involving my *donggi* over the weekend and there is an implicit agreement that we must hear these lectures ad nauseam. The first was committed by Yo-han and I can't help but feel partially responsible. I was scheduled for guard duty at the entrance of the joint ROK-US intelligence area in the basement of Headquarters on Sunday but I was called to put in overtime at the office and I had asked Yo-han to cover for me. While he was walking to Headquarters with his rifle slung over his shoulder, he accidentally pressed the trigger and set off one of the rounds we're given for guard duty. It was a blank but the *gocham* have been treating it as if it had been a live round.

The day before, Yong-ju went out on a weekend pass and failed to report back on time. The implication is that he broke the regulation of staying in the area and took a train home.[50] From what I've gathered, most of the conscripts in my company go home when out on pass, East Daegu Station being so close, but it's one of those things that you can do as long as you don't get caught, and Yong-ju got caught.

"Kids these days…" he continues. Sang-jun is actually a year older than

---

[50] I'm not sure if this was a base regulation or a unit regulation, but we were not allowed to stray more than 500 meters from the base during a weekend pass.

165

me, the only older conscript in the squad, which makes it a little less unbearable to sit through. The first two lectures were given to me by corporals five to six years my junior and I think it's ridiculous that these kids are preaching to me like I'm a child listening to his grandfather's stories.

"Don't get in any more trouble," he admonishes me before leading me back to the squad room to get ready for dinner. As we walk back, he pats me on the back to show that there are no hard feelings. I have to put up with this for eighteen more months? The thought is depressing.

D-571 (6JUL04): Afghanistan Application

I'm walking back to the squad room after lunch when I run into Ho-ju on the third floor.

"Chun, come with me for a second."

"Yes, sir."

We go to the same empty storage room that my *gocham* favor when yelling at me. I'm a little confused because it's usually one of my squad members that get on my case. The other *gocham* just insult or humiliate me and pass the responsibility of educating me to one of my squad members.

"Have you ever thought about going on *pabyeong?*"

"I don't know *pabyeong*, sir."

"Deployment. Going to Afghanistan."

"I haven't thought about it, sir."

"Think about it. It's a good experience."

"Yes, sir."

"They're going to take applications soon. Check the intranet if you're interested."

"Yes, sir."

Ho-ju's a thoughtful guy. As a private, I haven't expressed my disappointment at being unable to get transferred to the JSA to anyone. I haven't even let my face betray my frustration. I guess that's what fathers are for.

At the office, I check the intranet for the announcement. It's been posted today. I scroll down to the application requirements. I fit the rank requirements, and thankfully there are no health restrictions. I look at the positions and see that most of the Military Occupational Specialties call for large numbers of engineers, electricians, and plumbers. At the bottom of the list are the others, small numbers for drivers and administrative assistants. The last line is the number for interpreters—one. Only one interpreter from the Second Army. I ask Yeong-jun and he tells me that it doesn't mean one from Headquarters, our base, but from the whole of the Second Army. The Second Army encompasses the bottom half of South Korea, the entire rear area, comprised of at least seven full divisions.

The odds are not in my favor, but I decide to take my chances. I'll take any opportunity to leave this place. I read the application procedures and note that I have to get permission from my parents and my company commander. I'll have to go see Captain Jin again.

I'm standing in the phone booth with my notepad in my hand. I've just called my mother to let her know that I'll be applying to the deployment in Afghanistan. She wasn't happy about it but she knows there's nothing doing when I've made up my mind. It hurts when I hear the resignation in her voice when she says goodbye but I tell myself this is the last time and it's something I have to do. I know money is tight, and I can't let her continue to pay off my college loans while I'm here.

The problem is the next call. I have to call my father. The officer at the Personnel Office told me I had to get permission from both parents, regardless of their marital status. I pick up the receiver and dial his number.

"Who is this?"

"Hi, Dad," I answer, the word strange as it rolls off my tongue. "This is Young."

"Oh, Young. I'm a little busy right now. Can you call back later?"

"No, I don't think I'll be able to call later. It'll only take a second."

"All right. What is it?"

"I'm just calling to let you know that I'm going to apply for a deployment to Afghanistan." That's how I chose to phrase it when I practiced what I'd say. I don't mention that I need his permission.

"What? Young, I don't think that's a good idea."

"Sorry, Dad, but I've made my decision. I'm just calling to let you know."

He starts to respond but stops himself. "All right, Young, if that's your decision. I've got to go now."

"Okay. Goodbye."

Two down, one to go. Captain Jin. I've saved the most difficult for last.

At evening call, the officer on duty has us watching the news until he comes for the personnel report. The news story of the day is Kim Sun-il. There have been a lot of beheadings in the Middle East during the past few months, but this is bigger news here because he was Korean. The story has been dominating the news for the past couple of weeks.

From watching the news, I've learned that Kim Sun-il was working as a private contractor in Iraq, as an interpreter. He was kidnapped and his captors had demanded that Korea withdraw its troops. There have been many reports of protests urging the government to agree to their demands, but the government recently announced that it was going to refuse the kidnappers' demands.

Today, the news is reporting that it's been confirmed that he's been killed. *Chamsu*, the tagline reads. Decapitated, my dictionary tells me. On the screen, they show a video still of Kim in a black hood, kneeling before his armed captors.

Have there been any beheadings in Afghanistan recently? I can't remember hearing of any but I'm not sure. Regardless, the impeccability of my timing never ceases to astound me.

At the office in the morning, I read a report about two American soldiers that were found decapitated a short distance from where their vehicle was found in Afghanistan. I'm reminded of an odd comment from Il-su a week ago, before I'd even heard of the deployment. He commented that my neck looked skinnier. The thought of having my head cut from my body is disturbing and with my luck, who's to say that it won't happen, but even I'm unable to change my mind once I've made it up.

Now I'm standing in front of Captain Jin's door. I don't want to go in. I've stayed under his radar since the whole Seattle P-I debacle but he seems like a guy who'd carry a grudge.

I take a deep breath. It's better to just get through this quickly. I knock on the door.

"Private Young Jin Chun. May I enter, sir?"

"Enter," he says from the other side of the door.

I enter the room and salute.

"What do you want?"

I look at him carefully. He looks displeased but no more displeased than he usually does as he walks around the base.

"I want to apply for Afghanistan deployment, sir. I... the Personnel Office told me I need the commander's permission, sir."

"Afghanistan?" He pauses to think and his face lights up slightly, the semblance of a grin barely forming at the corners of his mouth. "Hmm. Good. That sounds like it will be a good experience."

"Uh... yes, sir."

"You have my permission."

"Thank you, sir."

I salute and close the door behind me, confused. I can never guess how our meetings will go. I had expected open antagonism. I hadn't expected that he could be rational. Nothing in any of our previous meetings gave any indication of his rationality, but it turns out he can be rational when it means getting rid of someone like me. Conscript of interest? I'm more like a thorn in his side, one that he obviously is happy to let go.

I'm on a train to Suweon for an interview for the deployment. I feel good. It's a result of leaving the base even though this is not a furlough or weekend pass. It's also because I've got my new rank insignia stitched onto my uniform. I'm going to the interview as a private first class, two horizontal black bars versus the skimpy single bar of a lowly private. I didn't earn it, per se—promotions are automatic for conscripts[51]—but I certainly feel as if it's been earned. The only damper on my mood is my company.

"Wake me up when we get to Suweon," Private Ja-hong says beside me.

"Yes, sir."

Of all the people to apply for the same deployment, it had to be Ja-hong, my most prolific tormentor. There isn't a private in our company who hasn't had the misfortune of his angry tirades. If we both pass our interviews, there will be much rejoicing in Daegu and much sadness for me in Afghanistan.

As we come out of Suweon Station, my eyes are drawn to a small group of protestors carrying poster boards and candles. When we get closer, I can read the slogan on the posters. *Pabyeong bandae.* They are opposing the deployment of troops overseas. I chuckle to myself at the irony, glad that they don't

---

[51] Promotions are given strictly according to time served. At the time of my service, the length at each rank was as follows: six months at private (PVT/PV1/PV2), six months at private first class (PFC), seven months at corporal (CPL), and five months at sergeant (SGT). There is no merit involved, save the merit of waiting and putting up with shit.

know the reason for my trip to Suweon.

After a short bus ride, we arrive at the interview center and check in. There are hundreds of conscripts milling around the dusty area in front of two trailers. As I walk over to the bulletin board to check out the competition, I feel the other conscripts sizing me up. I look at the list of applicants for the interpreter position, and there are ten names from units spread all over South Korea. I'm the only one from the Second Army.

Ja-hong is applying for one of the administrative-assistant positions, and it's a relief when we are separated into groups to form lines for our interviews. My group is the last to be interviewed, and Ja-hong tells me to meet back in front of the bulletin board once I'm done.

The guys in line keep giving me and each other dirty looks. According to the bulletin board, there are ten of us and six positions. There's a sixty-percent chance of passing, and yet it's clear that the flames of competition are burning brightly within each candidate. One thing that is stoking the flames is that the roster also listed our qualifications. One corporal was studying English Lit at Seoul National University, the top university in Korea. Another was studying at Rutgers. My qualification is following me whether I like it or not: 22 years living in the States.

The first five enter the trailer, and the rest of us are the last conscripts to be interviewed out of the entire body of applicants. Nobody says a word. I just want it to be over with. We have to return to our respective bases by 2100, and the longer this takes, the less free time I'll have, considering the lengthy trip back down to Daegu.

The first five file out and we enter the room. At the front is a long desk where two majors and a lieutenant are sitting, shuffling papers and discussing the previous group. In front of the desk are five chairs lined neatly in a row where we take our seats. I'm seated in the second seat.

The first applicant is a mess. The lieutenant begins the interview with several questions in English and the corporal does a poor job, eventually answering the last question in Korean, explaining that he was majoring in French at the Hanguk University of Foreign Studies. I wonder if they'll need French interpreters but figure that there's one less person to worry about, seeing as the questions were posed in English. I'm also feeling fairly confident because only one question was posed in Korean.

"Private Young Jin Chun?"

"Yes, sir."

"You've lived in America for 22 years?" the lieutenant asks in Korean.

"Yes, sir."

"Why are you applying for this deployment?" I'm a bit unnerved that he's continuing the interview in Korean but I was expecting the question.

"I want to spend the rest of my military service more productively, sir." Even I am surprised by the fluidity of my answer. It seems typing up all those reports at Headquarters has allowed me to speak in their jargon, the words and expressions that the officers use most often.

"Do you have any interpretation experience?"

"Yes, sir. I interpreted during an ROK-US exercise a couple of months ago, sir." It's not a lie. The question was about my experience, not my performance.

I'm doing well. The majors are grinning at each other.

"Okay, this will be the last question," the lieutenant says, switching to English. "What do you think of the deployment of Korean soldiers in Afghanistan?"

It's a simple enough question. "I think... uh... I think that it's... good. It's good to support... to work together for the Afghanistan people... the people in Afghanistan." As I speak, I feel myself falling to pieces. What's going on? Why can't I speak in English?

All three of the officers start whispering amongst themselves, confused expressions on their faces. Please ask me another question. Give me a chance to redeem myself. The whispering stops and the lieutenant regains his composure. "That'll be all, private," he says and moves on to the next applicant.

What just happened? It's true that I haven't spoken much English in the last six months, and I'm not familiar with bullshitting in military English, but there's no explanation for such utter ineloquence. Even my elementary-school students at the *hagwon* could have answered with more elegance.

I sit through the rest of the interviews, the pangs of my inexplicable failure making me sick. The next three applicants do reasonably well, which is disheartening because I needed to do better than at least two of my group of five to be reasonably confident.

After the last applicant is finished, we file out of the room, and I find Ja-hong at the appointed place.

"How'd you do?" he asks, smiling.

"I really don't know, sir."

I've been nervously checking the intranet all day, refreshing the page every couple of minutes. The results are supposed to come out today and it really could go either way. I can barely eat lunch, even though it's one of those rare occasions where they are serving something resembling beef. For the first time after lunch, I'm itching to head back to the office.

It's shortly after 1330 that the results are posted on the intranet. My hand is trembling as I move the cursor and click the link. I slowly scroll the page down. The administrative assistant results pop up first. Pfc. Gu Ja-hong. The bastard made it. At least if I don't make it, he won't be around in Daegu for a while. I scroll down a bit further where I know the results for the interpreters will be.

Pfc. Young Jin Chun.

I made it. I can't believe it. I stifle my expression to a whisper of thanks to the powers that be.

"Did it come out?" Yeong-jun asks. He knows that I've been anxious all day because of the results.

"Yes, sir," I say, unable to mask my smile. "I made it, sir."

"Congratulations, Chun."

"Thank you, sir."

"I guess you're not going to be here for much longer. Make sure to tell the officers before you leave."

"Yes, sir."

I show up to the office for the rest of the week and inform all of the officers, including the chief, of my deployment orders. Most of them are happy for me; Mr. Choi, our civilian contractor, and Yeong-jun take me out for a cup of vending-machine coffee so they can give me some parting remarks. During the past four months, they've been the ones in the office to whom I've been able to speak candidly and who have treated me like a person with emotions and feelings.

Every night after lights out, I inform the night watch I'll be studying and head to the break room with the Defense Daily, the Army newspaper, and my dictionary. I realize that I can never cut it as an interpreter at my present level of ability and am doing as much as I can with the little time that I have. I stay until midnight, when the night watch comes to kick me out.

Life at the company has improved considerably, mostly because I don't let it affect me. Another guard duty on top of the five we already have? No problem. Manual labor on the weekend? I don't mind. *Mishing*? Why not? The fact that I'll be gone in less than a week is empowering. I do feel sympathy for my two new charges, privates who came to fill in my squad's depleted ranks, and try to teach them everything I can, everything I've learned over the past four months at SROKA, most importantly how to stay out of potential trouble and whom to avoid. I'm a fount of information because I've been punished for almost everything possible.

I'm on the last shift of our newest guard duty, sitting at a table in front of the base personnel office. The sergeant I'm on duty with is sleeping soundly, and the mosquito coil on the table is dropping its ashes, gray tendrils of fragrant repellent swirling up into the pale blue of the breaking morning. It's going to rain today.

After morning call, breakfast, and the morning cleaning of the company, I put on my grade-A uniform and boots and report to the office to pick up my furlough papers. The company first sergeant, Command Sergeant Major Park, has given me and Ja-hong a two-night, three-day furlough to get things in order before leaving for pre-deployment training on Monday.

I spend the first night with my relatives and again leave the apartment early the next morning to wander the streets of Seoul. After a couple of hours, I find myself in Yeoksam-dong, in the middle of the financial district. I spot a sign for the administrative office of Yeoksam-dong and, on a whim, decide to stop by to ask for a citizen-registration card. I've been in the Army since January and will be going to Afghanistan as a Korean soldier, I might as well get my identification card as a Korean citizen. I can't figure out which paperwork to fill out, so I approach the counter.

"How may I help you, sir?" the clerk asks politely.

"I want to get a citizen registration card."

"Can I have your citizen registration number?"

I hand the clerk the slip of paper I have it scribbled down on. The clerk takes it and starts clacking on the keyboard furiously with a confused look on his face. His expression is eerily similar to that of the clerk at the Immigration Office in Mok-dong and that of the immigration officer at Osan Air Base.

"I'm sorry, but the computer shows that you have dual citizenship. If you would like a citizenship-registration card, you're going to have to cancel your American citizenship."

The card isn't a necessity. It just means that I'll be able to get into clubs without paying the foreigner cover and get a cell phone without having to pay the two-hundred-dollar security charge. I just figure that I'm serving in the Korean Army, and the least they can do is allow me the same privileges and identity as the other six hundred thousand conscripts.

"Listen, I'm in the Army now. Can't you do anything for me?"

Looking at me with the same confused expression, the clerk asks, "What are *you* doing in the Army?"

What am I doing in the Army? The sheer absurdity of the question has rendered me completely speechless. *That's what I've been trying to figure out this entire time*, I want to scream. I should be the one asking the question. You should be the one with the answer.

I manage to control my anger and ask, "What about a passport?"

"I'm sorry but it's the same situation. If you want to cancel your American citizenship, you'll have to go to Immigration."

I don't dignify his statement with a response. I turn and walk straight out the door.

As I walk back to the main street, I'm left thinking. There is clearly something wrong with the system, with one person saying that I have to serve in the Army and another saying that I can't have the rights of a citizen who has to serve in the Army. This is not only the wrong end of the stick, it's been shoved deep up my anus in a supreme case of sodomy by the government. All of the obligations, none of the rights.

It's the early afternoon, but I walk to Gangnam to try to find a bar that's open. I need to wash the bad taste out of my mouth.

The bars aren't open yet, so I opt to go to an internet café instead. Having nothing to do, I download the video of the beheading of Kim Sun-il out of morbid curiosity. Jason told me that he had watched it and it was gruesome.

The video begins with the same scene as the video still on the news. Kim Sun-il is kneeling on the ground, a black hood covering his face. Behind him, his captors are standing, masked and holding their rifles. All of a sudden, one of his captors steps forward, producing a long, curved knife. He grabs Kim and raises his arm, the knife poised for a hefty strike.

When I heard of the beheadings, for some reason I assumed that they were done swiftly with one clean stroke. The reality is much more horrific. The man with the knife hacks repeatedly at Kim's neck, Kim Sun-il screaming the entire time. It's painful to watch and painful to hear. Kim's screams echo in my head.

174

I turn off the video. I try to distract myself by playing games but the ghastly scenes keep popping up in my head and I can't un-see what I've seen. I imagine myself in Kim's situation, kneeling on the ground, the knife repeatedly chopping into the muscles and ligaments of my neck.

I can't be here anymore. Even though my hour isn't up, I pay and leave the internet café to get some fresh air and renew my search for an open bar.

The return to Daegu is not half as depressing as it had been returning from my 100th-day furlough. The debacle at the Yeoksam-dong Office and the gruesome video are in the past. Tomorrow is Sunday, and I'll be leaving Daegu the next morning.

Sunday passes in one happy blur. I go to the PX twice, with my *donggi* for lunch and with my two charges for ice cream after dinner. None of the *gocham* comment on my absence from the squad room or my frequenting the PX.

On Monday morning, I wake up to reveille with a smile on my face. After morning call, I inform the corporal in charge of cleaning duties that I'll be leaving and head straight to the squad room to pack. I completely empty my locker, dumping everything into my duffel bag, removing all traces of my existence as a member of the 15th squad.

I say brief goodbyes as I walk down the hall, as I get my orders, as I walk out of the doors and away from the company. I smile as I say my goodbyes, in part because I know that many of these people I'll never have to see again and in part because this feeling is almost as if I've finished my service.

Pre-deployment Training
1113th Field Engineer Group
Ansan, Gyeonggi Province, Korea
Korean Support Group, Dasan Unit, 2nd Construction Company
19 July 2004 - 2 August 2004

D-558 (19JUL04): Not in Daegu Anymore

The 1113th Field Engineer Group in Ansan is built into the side of a mountain, a massive concrete block engraved with the unit name marking its entrance on the small country road. The gravel road leading up from the main gate is a steep grade, and along the path is another concrete block with a common Army slogan in black spray-painted lettering: "Make the impossible possible."

There is a long line of conscripts with duffel bags slung over their shoulders, and Ja-hong and I join their ranks. Ja-hong has been in a surprisingly jovial mood since we left Daegu.

"This place is pretty shitty, isn't it, *hyeong*?" It's the first time he's ever used the informal and familiar address toward me, something *gocham* don't normally do.

"Yes, sir."

"You don't have to speak to me so formally. We're not in Daegu anymore."

"Yes...."

When we reach the desk at the front of the line, we check in and are given our unit assignments. 2nd Construction Company. Ja-hong is assigned to the Support Company. Despite his unexpectedly relaxed attitude toward me today, it's a relief that we'll be in different companies.

We walk to the area of the base set apart for the deployment group, and it's a small cluster of decrepit tin buildings around a small dirt courtyard. Above the entrances to the buildings are hastily taped sheets of paper reading 1st Construction Company, 2nd Construction Company, *Tomok*[52] Company, Support Company. Off to the side is a small shack that serves as the unit bathrooms, and there are a few conscripts on the roof of the building hanging their laundry on clotheslines.

The barracks are old, Korean War-era barracks like the barracks at the mobilization-training center, a single room two or three times as long as the squad room from boot camp and much barer. The barracks are meant for temporary use, quickly built with long wooden shelves instead of lockers.

"Put away your things and change into your PT uniforms," an officer barks at the door. "We're going for a run."

I take a spot against the far wall, change into my PT uniform, and throw

---

[52] *Tomok*: Civil Engineering.

179

my bag under the wooden shelf. I scoot out to the edge of the raised floor but realize I didn't take out my sneakers. I scoot back and rummage through my duffel bag. Where are they? All around me, the rest of the recruits are running out the door. My sneakers aren't in my bag. I must've left them in Daegu.

Shit.

"You aren't going to hurry up?"

Having no choice, I lace up my boots and run out to join the formation.

After the run and mental education, I find that my duffel bag has been tossed aside to make room for a captain, our company commander. He's a tall, lanky guy with large, round monkey ears and an extended simian upper lip.

"2nd Construction Company, *jip-hap*," he orders. His voice is warbled and high-pitched as he addresses his company for the first time.

Once we're seated three to a row, the company commander, Captain Park, introduces the company noncoms.

"This is Master Sergeant Kim. He'll be the company first sergeant." Master Sergeant Kim is short and severely balding, with leathery skin and very long skinny limbs that also make him appear very chimp-like.

"And this is Staff Sergeant Kim, who will help out with the company administration." The staff sergeant is a tall kid with squinty eyes, a sickly pallor, and a full head of hair. He gives us a goofy smile. Career enlisted begin at staff sergeant; the lowest four enlisted ranks are reserved for conscripts.

Captain Park orders us to briefly introduce ourselves and gives us time to get to know one another. While the others get up and start to mingle, the first sergeant approaches me.

"Hey, you're from SROKA Headquarters?" he asks.

"Yes, sir."

"I was serving at the 50th Division."

"I understand, sir," I respond, smiling slightly. We were neighbors. The 50th Division is situated in Yeongcheon, just outside of Daegu.

He doesn't return the smile or even say anything more. He's just standing there in front of me, standing there and giving me a dismissive look. I thought that he was establishing common ground between us but it's as if he's saying I know where you're from, a place of comfort, and it's a bad thing. He walks away without saying another word.

The other recruits in the 2nd Construction Company are all from engineering units, civil engineers, electricians, and plumbers, salt of the earth, completely different from the conscripts I've met at Headquarters Company in Daegu. On the whole, they are young, just kids, but a better sampling of the population. They remind me of my squad in boot camp: tall kids, short kids, fat kids, skinny kids, pale kids, dark kids, kids with glasses, most without, fair kids, ugly kids, city kids, country kids.

I feel out of place. Private Chun, the company interpreter, the old kid, the kid from headquarters, the kid who runs with his combat boots on, the American.

D-554 (23JUL04): Captain Park

Captain Park is giving a lecture on concrete, on how different mixtures of the ingredients and water are necessary for differing purposes and climates. I don't mind sitting through the lecture because nothing is expected of me, and learning about concrete isn't so uninteresting.

One thing that is making me a tad uncomfortable is the prickly glances that Captain Park occasionally sends my way as he uses his long monkey arms to draw diagrams on the large drawing pad next to him. I know the glances well—glances that tell me I don't belong.

There is no separate training for the interpreters, so I've been spending my days with the company. Tagging along.

Being naturally withdrawn and introverted on top of my inability to hold a conversation in Korean, I haven't gotten to know anyone in my company very well. Some of the others served at the same units and for others, it seems like having the same Military Occupational Specialty has served as common ground to form friendships. The only person I've had a brief conversation with is Private Jeong-su, a civil engineer in my squad who was studying at McGill in Canada before returning to come to the Army.

Not that the others are hostile toward me. It's been decided that conscripts in our company don't have to abide by the strict hierarchy we observed at our previous stations. As a result, we treat each other like people, courteously and civilly. It's a nice change from life in Daegu.

During the scant free time we're given after the day's training and dinner, most of the others congregate outside the barracks and have vending-machine coffee or smoke or do their laundry. My routine hasn't changed; I'm spending every possible moment studying Korean because I know I'm still completely unprepared and inadequate. I'm studying after dinner when Captain Park plops down next to me.

"Chun."

"Yes, sir."

"What're you doing?"

"I'm just studying Korean, sir," I respond, holding up my study materials for him to see.

"Good, good," he says, pausing awkwardly. "Where did you say you were you stationed before?"

"SROKA Headquarters, sir."

"You worked in an office there?"

"Yes, sir."

"You know how to use PowerPoint?"

"Just a little, sir."

"Good," he says, getting up. "Come with me."

I follow Captain Park out of the barracks to a small trailer where a few desks and computers have been set up. A major is sitting at a desk, and there are a few conscripts at work at the computers, one of whom is Ja-hong. Captain Park tells me to wait and goes to talk with the major.

"*Hyeong*, what are you doing here?" Ja-hong asks me in a whisper.

"I have no idea. They have you working overtime already?"

"Yeah," he says, frowning.

Captain Park calls me over to the major, introduces me, and walks out the door. The major looks me over. I get the feeling that I've been pimped out again.

"So you know how to use the computer?"

It seems like a ridiculous question. It's the 21st century. I say I do, sir.

"Follow me," he says and sits me down at an empty computer. The Korean word-processing program is open, and it seems that someone has been making an organizational chart. "Make this look pretty."

"Uh… yes, sir."

I'm confused because this isn't PowerPoint. I'm disgruntled because I don't want to be sitting in front of a computer again. I thought I had left it all behind me. I look at the clock. 2130. The squad is probably having evening call right now. I'll just finish this off quickly so I can get to bed by lights out.

The organizational chart has been done sloppily. If I had done something like this in Daegu, Beaver would have given me hell. I get to work, playing with the lines, inserting and merging cells, and tweaking the spaces between letters, all the while watching the clock. When the clock hits 2200, I'm almost finished. I make it look presentable and inform the major.

He comes at looks at the screen over my shoulder, pats my back, and says, "Good job. You can return to the company." Thank God there are no corrections.

"Thank you, sir."

"And Chun...."

"Yes, sir?"

"Report here during the days, starting tomorrow."

D-553 (24AUG04): Major Jeong and Captain Bang

My approach last night had been a mistake. Throughout my first day at the Tactical Operations Center, I've noticed that I'm the only one being put to work. The other administrative assistants from the Support Company come and go, but it doesn't seem as if they do much at all.

The major, Major Jeong, is the unit executive officer and S2/S3 chief. He has dark skin and a full head of well-groomed hair, parted on the right, and he smiles and laughs easily while he assigns me more work.

"How's it like working for the *galchi*?" Ja-hong asks when I run into him after lunch.

"*Galchi*?" I ask.

"Yeah, he looks like a *galchi*."

Hairtail or scabbard fish, the dictionary tells me when I look it up later. I don't know what a hairtail looks like, but the chief doesn't look like a fish to me.

In the afternoon, Major Jeong has an administrative assistant from the Field Engineer Group come to sharpen my skill with PowerPoint. After dinner, the major has me return to start work on a PowerPoint presentation. When he decides to turn in, he hands the baton to the Operations Officer, Captain Bang, a hulk of a soldier, tall and bulky and clean-cut like a football player from the 1930s.

It's now well past midnight, and Captain Bang has me typing up a report. It's just the two of us. All of the other conscripts have been sent back to the barracks to sleep.

"How's the report coming along?" Captain Bang asks, reclining in his chair, his thick arms folded behind his head.

I don't catch the sigh before it escapes my lips. "I'm almost done, sir."

"Chun," he says after a moment of reflection, "do you know the expression, *bu ik bu, bin ik bin*?"

I stop typing and look at the captain. "No, sir."

"It's taken from Chinese characters. It means the rich get richer and the poor get poorer."

He pauses so I tell him I understand.

"You're here working and everyone else is sleeping. In the expression, you're the rich man."

"I understand, sir."

I wait for further explanation but he's finished talking. As I finish typing up the report, I think about what he said. I think he meant to say that I'm here typing in the middle of the night because I do good work. Had I not done a good job last night, I wouldn't be in this situation now. Major Jeong could have had any of the other conscripts in the office work on the presentation and type up his reports. He could have had any of them learn Power-Point from the conscript from the Field Engineer Group. The problem is that the reward for good work is even more work. I can't tell which end of the analogy applies to me, but it sure feels like the butt end.

D-551 (26JUL04): Power Plays

The one consolation of working late nights is *ochim*, meaning that if they work me past a certain time, they let me sleep in until lunch. The downside is that usually around 0100, Captain Bang will make a decision as to whether to send me back to the company to sleep so that I can report to the Tactical Operations Center the next morning. They've had me working the past week with an average of five hours of sleep a night.

Last night, they had me work until past 0430. There's an important presentation coming up, and Major Jeong had me working on his PowerPoint slides, the urgency of getting the slides done necessitating the late hours and allowing me *ochim* the next day.

Sleep in the morning is restless. There are around fifty conscripts and officers in this barracks, and the sounds of them getting ready for the day and ordering each other around hardly allows for sleep to set in. I hear the whispers, too. The other conscripts resent me for being able to sleep in. As if I needed another reason to not fit in. They don't know that I work late because they're deep in sleep at the hours I return.

"Hey. Hey. Wake up."

I crack open my eyes and see a giant of a conscript towering over me. I recognize him solely by his height. He's one of the guys from 2nd squad. "What?"

"It's lunch time."

"I'm not hungry. I was up late working."

"Sorry, but Captain Park told me to wake you up."

Damn it. I sit up and wipe the sleep out of my eyes. I check my watch. It's 1130. This is a power play, I know. Captain Park has sold me to the unit S2/S3 but still wants to show that he has control over me. A pimp has to keep his whores in line.

I'm jolted awake by a hard bump, my head nearly hitting the roof of the jeep. We must almost be wherever we're headed. I didn't get any sleep last night. Today is the day of the presentation, and Major Jeong had me up all night finishing the PowerPoint. I managed to get a little sleep on the highway, and I know by the sound of the engine idling that we're in the city now.

The jeep pulls into a large military establishment, the words Army Consolidated Administrative School in big blue letters in an arch above the entrance. The jeep stops in front of a two-story building, and we go up to a briefing room on the second floor. Major Jeong tells me to set up the laptop and get the presentation ready so he can do a run-through before lunch.

I'm setting up the computer when I hear footsteps out in the hall and a group of conscripts pass by the room. One of them stops and peeks into the room. It's Johnny.

"*Hyeong!*"

"Johnny, what are you doing here?"

"I'm the interpreter for the medical unit. We've been here for about a week." The deployment consists of a large engineering detachment and smaller medical and civil affairs units. The medical unit must've had separate

185

interviews.

"What happened to you after I left the Replenishment Unit?"

"I was sent to Gwangju. I was working for the divisional operations branch there."

"How was it?"

"Actually, it wasn't too bad," he says hurriedly and looks down the hall. "I gotta go. I'll see you around."

"Yeah, I'll see you around."

It's good to hear that he fared well after we parted ways at the 100th Replenishment Unit. I've always wondered what happened that day his attitude changed. I tell myself to remember to ask the next time I see him.

In the afternoon, Major Jeong delivers the presentation to the commander of the deployment, Colonel Park. I haven't seen him in Ansan; he must be working here with the medical unit at the ACAS. He's an imposing man, tall and well-built for his age, but there's something unsettling about him. It's his eyes. He has those crazy eyes that Captain Jin had back in Daegu, but whereas Captain Jin's eyes were full of anger and disdain, the colonel's eyes seem vacant, as if he's looking straight through me. He gives his comments on the presentation and sends us on our way back to Ansan.

It's dinner time when we return to the 1113th, and Major Jeong tells me to return to the office after dinner. We have to edit the PowerPoint based on Colonel Park's comments. When I report to the TOC, there are a few conscripts from the Support Company present.

Major Jeong gives me a list of corrections to make and entrusts the task to Captain Bang, leaving to go to bed after a long day. Captain Bang tells me to get to work and report back when I've finished. I'm working quietly when I feel a tap on my shoulder.

"Hey, who are you?" It's one of the conscripts from the Support Company, a kid with a weak chin, squinty eyes, and a large, hooked nose. The tone of his voice is condescending.

"I'm here from the 2nd Construction Company," I say pointedly, letting him know we're from different companies and he should leave me be. Members of different companies aren't bound by the rules of hierarchy.

"Hey, you should address me as 'sir.' I'm higher than you." He has the same two bars on his chest. He must've asked Ja-hong about my serial number.

I look at him blankly and turn back to my work.

"Hey, did you hear what I said?"

"Yeah, I heard," I say without turning from the screen. An awkward silence ensues. I can almost feel the anger rising in him as he walks back to his seat. The officers can make me work here—there's nothing I can do about that—but I'll be damned if I'm going to let these kids push me around.

D-549 (28JUL04): Private Gwang-hyeon

I'm in the Tactical Operations Center alone, working. There are no officers and no other conscripts, just me. Outside the barred window, I can hear the sounds of soldiers at play. Today, everybody has been given the day off to participate in a sports competition in order to promote camaraderie and mutual respect. As Captain Bang was leaving to join in, he explained, "Chun, someone's got to stay behind and keep watch over the office." That someone is me.

I have to keep watch over the TOC throughout lunch time until one of the conscripts from the Support Company shows up, and I hurry to the mess hall alone, hoping that they haven't started taking down the chow line. Most of the soldiers are finished with lunch and cleaning their trays when I walk in. I load up my tray and look for a seat. I don't mind eating by myself but I spot the PFC I argued with the other night—he's eating by himself—and figure I might as well be the bigger man and use the opportunity to patch things up.

"You mind if I sit here?"

"Go ahead," he replies, barely looking up from his tray.

He continues to avoid eye contact, his eyes on his food. It seems he doesn't want to make friendly so we eat in silence. As he's eating, I can tell that the bug up his ass is getting restless. He puts down his spork.

"Hey."

"What?"

"If you work in the office, you got to address me as 'sir.' I'm higher than you."

It's my fault for believing in diplomacy in a place like this. I'm angry at myself but angrier at this kid who won't let it go.

"No," I say through gritted teeth.

"What?"

"I said, 'No.'"

"Who the hell do you think you are?"

"I'm not in the same company as you. I don't even know you."

My steadfastness surprises me. Where did these balls come from? I was sure that I had been effectively castrated during boot camp. Even before the Army, I had avoided confrontation whenever possible, always choosing the path of least resistance because it was easier.

His face is turning red and he's shaking. I meet his stare, determined not to lose in this battle of wills. More than anything, I'm not going to put up with the bullshit I put up with in Daegu if it can be avoided.

He curses to himself so I can't hear, stands up with his tray, and walks away.

I shrug. I gave it a try. It looks like this deployment is not going to be peaceful after all, but I decide I don't really care. The deployment's only six months. There's something empowering about a short-term assignment.

The rest of the week goes by uneventfully. The members of the Support Company steer clear of me and occasionally glare at me from a distance. There's a general antipathy directed toward me and I find out the reason from someone I had never thought would side with me.

"Brother, you know that he's saying shit about you?" Ja-hong tells me.

The 'he' Ja-hong is referring to is the same conscript with the beak-nose, Private Gwang-hyeon. It seems he's taken the passive-aggressive path and has been telling his company members I'm an asshole.

"I figured as much. I don't really care."

Ja-hong is the only person who harbors positive feelings toward me, which I appreciate. It was awkward at first but I've begun to see him in a different light since we arrived here at the 1113th. It's strange what a change of environment will bring about.

I still haven't been able to get to know anyone in my company, either, spending very little time at the company, having to report to the TOC during the days and through the nights. The only time I'm at the company is when I'm sleeping in the mornings, and I know that more than a few of them harbor resentment because of that.

This marginalization, it's a different kind of marginalization than in Daegu, the primary difference being that people leave me alone. There's much to be said about being alone.

Another solace is that since the 1113th is relatively close to Seoul, I've had visitors on the weekend. My drinking friends and my former co-workers came with chicken and pizza and a bagful of books to keep me occupied in my isolation. My aunt and cousins also came for a visit bearing a much needed gift—a pair of sneakers.

Another nice surprise was receiving mail, something that has been rare and always sweet. The letters were from Sang-mok and Seung-su, my father and his subordinate at the company personnel office in Daegu. They found the address through the personnel channels and each sent me a short letter, but the best part was a postcard that had been sent to my address in Daegu.

The postcard is from Jen, another of my former co-workers at the *hagwon* in Bundang. It's postmarked from Vienna, and she's written "postcard 2" at the top. I look in the envelope, and there isn't a postcard 1.

You're special—you get two postcards. Anyhow, I'm here in Vienna. It's good to be home with mommy and daddy. Do you miss your mommy, too? And *Oppa!*[53] I'll kill you if you go to Afghanistan!! Are you insane?!! You want to leave me here all alone and leave for Afghanistan?!!! *Oppa*, I hate you! Just stay where you are, I'll go visit you in August!!! Deal? I miss you thi~s much! Love, Jen

I realize I've been smiling as I read. It's very much like her, the excessive saccharine of her tone, the tendency toward hyperbole, the erratic emotions evident in her use of punctuation. We had had a playful flirtation that the kids at the *hagwon* thoroughly enjoyed but nothing had materialized by the time my contract was up. I've often thought about her on the lonelier of nights, the way she would bat those long eyelashes and the way the high register of her voice would bounce up and down erratically when she talked to me.

Now that it's too late, I wonder why I didn't try harder when I had the chance, why I didn't even get her address. When Marc and Erin visited on the weekend, I asked about her and they told me she went off to work for the UN. She's now in Vienna and I'm stuck here.

---

[53] *Oppa*: Literally, older brother. Similar to *hyeong*, but *hyeong* is used when a younger male is addressing an older male and *oppa* is used when a younger female is addressing an older male.

Army Consolidated Administrative School
Yeongnam, North Chungcheong Province, Korea
Korean Support Group, Dasan Unit, 2nd Construction Company/Support
Company
2 August 2004 - 27 August 2004

D-545 (02AUG04): The Problem is Captain Park

After two weeks at the 1113th, we've now moved on to the second stage of our training at the Army Consolidated Administrative School. The ACAS naturally has nicer facilities, but they still have somehow managed to find the most worn-down barracks to house us. The barracks are surrounded by muddy yards, criss-crossed by clotheslines. The trees in the area must be the kind favored by the cicadas; their high-pitched screeches echo back and forth in the courtyard.

I don't see Johnny around, but I don't see much of anyone except the officers and conscripts in the TOC. If this stage of training is any different from the previous, I can't tell. The only difference from my time at the 1113th is a change in scenery.

Over the past weeks, I've learned that Captain Park is the least senior company commander, perhaps the least senior captain of the entire detachment. I know this because even though our unit is crawling with captains—the exceptions being the commander, the two section chiefs, and a first lieutenant with the Civil Affairs Team—it's obvious by the way that Captain Park comes running when the other captains call him. The subservience and degradation start from the privates and go all the way up the chain of command to even the officers. While it's fun to watch Captain Park squirm, his low rank is probably the reason he pimped me out to Operations and Intelligence Branch, to curry favor with the major. Another disadvantage is that he usually chooses to take out his frustrations on me.

I'm in the office after lunch, ready to work. I'm alone—the officers usually take their time coming to the office after lunch—I've got a cup of instant coffee and the report I need to type up laid out in front of me and am opening the word processing program when a private from my squad peeks into the office.

"Chun, Captain Park wants you to return to the company."

"What is it?"

"I don't know. Let's hurry."

When I report to the company, everyone is filing outside in their PT uniforms. Captain Park tells the two of us to change into our PT uniforms and report outside as soon as possible.

"Captain Park, I've got to be in the office, sir."

"No," he says adamantly. "No exceptions today."

"But, sir…."

"No exceptions."

I change and fall into formation outside the barracks. Staff Sergeant Kim leads us in stretching and once we're warmed up, Captain Park announces that we're going for a run. Eight kilometers, he says, in order to prepare ourselves for the conditions in Afghanistan. The day is sweltering hot and palpably humid, severe even for the ordinarily hot and humid Korean summers.

Eight kilometers amount to a little more than three laps around the school. Halfway through the first lap, it feels like I'm breathing through a wet rag. Halfway through the second, I've taken off my shirt and am wringing out the sweat as we go. By the last half-lap, we've given up on singing war songs and run in silence. When we return to the barracks, everyone is completely drenched in sweat from head to toe, drenched down to our underwear. I can barely stand as we cool down with a series of stretches.

"Good job, everyone," Captain Park says. "Hit the showers."

I drag myself back to the barracks along with the rest of the company. Some of them are jogging to be the first in the showers and I let them. I take my time because my breath still hasn't returned to me. I grab a change of underwear, my towel, and toiletry bag and am about to head to the showers when Ja-hong shows up in the barracks.

"Brother, Captain Bang wants you back at the TOC."

"Okay, let me just take a shower first."

"I wouldn't if I were you. He's pretty pissed off."

A couple of days later, I'm again in the TOC alone but this time the officers won't be showing up. Colonel Park has called for another sports competition, and again I've been told to keep watch over the TOC. Hours pass before Captain Bang returns to the office, picking his teeth.

"Chun, go down to the field. There's food."

When I show up at the field, everyone is having a good time, talking and singing and playing games. The remnants of a feast are strewn out all across the ground and there are white *makgeolli*[54] bottles everywhere. I pass through

---

[54] *Makgeolli*: A cloudy, white Korean rice liquor. Several years ago, the Ministry of Agriculture, Food, and Rural Affairs held a naming competition for the drink to use in foreign promotion and nonsensically decided on the name "drunken rice."

the crowd of faces deep red from the rice liquor as I make my way to my company. When I show up, Jong-hun, my squad leader, hails me.

"Get some food," he says, pointing to what's left over from dinner.

Given how cold and hard the rice is and how drunk everybody seems, it's been a while since dinner. I scoop a generous portion of rice, but there's very little to eat it with, nothing more than scraps and white flecks of congealing fat. I search for some alcohol, but all of the bottles are completely empty. I take my plate of rice and scraps and sit off to the side beneath a tree for the shade.

I'm trying to swallow my second mouthful of cold rice when Captain Park stumbles over to me, red-faced and holding a bottle of *makgeolli*.

"Chun, where the hell have you been?" he asks, his speech slurred. He knows damn well where I've been. He found me without problem when we had that run.

"Working, sir."

"Come here, you little bastard," he says. I put down my plate and step forward and he throws his arm around my neck, squeezing a little too tightly.

"You... *hic*... you know what your problem is?" His breath reeks of alcohol and spittle sprays from his mouth as he talks. He's pointing at me with his other hand for emphasis, wagging his finger, the bottle dangling in his grip. "You act like you're not a part of... *hic*... this company."

I want to argue that it wasn't my decision to work at Operations and Intelligence, but all I want right now is to get away from him. I tell him I understand, sir.

"Try harder from now on," he says, breaking his grip around my neck and slapping me hard on the back. He stumbles off in the direction of the other company commanders.

I sit back down and pick up my plate, but I've lost my appetite.

D-526 (20AUG04): Passports

Hope has stuck out its turtle-head once more, the realization of that hope coming with the flash of the camera. As the date of our deployment nears, Personnel has been working on getting our documents ready, which includes all four companies taking passport pictures. The flash triggered a memory of that day at the Yeoksam-dong Office. I can't get a passport. The

195

government doesn't give passports to people with other citizenships. The government does send them to the Army. Maybe, just maybe, this will be the catalyst that forces the government to get its story straight and let me go.

Of course, this hope is accompanied by fear, fear that the government denies me a passport and I'm unable to go on deployment, but I've become accustomed to fear. Hope is something that I'll take when it comes. Besides, the unit needs me. If I'm not there, who else will hold down the office?

I share my hope with Ja-hong as we have a cup of vending-machine coffee under the stairs, out of sight of the officers.

"That's crazy," Ja-hong says. "What're you gonna do if they let you out?"

"It's easy," I say, sipping on my coffee. "I'm going to get an apology." I smile and rub my fingers together so he knows what I mean. Monetary restitution.

"Crazy. That'd be awesome."

"Yeah, wouldn't it?" I crumple up my Dixie cup and throw it in the trash. We've been playing hooky for long enough. Time to get back to work.

"Hey, wake up." I open my eyes to see a corporal from the Civil Engineering Company standing over me. "You have a phone call. It's from the American Embassy."

I've only had an hour or two of sleep due to another late night last night, but I'm wide awake now. I jump out of bed and follow the corporal to the TOC. It's Sunday, and the office is almost completely empty. The corporal points at the phone on the Operations Officer's desk. I'm so nervous I'm shaking as I pick up the receiver.

"Hello?"

"Is this Young Jin Chun?"

"Yes, sir." I can hardly contain my excitement. I'm like a little school girl awaiting a confession of love from her crush.

"This is Christopher Warren with the U.S. Embassy."

"Good afternoon, sir." Mr. Warren, don't keep me waiting. Say the words I've been longing to hear.

"You're an American citizen, correct?"

"Yes, sir."

"And you're training for a deployment to Afghanistan?"

"Yes, sir." Come on. Get on with it.

"Did you volunteer for the deployment of your own volition?"

196

I'm confused. I don't understand where he's going with this line of questioning.

"Uh… yes, sir."

"I'm calling to confirm that it is your decision to go to Afghanistan. Your mother contacted the State Department and the State Department contacted the embassy. Just to clarify, it is your decision, correct?"

"Yes, sir."

"All right, that's all I need. Thank you for your time."

That's it? You tease!

Dumbfounded, I stare at the receiver in my hand. What was that? The American government is fine with me being forced to serve in a foreign army as long as I'm not forced to go overseas on deployment? It's not only the Korean government that needs to get its story straight.

I shouldn't be surprised by the indifference. Like any other rational American facing unbelievably absurd difficulties abroad, I had first turned to the American Embassy when this whole farce began.

I went to the embassy full of bright-eyed hope like a child. The bully had given me an ultimatum, but my father was stronger than his. I waited my turn, and when my number flashed on the display, I walked up to the counter with my blue passport and draft papers in hand.

"Hi," I said to the austere-looking Korean lady on the other side of the Plexiglass. She looked up but didn't respond so I went on. "I'm American, but I got these papers—"

She cut me off with a glare and a single raised finger before I could finish. Reaching under the counter, she pulled out a book and tossed it under the divider.

"You can find the number in there."

"B-but…."

"It's not our problem. Work it out yourself."

I opened up the book and it was full of phone numbers and Korean words.

"But I can't speak Ko-," I managed to get out before she shot me another glare and pressed the button for the next number.

At the time, I felt betrayed. I went to my figurative father for help and he told me it wasn't his problem, that it was something I had to work out myself when there was nothing I could do myself to work it out. If it had been a lesson disguised as cruelty, I might have accepted it, but there was no way this was a lesson. It was just plain apathy.

I called my actual father after returning from the embassy and he gave me a similar response. "Just go," he said.

I'm in the yard outside the barracks the next day during lunch, hanging my laundry, when the Personnel NCO, Sergeant First Class Jang, comes looking for me. He has this strange expression on his face, a mixture of weariness and triumph as if he had just stormed and captured a heavily fortified hill singlehandedly.

"Chun, you caused me a lot of trouble today."

"What are you talking about, sir?"

He takes off his cap and wipes his brow in mock exhaustion. "I was out getting passports for the deployment and there was a problem with your passport."

Please tell me good news.

"Did you know that you can't get a passport?"

"Yes, sir," I admit.

"Geez, you could've told me before I left. I had to spend all day at Immigration arguing, but you know what?"

"What, sir?"

"I did it," he says triumphantly, his smile stretching across his face. "I got you a passport."

He's standing in front of me with his chest puffed out, waiting for me to praise him for effort.

"Uh… thank you, sir." I try not to betray my disappointment. It's over. My hopes of getting this mess straightened out have been dashed, this time broken into such minute pieces it can never be recovered.

"Geez, Chun. You could be a little more grateful," he says, walking off, leaving me to wonder exactly how he managed to get me a passport and if it was something that I had overlooked.

D-519 (27AUG04): Leaving on a Jet Plane

After six weeks of pre-deployment training, our time has come. We ship out early in the morning, boarding buses headed to Seoul Airport in Seongnam. Nobody sits next to me on the bus. Yesterday, Captain Park pulled me off to the side as I was packing my duffel bag and told me I'm no longer a part of the 2nd Construction Company. While I'm happy to be free from his lunacy, he's sending me to the one company that despises me, the Support Company. To make matters worse, I've been transferred in exchange for Corporal Yeong-rok, an interpreter and the squad leader of their administrative support squad, Gwang-hyeon's squad.

When the buses pull up to the airfield, I see a lone 747 parked on the runway, Asiana in white letters against a gray body. We assemble in front of the 747 for a ceremony to send us off. I take my place at the back of the line of my new squad. Gwang-hyeon gives me the stink-eye.

The ceremony starts with an address from some general, followed by the taking of pictures for PR, waving tiny flags and cocking our arms collectively, and ends with a lot of handshaking up until we climb the steps into the cabin of the plane.

It's assigned seating, and the Support Company Commander has stuck me in the rear of the plane, separate from the other company members. A small blessing. The man who travels alone gets more leg room and sole right to the arm rests. The highlight of the trip is the view. Unlike the West and their flight-attendant labor unions and non-discrimination policies, Korean airlines are very particular about whom they employ to work the aisles. If you're going to send boys to war, at least let them get their fill of ogling to last the six months they're in the desert.

When the meal service comes around, it's fish. I ask the flight attendant if there's a meat option. Sorry, she says, but she returns a little while later and takes me behind the curtained area in the back for cup ramen. "You have to eat back here because if the others see you, they'll all want ramen," she explains. "I understand, ma'am," I reply. Put a beautiful woman in uniform and I'll follow her anywhere.

I fall asleep somewhere over southern China.

Deployment
Manas AB, Kyrgyzstan
Korean Support Group, Dasan Unit, Support Company
27 August 2004 - 30 August 2004

D-519 (27AUG04): Manas

The moment I step off the plane in Manas Air Base, I'm met with the blinding brightness of a Central Asian sun unfiltered by the blanket of pollution that mars the skies in the developed world. It's a strange, foreign heat, very different from the Korean summer. It's definitely hotter but the climate is so arid the air licks the sweat directly from my pores. As we walk through the encampment, it's so bright it feels as if there are no shadows, and everything, including the plywood structures, has been bleached by the sun.

We take up residence in a community of small tents, their interiors crowded with bunk beds, and report outside for yet another ceremony, this time to signify the changing of shifts with the previous deployment. The members of the previous deployment don't appear very disciplined, non-regulation T-shirts visible around their collars and their uniform pants bloused low over their boots. It's an indication of a lax commander, and I find myself envious; our commander, Colonel Park, had us run laps with full packs the night before we left to make sure we stay disciplined.

After the ceremony, the Support Company Commander, Captain Kim, gathers the company and makes an announcement.

"We're shipping out to Afghanistan in a few days, but the date and time have yet to be determined," he says, smiling a broad smile on his very broad, boyish face. "While we're here, relax and explore the base, but you can't leave."

The other Support Company members wander off in small packs, and I take off by myself in as opposite a direction as possible.

Manas is the closest to heaven I suppose I'll get while in the service. The Americans know how to take care of their soldiers, and for a soldier in the Korean Army, it's overwhelming. I stop by the gym, and it has a full-size indoor basketball court and an array of new Nautilus machines and free weights. Next to the gym is a structure that houses a bar—only non-alcoholic beer—a pool hall and a large seating area with picnic tables, for bingo, a poster reads. I wander out around the outskirts of the base and find a couple gift shops with Soviet-era souvenirs, Lenin pins and flasks with sickles and hammers. I inspect a pair of spectacles that could've been a pair of Trotsky's, and look at the Matryoshka dolls lined up in neat rows in descending order, making a note to buy some souvenirs on the way back to Korea. The only thing that Manas doesn't seem to have is women.

At lunchtime, I'm ogling the selection at the D-FAC, what the Americans call their mess hall, saliva practically dripping from the corners of my mouth. This is what chow should be like. I decide on chicken parmigiana and take a seat at an empty table farthest away from the main group of Koreans. There are a few Support Company members at the adjacent table, but it was unavoidable. I recognize one from my squad. The others I think are drivers.

I try to mind my own business and my chicken parm but they're whispering very loudly.

"You sure we can do this?"

"Yeah. The guys from the previous deployment said they did it."

"No one got caught?"

"Nope. I heard it's easy."

They pause as if they just realized their voices have gained volume with their excitement and look around furtively, making sure no one's listening. They pay me no heed.

They lean in closer, in a huddle, and talk much more softly. I hear only bits and pieces—"taxi," "Bishkek," and "How much?"—but I have an idea what they're talking about. Young soldiers, just boys, are the same regardless of nationality, it seems. Sex. Prostitutes. They're planning to leave the base and head to Bishkek to sow their oats at a brothel.

"So, Bishkek?"

They nod one by one, their eyes darting from one person to the next.

I don't think it's wise to get into trouble at the beginning of the deployment, but I don't give a damn what they do. Besides, maybe a little sex will calm them down and make them a little more civil for a change. I finish off my plate and head back to the chow line for dessert. This is all the ecstasy I need for now. When I return to my seat, they're gone.

After lunch, I head to the gym for a light workout and return to the tent to read, enjoying the peace and quiet and lack of work. I take out the postcard from Jen and read through it a couple of times. I take out one of the books I brought with me, Charles Bukowski's *Factotum*. I'm identifying with Hank in his drifting from tedious job to tedious job and wanting nothing but to drink when the flap of the tent swings open. I scoot deeper into the corner of my top bunk but I take note of who's entering. It's the boys from earlier. They strut into the tent with the swagger and glazed eyes and big, dopey grins of high school boys who've just bedded a woman for the first time.

They plop down on the lower bunks and begin to chatter and giggle excitedly. They haven't noticed me from where they're congregated. It turns out it had been the first time for at least one of them. I can't help but feel a slight sadness and pity for these boys, just kids, going off to war and losing their virginities to Kyrgyzstani whores.

Bagram AB, Afghanistan
Korean Support Group, Dasan Unit, Support Company/2nd Construction
Company
30 August 2004 - 23 February 2005

D-517 (30AUG04): Faces of Death

I'm sitting in the back of an old Pathfinder, tightly clutching a borrowed Korean-made K2 rifle[55] to my chest. All around the vehicle, countless pairs of eyes are staring with rapt and undecipherable attention at us, at me, piercing through my cumbersome Kevlar vest from the crowded market streets. It's before lunch—I have nothing in my stomach to empty—and it's already the second time I'm fearing for my life.

Word came that it was time to board the American C-130 to Afghanistan at 0430. The inside of a C-130 is like the belly of a great steel whale, rounded and cavernous with thick, curved steel ribs lining the sides of the massive body. The seats are made of thick seatbelt-nylon which uncomfortably cradled my buttocks as I tried to make up for lost sleep. It was an exercise in futility, the deafening drone of the propellers echoing throughout the cabin, and the jerking and jolting of the plane were too unnerving to stay asleep for very long. Turbulence takes on a new element of fear when you're in a military transport over hostile territory.

I was drifting off a second time when I was again snapped awake by a sudden pop and hissing. I groggily looked down toward the rear of the cabin where one of the hoses that travel along the length of the plane above our heads had burst, spewing a steady stream of unknown vapor. I looked nervously at the others around me; their faces had also become ashen and queasy. Two American airmen rushed past me to the site of the burst, frantically examining the hose and shouting at each other over the roar of the engines. It didn't seem like an ordinary in-flight malfunction.

There had been news that the C-130 that transported the advance team had almost crashed when its landing gear failed to deploy. According to the officers, American soldiers on the ground climbed up on the roofs to take pictures of the impending crash. Luckily, the landing gear deployed just before the plane touched down.

One of the airmen ran off and returned with what appeared to be duct tape and wrapped up the hose. It stopped leaking, at least visibly, and the

---

[55] The Daewoo Precision Industries K2 rifle is the standard service rifle of the ROK Army. I used an M16 in boot camp and in Daegu, and I assume it was because the 37th Division is a small division, and the Headquarters Company is not really a combat unit. It's basically a copy of the M16 with a side-foldable buttstock.

airmen returned to the front of the plane. I held my breath and stared anxiously at the hosing until the C-130 landed in Afghanistan, unable to return to sleep.

The relief of planting my feet on solid ground in one piece and not a bloody mess strewn all across Northern Afghanistan lasts only for a moment. I haven't taken more than a step when I'm grabbed by our warrant officer in charge of maintenance, Chief Kang.

"You, you're an interpreter, right?"

"Y-yes, sir."

"Get in," he says, pointing at a jeep that is parked near the flight line.

The jeep zips through the base, and we pull into the Korean compound and stop in front of a row of huts covered with tents.

"Throw your duffel bag in a hut, pick up a bulletproof vest and rifle, and come back."

"Yes, sir."

As I pick up a Kevlar vest and K2 rifle, an uneasy feeling creeps into the pit of my stomach. Why do I need a bulletproof vest? Where are we going? What's more troubling is, from what I can gather, the warrant officer is held in low esteem by the other officers. I get the feeling that they think he's incompetent and a dolt. He doesn't have the charisma to inspire devotion, but I follow him because it's my duty to do so.

We get into a Pathfinder, the warrant officer in the front passenger seat and me in the back. The driver is a local national, stocky, bearded, and silent. We pull out of the compound and drive down a two-lane road through the middle of the base. At first, there are only massive communities of tents, but as we drive on, the communities pass behind, and there are only scattered Soviet-era buildings, bombed into disuse, red signs reading Danger: Mines swinging from barbed wire along the roadside. When we pass through the first checkpoint, my heart starts beating fast. We're not leaving the safety of the base, are we?

At the next checkpoint, the American guards stop us again.

"What is your business off-base, sir?"

Chief Kang stares dumbly at the guard.

"Sir, I advise you return to the base unless you have important business off-base."

The warrant officer doesn't respond, probably doesn't even understand, and I can't answer for him because he hasn't told me anything of our mission.

"Sir…."

"It's okay. It's okay," Chief Kang interrupts, waving his hand dismissively.

The guard is put off by the warrant officer's dismissive attitude and lets us pass. It certainly doesn't feel okay. The security at this checkpoint and the massive walls and obstacles and barbed wire tell me that there will be no more warnings. We're heading off-base and the clip in my rifle is empty. Why didn't they give us live rounds if we're headed off-base?

There's a local national on a scooter beyond the walls of the base, and Chief Kang tells the driver to follow him. I want to ask who the man on the scooter is, but it's not my place to do so. What if the one leading us into the valley of the shadow of death is the devil himself?

All I can do is nervously check the Kevlar plates in my vest. As we approach the busy marketplace, I'm acutely aware of all the stares of the residents watching us. I clutch the rifle tightly but know that if the bullets start flying, it'll be useless. What do I do if that happens? Could I make a break for it?

I look out the back of the Pathfinder. It's a long way back to the base. Would getting shot in the back be better than surrendering myself into their hands alive? I slowly slink down in the back seat, ducking down as much as possible.

The man on the scooter motions for us to pull over behind a dark sedan and quickly speeds away, leaving behind a thick, yellow fog of dust. Once the dust settles, I notice that the four doors of the sedan have flung open and four large, mean-looking local nationals have stepped out and are now headed toward our SUV.

So this is the end. I'll be found in a dark alleyway, days later, a bullet-riddled, headless corpse in stained underwear. There's nothing I can do but hope for a painless death.

One of the four men approaches the driver's side and the driver rolls down the window. They began talking in Pashto, I assume, and it doesn't sound like it's going well but it could just be me. At least they're talking and not shooting or dragging us out of the Pathfinder. The driver turns to Chief Kang and says, "He says to turn back." This time, Chief Kang doesn't argue. His face has the same scared-shitless expression I assume I have. "Okay."

The driver turns around and I can breathe again when I see the men returning to the sedan out the back window. Soon I can see the welcoming gates of the base and I know that this will not be the day I die.

D-509 (06SEP04): If You Can't Avoid It

Aside from the brief excursion on my first day here, things here are safe and monotonous, and I'm confused by the fact that I find it somewhat disappointing. Of course, I'd rather not be risking my neck out on patrols or clearing mines, but part of my reason for applying for this deployment was to spend the rest of my time doing something meaningful, something significant.

I had no reason to expect that life would be any different than it is. We are an engineering unit, and there was a reason why we sat through lectures on concrete mixtures. From what little I can gather, the primary objective of our unit is to lay concrete around the base. The Slovakians are also engineers, and maybe the Polish as well, but their primary duty is clearing mines. I remember mine-clearing training from boot camp, poking around in the dirt with my bayonet at forty-five degrees, and although I'm sure they're better outfitted, I don't envy their jobs.

As it were, I'd rather be outside laying concrete. Instead, I sit in the TOC typing up countless drafts of reports that are of no consequence to anyone, six days a week, leaving the TOC only for meals, a little sleep, and the base-wide meetings with the Liaison Officer, Captain Ko, and the force-protection meetings with the Operations Officer. Our presence at the daily morning briefings is nothing more than a formality; every morning, my duty is to say "Nothing to report" when the unit XO addresses the coalition teams at the end of the meetings.

I have a feeling the base administration doesn't feel we're worth the trouble. They've singled us out on an issue of pallets several times during the briefings and once afterward. The base command sergeant major, Sergeant Major Ashe, threatened to come to our compound with a tractor and tear them out himself. I've brought it up to Major Jeong, but he told me to forget about it. I looked around our compound but realized I have no idea what a pallet is.

An officer from the medical unit also shows up to the meetings with an interpreter, but it's not Johnny. It's some tall kid with glasses and no facial expression. I haven't seen Johnny around the D-FAC during meal times, either. Now that I think about it, I haven't seen him since that first trip to the ACAS. I wonder what happened to him.

The Support Company hasn't warmed up to me any. They've taken to shunning me and with my duties at the TOC taking up most of my time and only me and Ja-hong in the TOC, it's not much of a problem. I'm stopping by the B-hut to pick up some things before dinner when I see Gwang-hyeon and a couple of squad leaders lying in wait outside the door.

"Hey, Chun. Come here." It's my squad leader, a short, nervous corporal working design with the Construction Officer.

"What do you want? I'm on my way to dinner."

"We have something to say."

"What?"

"Look, you're part of the Support Company now," the squad leader of the motor pool cuts in, "and so you have to follow our rules. You have to observe the hierarchy."

I'm tired and cranky, and I only have a short meal break before I have to head back to the TOC for more work. I see the shuttle bus to the D-FAC drive off and now I have to wait for the next one. I don't have the energy to deal with their bullshit.

"I don't see why. What's the point?"

"It's how things are done here."

"I don't see why it has to be this way."

"You're just a PFC," Gwang-hyeon interjects, visibly agitated.

"You're one, too."

"I started before you."

"So what?" His growing agitation is making this almost fun. "Look, I have to go to dinner." I turn and walk away. I don't wait for the shuttle bus to return. I decide to walk to the D-FAC to calm myself down.

My mood hasn't improved by the time I report back to the TOC. Captain Bang tries to banter with me while I work but I only afford him curt, disciplined replies. I feel slightly bad about it because Major Jeong and Captain Bang are fairly nice to me when they don't have to be, which is a rare quality among officers.

I work quickly, wanting to wash up before lights out. It isn't until it's dark out that he sends me off. As I'm walking out the door, Captain Bang stops me.

"Chun."

"Yes, sir?"

"Have you ever heard of the expression 'If you can't avoid it, enjoy it'?"

"No, sir."

"Think about it."

"Yes, sir."

I stop by the Port-o-Potties to drain my bladder and head toward the squad B-hut. I don't like spending any more time there than I have to, but all I want to do right now is to go to bed.

When I open the door of the B-hut, the frame of Captain Kim, the commander of the Support Company, is blocking my way. He shouldn't be here. It's past the time for evening call.

"Chun, get in here."

"Yes, sir."

He moves slightly and I squeeze in and sit on my cot.

"I want you to conduct maintenance of your rifle. When you're finished, you must get approval from me."

Damn. So much for going to bed on time for once.

I rest my rifle on my mattress and pick up what's left of the cleaning tools, an old toothbrush, its bristles worn and gray, a tattered rag, and some toilet paper. I decide to take my time with the cleaning. I've given up on any chance for rest. I can wash up after lights out.

Trying to take Captain Bang's bullshit advice, I put in my earphones and listen to music while I dismantle my K2 and lay out the pieces across my mattress. I hear the other squad members whispering about me, nothing nice, so I turn up the volume.

D-507 (08SEP04): Sergeant Luvaas

"This is Private First Class Chun," Major Jeong announces to his guest, a tall American soldier, a sergeant, with closely shorn hair and soft features. "He's almost American." Almost American? What's that supposed to mean?

"Chun, this is Sergeant Luvaas from the 109th." The 109th Engineer Group is the unit to which our engineering unit is attached. I'm relieved the major bothered to say the sergeant's name. Loo-vahs. I'm positive I would've butchered it. "Take him to D-FAC for lunch today."

"Yes, sir." I guess entertaining the major's guests is now part of my duties, too. Major Jeong takes his leave, walking out the back of the TOC. I save the report I was working on and gather my things.

"Sergeant, you mind walking?" I ask. There's a shuttle bus to the D-FAC but I prefer walking instead of sitting on the bus while Support Company members give me the stink-eye.

"I don't mind," the sergeant says, and we start across the dirt parade ground.

The Korean compound is located almost in the exact center of Bagram Airfield, between the 109th and the Slovakian and Polish Engineer compounds. Even in Afghanistan, we use the parade ground for our morning calls and ceremonies and all of the offices and B-huts, the plywood structures covered with tents that serve as our barracks, make way and lie around its periphery.

"What did the major mean when he said you're almost American?" the sergeant asks.

"I don't know. I am American."

"What? How'd that happen?"

"It's a long story."

I give Luvaas an abridged version of the events leading up to my conscription as we pass the guard post of the compound and walk up Disney Drive,[56] the only road down the center of the base. I tell him about finding out for the first time that I had Korean nationality and about how I tried to get out of the obligation and how I was a specialist in the U.S. Army for a day, only to get caught at Osan Air Base, and how I ended up in Afghanistan.

"Damn, that's a crazy story," Luvaas remarks.

"Yeah, a damn crazy story."

We take a shortcut through another B-hut community. The D-FAC is next to where the Korean medical unit is situated, toward the edge of the base to allow access for local nationals to get medical treatment.

"You ever have Korean food before?" I ask.

"Yeah," Luvaas says. "My mom is Korean." I wouldn't have guessed that he was half-Korean. He must take after his father. He tells me in South Dakota—the 109th is from the South Dakota National Guard—there are a few Koreans, and his mother spends a lot of her time at the local Korean church.

The Korean D-FAC is a blessing and a curse. There are no cooks among us and so the Army has contracted the meal services to Korean civilians from Kyrgyzstan. On the chow line, the food is actually decent—there is meat in

---

[56] Named after Army Spc. Jason A. Disney of Fallon, Nevada, who died in Bagram in 2002.

a form that looks like meat—served by two college-aged women. To a soldier, the beauty of any woman is amplified due to the lack of a frame of reference, and the chow line is often sluggish as the others try to hit on them. It's a vast improvement over any mess hall in Korea but I can't help but eat begrudgingly because conscripts are barred from visiting the American D-FACs.

Luvaas and I get in line and load up our trays and take a seat. It's not so bad to have company when I eat. I usually eat alone. The Support Company hasn't warmed up to me in the slightest.

We're eating when the loud *clack* of a rifle hitting the ground reverberates through the monotony of silverware against metal trays. Luvaas jumps in his seat.

"You okay?" I ask.

"What the hell was that?"

"Somebody probably just knocked over his rifle." It's a usual occurrence at the D-FAC—many of the conscripts are not used to having to carry their rifles with them at all times and prop them against tables or chairs, inevitably knocking them over every once in a while.

"But... it's dangerous."

"Yeah, I know."

"There was a guy a while back who accidentally knocked over his weapon and ended up shooting someone."

"Well, you don't worry about it here. They don't give us live rounds."

"What?"

"Yeah, I know it's a base regulation, but I think they don't trust us with live rounds. Only one Korean has died in Afghanistan and he died at the hands of another officer. Apparently they got into an argument and the one shot the other in the face."

"Still, it's the rules."

"I know."

"Geez."

I understand Luvaas' irritation. The others don't know that it's a base regulation and treat their rifles like props, which is essentially what they are without ammunition. All of our ammunition is locked up in the TOC, the key around the Operations Officer's neck.

There's a concept that Koreans like to pride themselves in called *nunchi*, which is basically some sort of social awareness, taking subtle hints to gauge others' feelings and perceptions. Unfortunately, this social awareness apparently only applies when they're with other Koreans. It's only been a week since we arrived on those C-130s and I'm afraid we've already established ourselves as a public nuisance.

The knocking-over of rifles is a minor issue since we are restricted to eating at the Korean D-FAC, but it's only the first of many things. Every morning, we blast our reveille over the loudspeakers promptly at 0600 and go on our daily run up and down Disney, singing our war songs at the top of our lungs, oblivious to the half-awake American soldiers glaring at us from the doors of their B-huts with expressions full of anger and spite. I want to shout my apologies but would never be heard over the renditions of Cool Guy and The Scent of Home. Instead, I keep my head down and run in shame.

I've learned to walk right back out the door of the monstrously big BX[57] or the Northface store at the first sight of another Korean soldier. The others don't understand the concept of personal space or the American brand of social etiquette. They bump into people without a Sorry or Excuse Me, monopolize public areas, and consume everything in sight like a swarm of locusts. The other day, there was a new shipment of DVD players, and my comrades snatched up every single one, only to return all of them the next day because the region code was different from the one for Asia. I had been unlucky enough to be nearby and was asked to translate why forty Koreans were standing at the refund counter with forty DVD players.

I'd like to give a lecture on American etiquette during one of our mental education sessions, but nobody would allow that or listen to a lowly private, and to be honest, I only care because I'm the only one who knows how much everybody despises us.

D-503 (12SEP04): Unwanted

I don't blame the Support Company for hating me. They're the same as all those kids from my childhood when I was always the new kid, which was only a good thing if you were pretty or handsome, and they'd make it hard

---

[57] BX: Base exchange, the Air Force equivalent of the Army's PX (Post exchange). Bagram is technically an Air Force base.

for me to fit in, and I'd get tired of trying and become withdrawn and unap-proachable. I have tried in my own ways, but now I'm back in the comfortable zone of estrangement. I learned that being estranged is not such a bad thing back in Daegu.

After the last confrontation, the others have left me alone. Gwang-hyeon assumes a sour expression whenever we run into each other, which isn't in-frequent since he's the commander's orderly and the commander's office and quarters are next to the TOC. But there haven't been any repercussions alt-hough I still haven't bent to their rules. They don't know what to do with me, and their passive-aggression hasn't had much of an effect on me.

I'm in the TOC after the morning briefing when the Support Company commander pokes his head through the door and waves his hand downward, beckoning me outside. I walk out the TOC and meet him just outside the door.

"Chun."

"Yes, sir."

"I'm going to send you back to the Construction Company," he an-nounces. "We need Corporal Yeong-rok back to be the squad leader of the administrative support squad. You understand, right?" I know it's an excuse. I'm not good for the company, and so they're shuffling me yet again.

"Yes, sir."

"You can pack up your things at lunch and head over. I've already talked to Captain Park."

During lunch, I head back to the squad B-hut to pack my things. The others are playing cards or listening to music. It seems like they know I'm leaving but no one says a thing. As I pack, I can't find my mess kit. It's not in or near my pack or anywhere under my cot. I start circling my cot when I notice that the others are giving each other furtive looks. Really?

"Hey, you seen my mess kit?" I ask the slight kid from Construction whose cot is next to mine. His status in the squad is fairly low and we've talked on an occasion or two during the pre-deployment training.

"Uh…," the kid hesitates, looking from me to the where the others are sitting in a loose huddle on the other side of the room.

"Have you seen it or not?"

"Uh…."

"Forget it." It's petty and I don't want to deal with it so I sling my pack and duffel bag over my shoulder and head out the door.

My reception at the Construction Company is not much better than my farewell at the Support Company, even though this was my original squad. They don't know me, and I don't know them. They've spent every day for the last two months together, trained together, poured concrete together, wandered Manas together. I've only ever talked to Private Jeong-su, and it was a single short conversation during the first week at the 1113th.

The squad is silent, their eyes frozen on me as I unpack my things in the one vacant spot. Once everything is in its place, I pick up my notebook and head out the door.

D-491 (24SEP04): Rockets over Bagram

The first rocket attack was followed by another the next day. The second hit in the 109th Engineer's compound, maybe 100 yards away from where I was in the TOC. There was a very slight tremor, an unusual quiet, and then the Giant Voice calling out the Amber Alert in the night.

I'm in the TOC working on the morning situation report, and I think about my conversation with Sergeant Luvaas and Captain Koepke, the 109th's Operations Officer, the previous day.

The rockets are only four to five inches in diameter. In every report I type up, there are reports of rocket attacks at American bases across the country. 107 mm and 122 mm rockets are the types favored by the Taliban. Not too familiar with the metric system, I never bothered to do the conversion to inches.

When I was running to the squad B-hut to grab my Kevlar and helmet, I didn't see any thick clouds of smoke billowing up from the 109th. I looked in the direction of the tremor, but there was no indication that anything had happened at all.

Most of the casualties I type up in the report are not from rocket attacks. The biggest danger is IEDs, improvised explosive devices, which is what the Army calls these makeshift bombs the Taliban makes using fluorescent light fixtures and cheap wristwatches and unexploded ordnance, usually mines. They plant them along the roads to attack military transports in transit.

There is almost no reason for us to leave the base. After that first day, I've only left the base on one other occasion. I was with Captain Bang, and he thankfully had the presence of mind to make sure we were carrying live ammunition while we drove around and handed out bottles of water to the kids that swarmed the vehicle.

I asked Captain Koepke whether the people who fire the rockets are usually caught.

"It's impossible to catch the local nationals responsible," he replied. "They prop up the rockets on piles of rocks during the day and set a long fuse. By the time the rockets are fired, they're long gone."

"How do you know that the local nationals here aren't the same guys that are firing rockets at us, sir?" The first week on base, I had to go down to the checkpoint at the front gate to pick up the local nationals that operate our construction equipment. I run into them on my way past the Motor Pool, and they seem fairly friendly although they usually keep to themselves.

"There probably are some."

"Sir?"

"You don't need to worry. Basically, they can make more money working here than firing rockets for the Taliban."

For lunch, instead of going to the Korean D-FAC, I take the shuttle up Disney to the BX to get some Burger King with Jeong-su, my replacement as the company interpreter. He's become my first friend on this deployment aside from Ja-hong, and we've bonded over music. Just before the deployment, we were told we could bring instruments, and he brought a drum practice pad, and I brought my guitar. He's the one who told me the church on base allows soldiers to jam using the church equipment when there are no services. It also helps that he can speak English.

We're talking about trying to find others to fill out the band when an American on the shuttle bus interrupts us.

"Hey, where'd you guys learn to speak English?"

I don't reply. I've had to answer that question my entire life and the answer here would lead to sharing my story, which I've done countless times since I started the service eight months ago.

"I studied at McGill University," Jeong-su replies. "You know where that is?"

"Uh… no," the American says, a bit flustered.

I'm okay with letting the conversation end there, but Jeong-su lets him off the hook by asking, "What unit are you with?"

"Actually, I'm not stationed here. I'm on my way back to the States."

"Oh, where were you stationed?"

"Forward Operating Base Ghazni."

"Were you here the other night for the rocket attack?" I guess it's still on Jeong-su's mind.

"No, I got in yesterday. But we get rocket attacks all the time in Ghazni. I mean, all the time."

Jeong-su and the guy continue their conversation but I stop paying attention. Instead, I try to imagine what it must be like at the other bases here. Although we've had two rocket attacks in the past week, we've been here for three weeks without any other incident, whereas there are incidents all over the country every day. Bagram Airbase is huge, and the Korean compound is located almost in the very center of the base. They really chose the safest compound in the safest airbase in Afghanistan.

The first weeks, I'd lie awake at night, listening to the buzzing of the propellers of the planes on the Flight Line and imagining the roar getting louder until a plane crashed right into the squad B-hut. An American soldier told me that because Bagram is surrounded on all sides by the Hindu Kush mountains—"like a bowl," he said—a Taliban plane flying in wouldn't get picked up by the radar until it was too late. I don't know how reliable the information was, or if the Taliban has planes to spare, but it occupied my mind in those moments before sleep came.

Once the third rocket hits a few days later, I accept it as a fact of life here in Bagram. The date of the first direct presidential election is rapidly approaching, and the Taliban has vowed to disrupt the election. As I run to the B-hut to get my Kevlar and helmet, I realize that I'm actually enjoying myself. I feel like an actual soldier instead of what I am, nothing but an incompetent desk jockey.

D-487 (28SEP04): Thanksgiving for Nothing

By the time *Chuseok*, Korean Thanksgiving, rolls around, at least some of the others in the squad have begun to warm up to me. I remain closest with Private Jeong-su, and he's proven to be the closest thing I have to a friend here. I've had a couple of conversations before lights out with Corporal Gi-hwan, who sleeps in the cot next to mine, and with Corporal Jun-mo when I run into him at the pitiful excuse for a gym we have on the compound. I rarely see my squad but, after the first couple of weeks, they've welcomed me as one of their own.

Again I wish I had never taken the linguist test. I wish I had just been sent to some infantry division in the countryside to dig holes like everyone else. My squad in the Support Company was composed of the same ilk that abounds at SROKA. Privileged kids rotten from the inside for whom having so much has left them insecure.

The holiday is one of two long Korean holidays, but they're only giving us one day off. Of course, I'm not expecting any time off, especially because Colonel Park has called for a sports competition in the afternoon after the ancestor-worship ritual at the D-FAC.

I watch from the door of the TOC as the companies play tug-of-war and *ssireum* and hacky sack and *jokgu*.[58] I miss the team sports, but Captain Bang relieves me in time to participate in *ssireum*, Korean sumo. After losing, I look forward to some rest before I have to report to the TOC to relieve Captain Bang for dinner, but the first sergeant grabs me and tells me to clean the grills for tonight's dinner.

It's clear that the first sergeant has singled me out for this task. The other guys from the company are lounging around, watching the competition or smoking off to the side. Captain Park has been on my ass because he has no control over me and it seems he's recruited the first sergeant to give him a hand.

Cleaning the grills means digging holes in the rocky area behind the showers to bury the ashes and scraping the grills clean with jagged rocks that are scattered across the parade ground. I'm spraying down the grills when the first sergeant approaches me and mumbles something to me.

"I didn't hear you clearly, sir."

"Goddamn, learn to understand Korean," he scolds, this time loud enough to hear, punctuated with an exasperated sigh.

The comment is infuriating. It's not like I haven't been trying. One of the few books I brought along with me is a book on Korean grammar. Only I haven't had much time to read it between guard duties and TOC duties.

"I said don't spray so close to the lights for tonight."

I look around and see a metal frame with flood lights attached to it sitting off to the side, a good four feet from where I'm spraying. I don't respond.

---

[58] *Jokgu*: A sport that is a mixture of volleyball and soccer, played on a tennis court and popular among soldiers.

Instead, I stick my finger into the opening of the hose, spraying water everywhere, hoping to hit the lights. I'm too angry to be subtle about it.

"Stop," the first sergeant says angrily.

Again, I don't respond. I drop the hose to the ground and walk away. I'm too tired to deal with him today.

I trade shifts with Captain Bang again for dinner, and this time he relieves me in time for me to have some hot food. There are steaks and hot dogs for dinner, courtesy of the Class IV Yard. The rest of the company has finished eating, and most of them have called it a night, but the coals in the grills are still hot, and I make myself dinner.

The next day, the base executive officer, Brigadier General Jacoby, and command sergeant major, Sergeant Major Ashe, confront us over the issue of pallets again after the morning briefing. They know I'm the interpreter and they address me directly.

"Tell your commander that you need to return the pallets by the end of this week or we're going to come with a bulldozer and dig them up ourselves."

"Yes, sir."

When I return to the TOC, I bring up the threat to Major Jeong, but he dismisses it as usual. I want to tell him that it's not an empty threat, that unlike the fights I've seen in Korea, American culture requires a man to back up his word with action, but I know my words will have no effect. I hope I'm not around when the bulldozers come because I know he'll need a scapegoat, and my inability to persuade him will earn me another verbal thrashing.

Later in the day, I'm sitting in the TOC when our command sergeant major, Master Sergeant Kim, peeks in through the door.

"Hey, come here."

"I can't, sir. I have to watch the TOC."

"It's okay. It'll only take a second."

I follow him behind the TOC to his office and when he opens the door, I see the Sergeant Major Ashe stewing in his own juices. I didn't hear the bulldozers or see one outside, but he must be here about the pallets. I steel myself for a berating because there is nothing I can do. The words will be directed toward the officers, but as their ears and mouth, I'll be the one who suffers from their venom.

After a couple of short exchanges, I discover that he's not here because of the pallets. There's nothing reassuring about it because he's here for something completely unbelievable. It's about the steaks for dinner yesterday, steaks that apparently the Master Sergeant Kim stole from the Class IV Yard by browbeating the guys at the yard with an aggressive lack of English and It's okay's and false permission from Sergeant Major Ashe.

"Where the hell do you get off using my name to steal from the US Army? I should have you strung up for this."

Master Sergeant Kim has a dumb, proud look on his broad, ignorant face. "Tell him that we'll give him 100 cases of water."

"Uh, sir. I don't think 100 cases of water is enough."

"It's okay. Just tell him." Fuck my life.

"Sergeant major, he says that we'll repay you with what we have. We can give you...," I don't want to finish the sentence but Master Sergeant Kim tells me to hurry up. "... water."

The sergeant major looks like he's going to explode, lips drawn to a thin line and his face turning shades of red and purple.

"You have to be fucking kidding me."

"Tell him that we have a delivery of water coming in next week."

Before I can pass on the next message, Sergeant Major Ashe spits, "God damn Koreans," and stomps out the door.

I look at Master Sergeant Kim and he still has this dumb, self-satisfied look on his face.

D-476 (09OCT04): Election Day

It's quiet on base today. There are no local nationals around; the construction equipment in our yard sits quietly without the local nationals to attend them. There are very few people on Disney as I cross to head to the D-FAC after the morning briefing. The shuttle bus isn't running. It's Election Day.

They've been expecting insurgent attacks to reach a head, and it seems they've shut everything down for the day. There have been a couple more rocket attacks in the past few days, and there was a bomb scare last week. There was a tip that one of the jingle trucks—the trucks the locals drive around, colorfully painted and overly decorated with chains and sashes— would be used as a Vehicle-Borne Improvised Explosive Device, and the guards had all the trucks taken to a remote location and inspected before allowing them on the base. They managed to identify the truck before it could cause any damage. One of the trucks was missing a gas cap and they reportedly found batteries in the fuel tank.

But today is quiet.

Everyone is inside, which is my cue to be outside. I walk Disney and enjoy the peace and quiet. In the distance, the wind sifts the snow from one peak of the Hindu Kush to the next. Little black birds sit on the power lines and chirp to one another.

It's getting chilly out.

Hamid Karzai is the frontrunner for the election. According to hearsay, it is almost positive that he will be the new president of Afghanistan, the first president since the Taliban overran the country. It's a historic day for the Afghan people. The Taliban are fighting to regain control of the country, warlords vie for local dominance, and the poppy fields continue to grow, making Afghanistan the leading producer of opium in the world, but there is hope.

Around the base, I occasionally see members of the KPD, Karzai Protective Detail, mercenaries charged with protecting the probable next president. They stroll around the base in T-shirts and cargo pants and Kevlar, holding massive rifles and holstered sidearms. They almost without exception have big bushy beards. They're not around today, either, probably busy protecting Karzai wherever he is at the moment.

When I get to the D-FAC, it's almost completely empty. It's nice to be alone. I'm effectively alone all the time but always surrounded by people.

I load up my tray and take a seat and eat lunch in peace for once.

D-473 (12OCT04): Stepping on Mines

I've been getting along with the other guys in the company, but I still spend most of my time on my own. I wonder if it's because I've become comfortable with being alone. Perhaps I've always been this way.

Getting to know new people has always been draining for me, and with my patience wearing thin because of overwork, there's very little left to deal with the sudden attention and having to field the same questions again and again.

"You're American?" is the usual opener.

"Yeah," is my reply.

The follow-up is "Why did you come to the Army?"

"It wasn't my choice. It's a long story." The hint that I don't want to get into it is usually lost on the asker.

"You're like Yoo Seung-jun. You know Yoo Seung-jun?"

The reference irritated me the first time, and it has only gotten worse. Yoo was a singer/rapper who became the nation's golden boy when he proudly announced on television that he would do his military service at a time when many celebrities did everything in their power to avoid the service. He fell from grace when he was naturalized as an American citizen, giving up his Korean citizenship and its duties in the process.

"It's different. I was born American, and I'm here, aren't I?"

"Yeah, I guess you're right."

After a while, I stop explaining the difference and just smirk when they make the reference. After he was naturalized, it became a huge social issue. Yoo was branded a draft dodger and barred from returning to Korea. I don't know what the legal justification for his blacklisting was, but it doesn't seem like the Ministry of Justice considered something as trivial as the law and reason when barring my leaving Korea.

The result of the outrage directed at Yoo was a tightening of the conscription regulations. Apparently, it had been fairly easy to get an exemption because there were so many people volunteering after the Asian Financial Crisis in 1997. Because of Yoo, the tattoo restrictions were thrown out, and I assume an inability to speak Korean was also stricken from the list of excluding factors. That was 2002, the year I came to Korea. I came not knowing the situation and inadvertently stepped on a mine.

During my first week, while waiting at the front gate to pick up the local nationals that operate our construction equipment, I walked out to the fence that separates the base from the city of Bagram.

Outside the fence, a lonely tractor was chugging slowly through the dusty fields. In front of the tractor, a woman in a burqa and two small children, probably no more than five or six, were walking slowly, dark figures against the backdrop of the bleached earth.

"You know why the woman and kids are walking in front of the tractor?" an American guard asked me, also looking out into the fields.

I shrugged, not taking my eyes off the scene. "Why?"

"The fields around the base are full of unexploded ordnance and mines that never got cleared. These people are poor, and that tractor is worth more to that farmer than his wife and kids."

The guard wandered off and I continued to watch the tractor as it made its way up and down the field. It's a cruel world. The woman and children have to risk their lives and limbs for the sake of their patriarch; the man has to subject his family to such risk because he's too poor to work a nicer, safer field; and the ones who laid the mines are long gone, leaving behind a legacy of pain.

D-464 (21OCT04): Let It Be

Captain Park and the first sergeant are stepping up their efforts to make my life difficult. They've chosen me as the one person from the company to do the 24-hour TOC duty on Sundays while keeping me in the rotation for the regular company guard duties, including front-gate and night patrols. The guys from the other companies put on 24-hour TOC duty have been exempted from regular duties. This means that I have no guarantee of any night without guard duty, at least going through the rotation every other day.

The front-gate patrol is not such a bad guard duty. Two hours standing at the entrance of our compound on Disney, it's boring and somewhat useless, but it's an excuse to get out of overtime for a couple of hours.

I'm returning from the first shift at the front gate, and the guys are lounging around the B-hut. Jong-hun, our squad leader, sees me walk in and asks, "Hey, did you check the duty schedule? It just came out." Everything from Jong-hun is only a suggestion.

"I'm good. I just got back from duty," I say, taking off my helmet and utility vest.

There are only two duties and twenty-three guys in the company but as I change, I have a strange nagging feeling, so I stop changing and head out to check the schedule anyway. Not seeing my name on the list always makes me feel good.

A few of the guys from second squad are huddled around the duty sheet. It's not hard to spot Gwang-su, a good foot taller than everyone else.

"Hey, Gwang-su, I'm not on there, right?"

Gwang-su turns to the schedule and runs his meaty finger down the names from top to bottom.

"Yup, here you are. Two to four, night watch," he says in his booming baritone.

Two shifts in one night is unheard of. Four shifts in four days is malice. I would take it up with the first sergeant if it was a mistake, but I know it's intentional.

I've been on edge lately. The staff officers have been piling on the work as well, work from other offices. The Personnel Chief, Major Ju, had me interpret another absurd transaction, this time with a local national who came to fix the copier. "Tell him we'll pay him twenty dollars and call it even." "But, sir, he's asking for a hundred fifty." He also had me draft a contract for the long-term rental of our construction equipment because any error could cost the government a lot of money, even though Seung-ju, the S1/S4 interpreter, is practically fluent in English. The Personnel Officer keeps hounding me to teach him English and the Construction Officer wants me to help him when he goes out to the construction sites because there are no interpreters attached to the Construction Branch.

All work and no play is a good reason not to give a conscript bullets. I haven't seen the inside of my squad B-hut much in the past week. Major Jeong has me working at all hours on yet another big PowerPoint presentation. The presentation is not part of my regular duties at the TOC, and so he has me work on it after hours. The least he could do is make me work on it during mental education on Wednesday afternoons, but I have a feeling he thinks it's kindness to let me have time off to listen to bullshit.

"If you have great expectations, you will face great disappointment."

Captain Promotable Lee, the Public Affairs Officer, stares down at us from his makeshift pulpit, his beady eyes scanning the faces of a hundred tired conscripts crammed into a room built for fifty. He pauses for effect to let this invaluable lesson to sink in. From what I can gather, this session of brainwashing has been called to remind us that although Bagram has much to offer, we're only conscripts and should act accordingly. His message is basically this: Don't get used to it. Conscription and privation go hand in hand.

The lesson grates on my American senses. "Aim high" and "Be all that you can be" are the mottoes of the armed forces I grew up hearing on the television. "Don't expect anything" seems to be the motto of the Korean

Support Group. They've taken the line of President Kennedy about asking not what your country can do for you to the extreme.

I look around me but see that no one else cares. It's the usual bullshit, and this isn't boot camp. Only a few people look toward Captain Lee. The rest have their heads bowed, out of boredom or slumber. Captain Lee goes on.

"If you were born in America, you wouldn't have to be here."

I assume he means that, as Korean males, conscripts should accept their lots in life. If the others were born in America, they would be American soldiers and entitled to welfare. It is then that he notices my cold and indignant stare.

He clears his throat with a nervous cough. He knows damn well that I'm an American. "Anyway…."

He fumbles through the rest of his speech, mixing metaphors about the tortoise and the hare and something about highways.

I'm walking back to the B-hut, hoping to salvage what's left of my day. Major Jeong didn't tell me to report for work on the presentation after dinner, but I have a strong feeling he'll try to find me later. I need to gather my things and run off to the Americans' welfare facility to hide in the darkness of the movie theater.

When I open the door of the B-hut, the guys are sitting around, listening to the radio. I walk to my spot and start packing my bag.

"Hey, Chun." It's Jun-mo, a workout fanatic who's always walking around in his PT shorts and undershirt. "What does this song mean?"

I pause and listen. It's the Beatles' "Let It Be."

"*Nebido*," I say, using a dialect.[59]

"Huh?"

"Let it be. It means *nebido*."

"Oh, thanks."

I walk out the door to the guys singing the refrain in Korean—"*Nebido~ Nebido~ Nebido~ Ne~bi~do*—and I can't help but smile. It gets me thinking as I walk with hurried paces out of the compound. *Nebido*. Let it be. Here I am, an American, serving in the Korean Army. Let it be. Here I am, in the

---

[59] Standard pronunciation: *nebdweo*. *Nebido* is Gyeongsang Province dialect, the area where Daegu is located, but the expression was popularized in the past year by comedians.

middle of Afghanistan, worked to the bone by the staff officers, hated by my company officers, scorned by most of the other conscripts. Let it be.

I keep expecting the universe will correct its mistake, or that people in the Army will treat me like a human being, but I need to let go and accept that things are the way they are. There is no reason and no point thinking about it. I realize that the question I asked myself every night in basic—What the hell am I doing here?—I don't ask myself anymore. Maybe there was a kernel of truth in what the Public Affairs Officer said from his pulpit. Maybe having no expectations means not setting myself up for disappointment after disappointment.

I walk into the darkness of the welfare facility, the beginnings of peace germinating in my chest.

D-433 (21NOV04): Escape

Being on an American base, everyone has suddenly become eager to learn English. The good thing is that there are some Americans interested in Korean culture, and so I'm not the one they come asking.

I occasionally see groups of conscripts sitting around an American soldier around the compound or at the mess hall. The soldier is usually female, and I can't say I blame the others for that. The guys in my squad have befriended an American ranger named Chris, whom I dislike because he's a little creepy, and he's always hanging around the B-hut. The other day, the interpreter for the Civil Engineering Company told me Chris was taking a shower on our compound, even though his compound is not too far away.

On my way back from lunch, I spot my squad talking to a female American soldier of Asian descent, probably Korean-American. Human intelligence, I surmise because she's dressed in civilian clothes. I wave my acknowledgement to my squad but keep walking past. It's not Chris for once, but I'm not interested in making any more friends.

"Hey, Young," Jeong-su calls. "Come here."

"What's up?"

"This is the guy that I've been telling you about," Jeong-su says to the female soldier. It seems like I'm getting roped into another painful introduction.

We exchange greetings and she goes on, "So you're an American?"

230

"Yeah."

"But you were born in Korea, right?"

"No, I was born in Illinois. Where're you from?"

"Really? Actually, I was born in Korea but immigrated to the States with my family when I was young. Then how did you end up in the Korean Army?"

"It's a long story."

She looks like she wants to hear it so I give her the short version—coming to Korea to teach English for a year, finding out I was Korean, getting barred from leaving the country, reporting for boot camp, Afghanistan.

"Wow, that's crazy."

I give her a halfhearted smile.

"Did you try to get out of it?"

"Of course I did. I tried everything. I talked to the embassy and they ignored me. I talked to reporters and lawyers and they told me nothing could be done. I even considered finding a row boat and rowing to Japan. My last plan was signing up for the US Army, but even that fell through. Now that I'm in Afghanistan, I guess if I could just get to the US embassy in Kabul, I could probably escape. There are no governmental orders barring my leaving Afghanistan."

The female captain thinks for a moment. "You know, I could take you to Kabul if you wanted. Of course, you'd have to hide in the trunk."

I take a moment to consider her offer. Is she serious? It doesn't look like she's joking.

Is it worth it? Even if we make it to Kabul without hitting an IED planted in the roads by the Taliban, I'd be a deserter. Would the American embassy help me get home, or would they send me back here to face punishment? I'd have more faith in the embassy, but the past has taught me differently.

If I managed to make it home, I'd be an international criminal, forever barred from entering Korea on possible threat of prison and re-doing my military service. Of course, I don't know if I'd want to go back after all that's happened. But then again, I've been through the absolute worst of it, boot camp and life as a private, and it will all be for nothing.

"I'll think about it," I tell her but realize that I've already come to a decision.

The last stage of grief is acceptance, and I think I've finally made it. I don't think I'll ever be able to enjoy it, but at least I've finally accepted that I couldn't avoid it.

Sitting in Major Jeong's office nearing midnight, I'm questioning whether I've really accepted life as it is, but this is where I need to be if I'm going to turn things around. In one sense, acceptance is resignation, but in another, acceptance is power. Now that I've resigned myself to toughing it out for the full two years, I've turned my thoughts to what I can do within the confines of my service.

I've been re-visiting the regulations on overseas furloughs. I'm probably the Army's foremost expert on the regulations, having spent hours poring over them with dictionary in hand. The regulations only state that I need the permission of the unit commander. This was an impossibility in Daegu. It would certainly get shot down by Captain Jin before it could traverse the bureaucratic mess up to the commander of the Second Army, a four-star general.

I don't feel as if I'm asking for much, just a right that every other conscript gets at least four times during his service—the right to go home during a furlough. To see my family. To eat a home-cooked meal. To sleep in my own bed. It's not much, but the Army has been tight-fisted, and I know that I'll have to tread carefully to work this through.

Here in Afghanistan, I'll have to get permission from Colonel Park. Colonel Park is almost inaccessible, only emerging from his luxurious quarters for briefings and meals, and always accompanied by an entourage of officers. Besides, his demeanor is highly unnerving, and it doesn't seem as if he has much concern for conscripts. If I'm to get his permission, I'll have to go through Major Jeong, unit XO and Colonel Park's right hand.

"Try out a different color for the background," Major Jeong says from his seat beside me. "Something that will make the letters pop."

"Yes, sir."

After randomly trying out several colors, I manage to satisfy his need for a color popping. There is a silence as I start typing up the main text on the page, a silence I decide to use to see if all this work for the major has any benefit for my future.

"Sir, may I ask you a question?"

"Of course. What is it?"

"Do you think maybe I could get an early promotion, sir?"

"Huh? Why?"

I study his reaction. He doesn't look opposed to the idea, just curious. Emboldened, I go on, having rehearsed my speech earlier so that I can present my case despite still having the linguistic ability of a grade schooler.

"As you know, the American soldiers still call PFCs 'private,' and I think… it would be better to be a corporal in the base meetings."

Of course, embedded in that spoken argument was a reminder of all the hard work and sleepless nights I put in throughout the deployment. It was like hinting at the gift you want to receive before Christmas or your birthday.

"Why don't you ask your company commander?"

"Um… I don't spend too much time in the company and… I don't think he'd consider it."

Major Jeong thinks for a second and says, "When were you supposed to be promoted?"

"January, sir."

"Okay. Just leave it to me."

"Yes, sir."

There really is no benefit in getting promoted a month early—if anything, I'll probably be resented even more by the other conscripts—but I'm testing the waters. Before I can work out a trip home, I need to know the extent of my influence among the staff officers.

D-428 (26NOV04): A Monkey Wrench in the Plans

Something has crawled up Captain Park's ass lately, and he's been coming down on the company hard. Earlier in the month, he conducted an inspection of our B-huts while we were in mental education looking for infractions, taking note of the conscripts whose shoes weren't lined up neatly or whose uniforms weren't folded neatly with name tag facing front. I was one of the latter, but only because I had put my uniform in my laundry box to be washed. I have a feeling I'm the reason why, and I feel sorry that the others have to suffer as well. The punishment for the infractions was a full-pack march around the parade ground until he was satisfied.

He also commented on the lack of discipline in the company and ordered us to show up to evening call in our uniforms and read passages from the field manual. Another of the ways he's chosen to come down on us is the length of our hair. The first sergeant called me out on the length of my hair despite the fact that he couldn't see me hiding behind Gwang-su during evening call.

Despite the worsening of conditions in the company, I've managed to avoid punishment. I've never used my duties at the TOC to escape my company obligations before, but now I've decided I'm going to use it to my advantage. It's the primary reason why other conscripts don't like conscripts who work in the offices. I haven't abused my position before, but it's about time I did.

When called to do full-pack laps for the uniform infractions, I slip out the B-hut and report to the TOC.

"Chun, what are you doing here?" Captain Bang asks.

"I have to work on the presentation for Major Jeong," I reply. It's only partially untrue. I always have something to work on but I wasn't called by Major Jeong specifically.

The next day, I return to the B-hut to pick up some things before I head out for a late lunch when I hear yelling from behind the curtained partition marking Captain Park's quarters. I look under the curtain and can see the hands and boots of several of the company members. I also see Captain Park's boots pacing back and forth, lecturing the conscripts on the length of their hair. There's a pause followed by the heavy thudding of at least three conscripts against the wooden floor.

"Get up," Captain Park barks at them.

I see my company members pick themselves up off the floor and get back on their hands and feet.

I grab my notebooks and retreat back out the door as quietly and nimbly as I can and head straight to the container with the hair clippers. It's all coming off. Lunch can wait.

Chris is back. I didn't think he'd be back after the last time he came, when Jeong-su told him he wasn't welcome. The decision didn't have to do with his sexual orientation—the others have finally picked up that he's very likely homosexual—but more with the fact that he's a constant annoyance.

"You know, I was really hurt and angry when I left last time," Chris says to Jeong-su, "but I've missed you guys so much."

"No hard feelings," Jeong-su says. "What are you doing here?"

"I'm here to have English class with the captain."

Captain Park is lounging on one of the cots, watching television and

234

ignoring Chris. It seems as if he doesn't feel like having class.

"Commander," Jeong-su says. "Chris is here to have English class with you."

Jeong-su wants to get rid of Chris and our other annoyance with one swift stroke. Captain Park can no longer ignore Chris. He sighs and sits up.

"Chun, let's have class with Chris."

"I didn't hear you clearly, sir." I heard him, but it didn't register. Why would I go to English class?

"Let's have class. You, me, and Chris."

I can feel the anger rising in me at the prospect of spending any amount of time with two of my least favorite people on my only day off in almost two weeks, but I take a deep breath and suppress it.

"If you want me to teach you English, sir, you have to pay me hourly."

Captain Park laughs. He thinks I'm joking because the statement is borderline insubordination. I'm not.

"Fifty thousand won an hour, sir." I quote a price I think he won't accept. It's an insane thing to say to my commanding officer, but there's no way in hell I'm going to spend time with two of my least favorite people in Bagram.

"Are you out of your fucking mind?" He's not laughing any more. "You're in my company, and you'll do what I want you to do. If I want you to tutor me, you'll tutor me."

"Yes, sir."

"Let's have class."

"I'm sorry, sir," I say, looking at my watch. "I have to report to Major Jeong's office in five minutes." It's a lie, but abusing the hierarchy is the only way I'm going to get out of this. I quickly gather my things and head out the door, ignoring Captain Park's glare the entire way. I make a note to disappear at the slightest sign of Captain Park in the future. I don't know how long this is going to be effective.

The weather has been getting colder lately. Winter is coming. I'm working in the TOC when the first sergeant pops his head in and calls me out for a talk. Once we're outside, he tells me to follow him to his office in the 2nd squad B-hut.

"Sit."

"Yes, sir."

"I heard you asked for an early promotion."

I've been so busy with work I'd forgotten about my plan. I guess it must have come up in a briefing. "Yes, sir."

"Well, you can forget about it. It ain't going to happen. Got it?"

"Yes, sir."

"Early promotions are decided in the company, and you're worthless as a company member."

It's not untrue, but it's not something I want to hear. I consider talking back about how the reason I don't contribute to the company is because Captain Park pimped me out to the staff, but I keep my mouth shut.

"And keep your mouth shut. What happens in the company stays in the company. You better think about your priorities. Your duties are to the company first."

"Yes, sir."

"Try harder, got it?"

"Yes, sir."

It's not such a big deal that I'm not getting an early promotion, but I'm confused that things didn't work out. Regardless of how bad things are at the company, Major Jeong is our unit executive officer, second in command, and I was sure that he would push my promotion through. If he can't be depended on for something as trivial as an early promotion, my plan to request permission to go home is in jeopardy.

D-422 (02DEC04): A Hearty Fuck-you

Corporal Young Jin Chun, reporting one month early. It seems I was wrong about my plans, but this time the error was in my favor.

The first day of every month, we have a ceremony after breakfast for the men who are to be promoted. I've rarely participated in the ceremony, or roll call for that matter, because of my duties at the TOC. While all of the other squad members are getting changed and running out the door, I'm taking my time, gathering my notebooks before I head behind the B-huts to the back entrance of the TOC, out of sight.

I'm about to reach for the door handle when the door flings open and Jong-hun almost runs into me.

"Hurry up and put on your helmet and utility vest," he manages out between pants. "You're getting promoted early."

I'm confused. Not only did Captain Park and the first sergeant make it clear that I wasn't getting the promotion, the staff at the S1/S4 mocked me when I dropped off a report to the Personnel Chief later that day.

"You think you deserve a promotion?" the major laughed as he took the report from my hands.

"If anyone deserves a promotion, it's Seung-ju," the Personnel Officer added, smirking. Seung-ju is the S1/S4 interpreter although I've rarely seen him in the office.

I left the office filled with two strong emotions. The first was rage, considering all the work they've had me do, the absurd negotiations and the translating of their construction equipment contracts and other personal favors such as dictating the Personnel Officer's English books so he could work on his pronunciation. The second was disappointment because the two of them are the entirety of the personnel staff under whose purview promotions fall.

My name is called along with the others to be promoted. As I walk through the ranks in the formation, I can almost feel the resentment, mostly coming from the Support Company but also from my own company officers. Captain Park avoids my eye contact as I walk past him. I don't mind the animosity. I've become accustomed to it.

I purposely take my place next to Seung-ju, a December now-corporal. The Personnel Officer walks down the line, shaking hands and handing out corporal insignias. There's no strength is his handshake and no warmth in his expression as he congratulates me on my promotion as decorum dictates. I look up at the Personnel Chief up on the podium, and his expression is delicious. The third-highest ranking officer, and he's tasting sour grapes while I'm tasting payback.

"You're getting promoted, but this isn't going on your personnel record," the Personnel Officer whispers as he hands me the insignia. I shrug and smile. I don't care. It wasn't my purpose to begin with.

I turn my gaze to Major Jeong and he's smiling his full smile. Major Jeong may make me work late hours with little sleep, but now I know he takes care of the people who help him. It's good to have connections in high places.

D-421 (03DEC04): An Omen

"I'm sorry, son," the American major says, the overhead light blinding me from behind his looming head. "We can't save it. We're going to have to take it out. Unfortunately, we don't have the capabilities here to replace it."

I guess I'm not leaving Afghanistan unscathed after all.

"Is it going to be a problem getting by without it, sir?"

"No. You'll get used to it. Just take care of it when you get shipped back to Korea."

"I understand, sir."

I feel like I'm in an episode of *M*A*S*H*, stretched out in a war-time hospital tent with a US Army surgeon standing over me. The major has given me a little local anesthetic, but I'm fully conscious when he picks up a wrench-like tool, reaches into my open cavity, and takes out my molar.

Sitting in the TOC, I run my tongue through the gap between my second molar and second bicuspid, over the smooth gum and the rough stitches. The loss of the tooth is, like so many other things in my life, a result of bad timing, bad decisions, and a lack of choices.

"Did you throw your tooth on the roof?" Captain Bang asks.

"I didn't hear you clearly, sir."

"In Korea, when you lose a tooth, you throw it on the roof. Well, that's what kids do."

"Oh, I didn't know that, sir. They didn't give me the tooth."

I return to typing the force-protection report, again running my tongue through the hole in the bottom row of teeth. The tip of my tongue pulls on one of the stitches a little too hard and the slight metallic taste of blood mixes with my saliva.

"You know, people think that if you dream of a tooth falling out, it means someone close to you is going to die."

I know Captain Bang is only trying to keep me entertained while I type up his report, which is a kindness many officers wouldn't bother with. Nonetheless, there's something about this Korean brand of bluntness that confuses me.

Of course, Captain Bang doesn't know that it's been a concern of mine since the day I was sitting in the office during boot camp, shedding uncontrollable tears for all the bastards to see. The deployment's halfway through, and now that I know Major Jeong is on my side, I need to start working out the details for going home.

238

D-407 (17DEC04): The Comeback Kid

The TOC is quiet today. I open the door and look outside, and the compound is empty. I take a few deep breaths of the chilly December air. It's been getting much colder lately, cold enough to have to wear my field jacket during the days and my *ggalggari* during the nights. I had thought it would be dry and hot year round, but the nights I stand on front gate duty, I've had to take hand-warmers and stick them under my armpits and down my pants.

I sigh. I should be feeling peace, a wholesome, unadulterated Zen. The officers are nowhere in sight, and I have the TOC to myself. I've come to treasure these times that I've been left behind and left alone. But today is different. The others aren't outside playing tug-of-war or Korean sumo. They aren't feasting on steak or hot dogs. They're not even in the compound. They're down at the Clamshell for the USO tour.

While I can do without meeting Robin Williams or Wilson from Home Improvement, Lee Ann Tweeden, the cover model for this month's issue of FHM, is here, and more importantly, one of my childhood heroes, John Elway, the Comeback Kid, the engineer of The Drive, is here. No one else among our contingent even knows what American football is. "It's like rugby, isn't it?" Captain Bang asked when I pleaded with him for just a half hour off so I could go.

"The commander has prohibited everyone from attending the event," he explained. Colonel Park must've changed his mind because I'm fairly certain he's there, too, along with practically every other non-American from our contingent.

Having nothing to do for the first time in as long as I can remember, it's cruel that I can't enjoy it. It's unfair, the voice says weakly in the back of my head. I search for something to distract me. I can't find anything, but searching for a distraction is distraction enough.

I peek out the door again, and the officers are walking across the parade ground toward the TOC. Strutting. Laughing. Unfair, the voice says again. I close the door and sit in front of the computer.

The door opens with Captain Bang in the lead and the Personnel Officer in tow.

"What was that the guy was throwing into the crowd?" the Personnel Officer asks. "Rugby balls?"

"American footballs," Captain Bang answers knowingly.

The voice is getting louder, harder to ignore. I get up from my seat and approach the captain.

"What is it?" he asks.

"Could I return the company for a little while, sir?"

"Go ahead," he says, smiling. "Take your time. Come back after dinner."

"Thank you, sir."

The voice only begins to quiet when the door to the TOC closes behind me, and I trudge toward the squad B-hut. Sure, it would've been nice to get a football signed by John Elway, but it's only a thing, a possession. Let it be.

I walk into the empty B-hut and lie down on my cot.

It isn't long before the door flings open and the guys file in, apparently back from the USO event as well.

"Did you see the breasts on that girl?" Jun-mo asks the others, holding out his cupped hands well in front of his chest. "Hot damn!"

The guys start settling in, but the conversation is stuck on Ms. Tweeden and her melons. I put in my headphones, but I can still hear them talk about her produce. I put away my mp3 player and gather my things once again to head out in search for a place of peace and quiet.

I head out of the compound, cross Disney, and walk through the doors of the MWR.[60] I start toward the movie viewing area but change my mind and head upstairs to the small room with internet access.

I take one of the booths against the far wall and log on to my e-mail. I haven't received much e-mail since leaving Seattle, and even less since my induction. When I came out for my 100th-day furlough, I found that my account had been closed due to inactivity. I understand. What's the point in sending an e-mail to someone who may not be able to check it for months? Surprisingly, there's an unread e-mail in my inbox.

Hi, I sent you an eCard from Egreetings.com, the subject line reads. It's from Jen.

I click on the link and a cute flash animation plays on the screen followed by a short message. Happy Birthday and Merry Christmas, it starts.

Today is my birthday. That's what was really getting me down and what made today all the more difficult.

I read the message over and over. I check my e-mail and then read the message one last time before logging off and heading back downstairs toward

---

[60] MWR: Morale, Welfare, and Recreation building. A US Army facility with video rentals, a movie viewing area, and an internet café, among other things

the movie viewing area.

In the darkness, I let out a sigh and feel the heaviness leave my body. In the darkness, I regain my Zen. I was being foolish, giving an ear to the voice in the back of my head. What's done is done. The experience is temporary. Meeting people who couldn't give a damn about me. There are people who do who are waiting for me. The thought is comforting. The first sergeant criticized my frequenting the MWR, but this is my refuge.

D-365 (29JAN05): A New Year

It's a new year. 2005, the Year of the Cock. I know this because I get a reminder every morning with the rising of the sun. The local nationals that operate our construction equipment have gifted us with a couple of roosters and, being a city boy, I had no idea that roosters don't crow just once with the sunrise. They crow incessantly the moment the darkness in the sky begins to pale.

I was also wrong in assuming that Afghanistan is a desert. After four straight months of nothing but dry heat and cloudless skies, it rained the entire last week of 2004, flooding the parade ground, the parched earth unable to soak up the floodwaters. Even after the trucks came to drain the water from the field, there were still giant puddles spotting the parade ground.

The temperature has dropped even further, and the puddles have frozen into thick, dark, cracked patches of ice. The air conditioning units, with their ribbed caterpillar tubes that crawl into the B-huts, have been switched over to supply a steady flow of hot air. When it first snowed, the guys ran outside to have snowball fights and take pictures. Snow in Afghanistan, I hadn't thought it possible.

Unable to pour concrete because of the rain and now snow, the company has been having it easy, and even Captain Park seems to be in a better mood, having nothing to do.

When I stop by the B-hut to rest before lunch, I find the space crowded with guys from the other squads. They have expressions of shock and guilt and then relief when they see it's just me. They've installed satellite television, one per company, and the guys have recently discovered an Eastern European channel that features disinterested women performing an excruciatingly slow striptease over the course of a half an hour.

I squeeze past the horny kids that have taken seats on my cot and pack a few things in my bag before heading out. I was hoping to lie down for a bit, but being surrounded by people makes me uncomfortable, even more so when they're watching the closest thing we have to porn.

I walk out of the B-hut, and it's quiet on the compound, everyone at the D-FAC or inside where it's warm. I head toward the small space between one of the B-huts on the periphery and the sandbag walls and rest my back against the B-hut. Nobody's out, but I really don't want to be disturbed.

I open up my bag and take out a small and familiar red package, a Chocopie I've been saving since we left Korea five months ago, saving for this day. Today marks one year of service in the Army.

It's been a strange year, a year that's taken me from Jeungpyeong to Daegu and now Afghanistan. There are times when I still can't believe the turn my life has taken. Two years ago, I was a kid who had never left North America as an adult, and now I'm serving as a Korean soldier in Afghanistan. I still can't communicate at a reasonable level, and the culture remains a fathomless mystery.

I sometimes wonder if I'll ever completely understand. Maybe it's not meant to be understood, just done. Thinking only makes the time harder.

This time, I savor the chocolate and marshmallow. In Korean, they say that people eat age as they get older. And every Lunar New Year, Koreans eat *ddeokguk*, a soup with rice cakes and dumplings, saying that it represents getting a year older. This snack cake represents everything I've been through in the past year. I make sure to finish off every last crumb.

One year down, one to go.

D-360 (02FEB05): Bad News

"Hey. Hey."

I feel someone nudging my boot in the darkness.

"Wake up. Major Ju is looking for you."

Shit. How long have I been sleeping? I bolt out of the B-hut and dash the 50 meters to the TOC.

I burst through the door and Major Ju is awake, barely, and unhappy, his squinty eyes staring daggers at me. The shift change for the front gate is there, as well as a corporal from the 1st Construction Company in his orange PT uniform.

"Where the fuck were you?"

"I-I…," I stutter. I was supposed to be in the TOC while Major Ju slept through the night, but I've taken to napping while pretending to patrol the companies. My internal clock usually wakes me up after ten minutes, but I guess the fatigue from my workload has taken its toll. "I…."

"Sit down," Major Ju barks, cutting me off.

"Yes, sir."

I take my seat in front of the computer as he accepts the report of the shift change. I wonder why the corporal from the 1st Construction Company is here. I've seen him around often. He's usually in the B-hut gym, resting his back against the wall and curling a ridiculous amount of weight for such a small guy, probably no more than five-two. Maybe it's the way he talks, but I've always thought he was a hoodlum before the Army.

"You can return to Korea but there aren't any flights until next week," Major Ju tells the corporal. "Do you still want to go?"

"No, sir. I'll stay and finish the deployment, sir."

"Okay. Get some sleep," Major Ju says, patting the corporal on the back softly.

"Yes, sir."

The corporal salutes and exits the TOC. I want to ask Major Ju what he and the corporal were talking about but I don't want to bring attention to myself. Major Ju folds his arms and returns to sleep.

Before breakfast, Captain Park calls the company to gather in our B-hut.

"Yesterday, the Ministry of National Defense called the base. Does anyone here know Corporal Yong-hyeon from 1st Company?"

A couple of hands go up.

"His mother passed away yesterday. She was sick before the deployment, and the corporal knew that it was a possibility. The corporal can't go to the funeral, and so we're going to collect money and have funeral services here later today. If you see him, give him your condolences. That's all."

On the way to breakfast, the mood is somber. The shuttle bus to the mess lacks the usual energy and clamor. Unsure about Korean funeral protocol, I decide to ask Jeong-su.

"Korean funerals usually last three days, but I don't think they'll make him stay up for the whole three days."

"Stay up?"

"Yeah, the family of the dead person has to stay at the funeral hall for the entire time to accept condolences from visitors. They usually take shifts."

"What do we have to do later?"

"We'll collect money later and give it to him and bow to a picture of his mother. Don't worry. I'll tell you what to do when we get there."

After breakfast, I don't go to bed for *ochim* right away. Instead, I head out to the B-hut with the land lines to make an international call. I sit down in one of the booths and dial the number.

"Hello?"

"Hi, Mom. How are you feeling these days?"

As I walk to the restrooms to wash up before lunch, I see the corporal at the smoking area. He's by himself, hunched over, legs spread apart, elbows resting on his knees, taking long drags from a cigarette. I feel a need to say something to him although I haven't said more than a few words in passing to him at the gym. I feel sympathy and almost an affinity to him because he's in the exact situation I've been dreading since that day in boot camp, sitting in the administration office, bawling my pride away. He's handling it much better than I probably would. I decide against talking to him because I would want to be alone and think if it were me.

After lunch, I'm called from the TOC to join my company in paying respects. Jong-hun gathers money from the squad, and we give what we can. Jong-hun puts the money in an envelope, and we head single-file to the large B-hut we use for mental education.

We enter the B-hut as a squad. We put the envelope in a small coffee can and proceed to the far end of the room where a small makeshift shrine has been set up. I follow Jeong-su's lead, and we bow to the ground, on our knees with our foreheads to the ground, wait, and rise again. We walk over to the corporal and bow at the waist, pausing at the lowest point, and we leave the room so the next group can pay their respects.

I need to step up my efforts in finding a way home for my post-deployment furlough. I have to go home. The hope of being able to go home is what's been getting me through the deployment, and this bit of bad news hit too close to home. When I talked to my mother over the phone after breakfast, she assured me she was healthy, but it's something I need to see with my own eyes.

If I can actually work this out, the conditions are perfect. The post-deployment furlough is twenty-five days, more than enough time to not have to worry about losing days in travel, and I'll actually have money for a plane ticket home. If I hadn't come to Afghanistan, I would never have made enough in the two years for a ticket home even if I had saved up every paycheck.

I'm fairly certain that Major Jeong will help me get permission from Colonel Park, but the way home is fraught with many more obstacles and potholes and bandits of hope. A negative result of me testing the waters with the early promotion is that the inexplicable enmity that Personnel has harbored for me has now congealed, and they are utterly unwilling to help me. It was still worth it to see them eat sour grapes.

Thus far, I've checked with the various personnel offices in Korea, Immigration at the airport, and the embassy in Seoul. It was actually Ja-hong and Captain Bang who called on my behalf—my Korean's still not good enough for something this important—and the answers have been slightly positive but noncommittal. "They say you probably can go."

Probably is not good enough. I need confirmation. I'm in the office with Jeong-su, whom I've recruited for one more phone call to the personnel office at Army Headquarters.

I fidget while Jeong-su calls the number and talks with the officer. I listen to Jeong-su's questions and observe his reactions closely. He hangs up.

"He said you can go," Jeong-su says, smiling. "You only need to get the commander's permission."

I'll have to bring it up to Major Jeong the next time I see him.

"What about plane fare?"

"He said that you probably won't get plane fare."

It was a long shot, but as long as I can go, it's okay. I still feel uneasy, but I've done everything that can be done.

"Oh, yeah," Jeong-su adds, chuckling. "He asked why a conscript was asking instead of the Personnel Officer."

D-345 (17FEB05): Wrapping Up

The deployment is coming to an end. There's a sense that things are winding down, and it's a comforting feeling. The guys in the squad are in the

245

B-hut more often, and Captain Park has taken to leaving us alone, rarely crossing the divide between his area and ours.

I've recovered my mess kit. In the end, I had to weasel it out of one of the only guys in the Support Company with half a conscience and a weak will. "I wanted to tell you," he confessed, "but one of the *gocham* warned me not to." I told him it was fine; I haven't given the Support Company much thought and their feelings are inconsequential at this point in the deployment.

I also picked up some mementos at the bazaar: an Enfield rifle and a curved knife with a bone handle and engravings in the blade. Sergeant Luvaas held on to them for me until I had time to drop by the post office and send them to Seattle. I sent Christmas presents back home a couple of months ago, but these are for me.

We've been gathered in a meeting room at the 109th for a ceremony to signify the end of our deployment. Colonel Wetherill, the commander of the 109th, even put up a more than civil front as she commended us on our time here although I'm sure she despises us. She often butted heads with Colonel Park and Major Jeong because the Korean leadership considered our support group equal to theirs although we were only an attached unit.

"She's smiling," I remark to Sergeant Luvaas. "I'm impressed. I know she didn't like us much."

Luvaas and I often had front-row seats to the frequent tiffs between Colonel Wetherill and Major Jeong.

"Yeah, maybe she's glad you're leaving," Sergeant Luvaas jokes.

"I'm sure. Damn, I hope this ends soon."

"Hold on for a minute," Luvaas says enigmatically.

I'm not paying attention when I hear my name called. It's Colonel Wetherill.

"Get on up there," Luvaas says with a knowing smile.

I walk up to the front and Colonel Wetherill presents me with a certificate of commendation. "Good job," she tells me as she shakes my hand. "Thank you, ma'am," I say, confused. I translated for the major and lieutenant colonel at the 109th a couple times at the beginning of the deployment, but Major Jeong took over when he realized angry messages lose their potency when going through a third party.

By the end of the ceremony, I've received certificates of commendation from the 109th, the Slovakian Engineers, the Polish Engineers, and even one from our unit. They're only pieces of paper, but it feels nice to receive some recognition after all this time.

As I'm walking back to the compound, the Personnel Officer calls me over to tell me that I'll be on staff duty the entire time we're in Manas. I shrug. I don't care anymore.

Back at the TOC, my work is not over. The officers all have to submit research topics for the duration of the deployment, and Ja-hong and I have to compile them into a report by the time we leave. There's a lot of work to be done, but the end is in sight.

While I'm typing, Major Jeong walks into the TOC.

"You really cleaned up today," he jokes, patting me on the shoulder.

"Uh… yes, sir."

"You deserve it."

"Uh… thank you, sir." It's strange to get acknowledgement from one of our own officers. Major Jeong has worked me day and night, but he's a good person, a rarity among officers, especially an officer in his position.

"I have one more thing to give you," he says, handing me a piece of paper. I take it apprehensively. I thought that there wasn't any more work to do besides compiling the research papers. I look at the paper, but it isn't another report. It's permission to travel overseas from the commander for my furlough. "When you're finished compiling these reports, you're done for the rest of the deployment."

"Thank you, sir."

While it was nice to be acknowledged earlier at the ceremony, it's not something I expected or really felt I needed. This piece of paper is all I really wanted. I'm going home.

Manas AB, Kyrgyzstan
Korean Support Group, Dasan Unit, Support Company
23 February 2005 - 26 February 2005

D-339 (23FEB05): Manas Revisited

Manas, how I've missed you. No more rice for breakfast. No more duties. Just good food and freedom.

The others are excited, too, but for other reasons. There's to be a tour of Bishkek today, and there have been clandestine meetings among the conscripts of the unit to discuss including a trip to a brothel in the tour.

I'm reading in the tent, and the others are discussing, when Captain Park walks into the tent.

"The trip to Bishkek has been cancelled. We're going to go to the airport instead. You can buy gifts there."

The guys are not fazed. The moment Captain Park leaves, the guys start whispering their plans to make it out to Bishkek. One way or another, they're going to get laid while we're here. It's the Army mentality at work. Or maybe it's just hormones and months of deprivation.

It turns out that Manas International Airport is a ten-minute walk from the tent city. The moment we make it to the airport, we head to the front of the terminal and the others hail cabs.

"You coming?" Jeong-su asks, half-way in the cab.

"It's okay. I'm just going to stay here." Visiting a Kyrgyzstani brothel doesn't have enough appeal for me to jeopardize my chances of going home for the post-deployment furlough.

He shrugs and closes the door and the taxi takes off for Bishkek.

I walk around the airport alone, stopping by the gift shops while avoiding Captain Park and the first sergeant. I run into them a couple of times, but when the captain asks me where everyone else is, I shrug and say I don't know. It's not unusual for me to be alone, and he drops the matter. I get the feeling that he doesn't care now that the deployment is over.

The airport is clean and modern but practically bare, with very few shops spread out between the two floors. When I walk into the gift shops, I'm overwhelmed by the selection of vodka. Big bottles, small bottles, bottles shaped like flasks, bottles shaped like jugs, multi-faceted bottles like diamonds. I choose two bottles that have the most volume for the price and hide them in the bottom of a plastic bag underneath souvenirs I bought for no one in particular.

The airport having nothing else to offer, I return to the tent, stash my

251

bottles in my bag, and head out to a secluded corner of the tent city with a book and my journal. I don't want to be around when they return with stories of whoring.

Post-deployment Furlough
26 February 2005 - 22 March 2005

D-336 (26FEB05): Back in Korea

After landing in Korea, we head to an Army hospital for another physical—pissing on litmus sticks and giving blood samples to make sure we didn't pick up anything overseas—before returning to the ACAS for a final ceremony for the disbanding of the deployment unit. Everyone's families have come out to welcome their sons home. After the ceremony, the conscripts find their families and slowly everyone goes their own way. While everyone is talking with their families, I wander near the trees, away from the main group. It's not my time yet.

Once the group begins to disperse, I spot Jeong-su and Gi-hwan, one of the other interpreters who warmed up to me once the deployment wound down, and we make arrangements to meet up for drinks. I promised I'd buy them tequila once we returned to Korea.

It's the early afternoon when we find a bar in Shincheon that serves tequila. I have money for once and order a bottle of Jose, and we drink, still in our desert uniforms. Jeong-su leaves early to see his girlfriend, and the tequila destroys Gi-hwan. My mind is fuzzy and eyes blurry when I pay, counting the money over and over to make sure I have it right.

Gi-hwan's parents come to pick him up and I head to my aunt's house.

"Welcome back," my aunt says as I walk through the door.

"Thank you."

"Have you been drinking?"

"Yes, ma'am." I can't help but speak like a soldier when I'm out in the real world, the result of learning Korean in the Army. "I'm not feeling good. I think I'm going to go to bed."

"Okay. I made up your cousin's room for you. Good night."

"Good night, ma'am."

I fall heavily on the bed and pass out.

The next afternoon, I get out of bed, and my aunt sets up the table for me to have lunch. I sit down, the tequila wreaking havoc on my body after six months of sobriety.

"So how was it?"

"It was good."

"Was it safe?"

"Yes, ma'am. It's a lot safer than people think."

I'm working on my soup when I remember my last conversation with my mother. "Aunt, how is Aunt U-gyeong doing?"

My aunt pauses and looks at me with a deep sympathy, her brows knitted and her lower lip slightly pursed, the corners turned slightly downward. "Your mother didn't tell you?"

"No, ma'am."

"She passed away last week."

"I… I'm sorry," I mumble, feeling like a complete ass. I should've made time to see my cousins last night. I could've, if I hadn't gotten completely drunk on tequila.

I eat the rest of my lunch in silent penitence, wash my dishes, and head back to my cousin's room and close the door behind me. I need to call to check on my plane ticket.

D-333 (01MAR05): Immigration and Bad Memories

March 1st is a "red day" in Korea, a holiday commemorating one of the largest movements of passive resistance in history, when the underground resistance framed a declaration of independence against Japanese colonial rule in 1919. The day has taken on a special meaning of freedom for me. Last March 1st, boot camp had just ended, and we were preparing to head out to our prospective stations. This year, I'm leaving Korea on my post-deployment furlough, finally heading home after almost 400 days in the Army.

I'm not confident as I pass through security and wait in line for Immigration. I haven't had a good history with Immigration since coming to Korea. The first was when I applied for a visa and found out for the first time in my life that I had Korean citizenship. The second was Osan, where my fate was cemented.

I have my orders and both my American passport and my 1-year official Korean passport for the deployment. I've brought both with me because I'm not sure if I can use either.

The problem with my American passport is that I've been forced to illegally overstay, my work visa expiring shortly before my induction to the Army. The problem with my short-term Korean passport is that it was only to be used for travel to Afghanistan for the deployment. I didn't get a regular Korean passport because my visit to the district office before the deployment made it clear I couldn't get one.

The anxiety I'm feeling is the same anxiety I felt in that line in Osan AB. I had assurances then, too. I had orders for my departure. When I saw the immigration officers, my palms were sweaty, my heart racing. After the red flags came up on the computer in Osan, I was taken to the immigration office at the air base terminal. Nothing was said to me. They left me to sit in silence. As I sat, my eyes were fixed on the clock, and I watched the hands make their slow crawl until the plane was in the air, leaving me behind.

As I step up to the counter, I hand the immigration officer my orders and both of my passports. As expected, the officer doesn't know what to do with me and calls his supervisor.

"Come with me," the officer says, taking me out of line and leading me to a room off to the side. "Sit," he says, pointing to a chair.

The supervisor comes over and there is a great deal of chatting between the two officers and fumbling with the computer.

I look up at the clock. Thirty-five minutes until the gate closes and my plane home leaves without me.

Tick, tick, tick, tick.

Twenty-five minutes left.

Tick, tick, tick, tick.

Twenty minutes.

History is repeating itself. It's Osan Air Base all over again. The immigration office at Incheon reminds me of the one in Osan. Even the clock is the same as the one in Osan; standard bureaucratic issue, white face with black trim.

Tick, tick, tick, tick.

One of the officers approaches me with my documents rolled up in his fist. He tosses them into my lap and says, "Go. Hurry."

I sprint through the terminal, slipping through the slower foot traffic; take the shuttle to the international terminal; and arrive at the gate, out of breath and a sweaty mess. There is no one at the gate except two airline employees organizing the counter.

"Here," I say, handing the closer one my passport and ticket.

She takes my ticket, passes it through the reader, opens the cordon, and bids me a good trip. I've made it.

Return to SROKA
Daegu Metropolitan City, Korea
Second ROK Army (SROKA) HQ, HHC/Support Company
22 March 2005 - 28 January 2006

D-312 (22MAR05): Back in Daegu

It's a strange feeling, returning to Daegu. I can't put it into words because I'm not sure how I feel. It's not the deep midnight blue of my return from my 100th-day furlough. It's more of a numb and dull gray.

The sky was a similar gray the morning I left Seattle. It was hard to leave; I almost didn't. It was only until the plane had departed from the terminal that I stopped thinking, "There's nothing stopping you from staying."

There really is no place like home. When I met up with old friends, they did their best to welcome me back and keep my spirits up. Unfortunately, there was something a bit off; the Army had thrown off my wavelength, or perhaps mine had remained stagnant while theirs kept growing. But family will always be family. Jason picked me up at the airport, waiting at the baggage claim with a cheeseburger.

"What's it like?" he asked as we sped down the 405.

"It sucks" is all I could say. It was too monumental a task to put the past year and two months into words, and it was all I could say. He understood that I didn't feel like talking about it.

Mack greeted me at the door, his little pug ass wagging, even though I had left for Korea when he was a year old. I walked in, and my mother walked out from the kitchen, where she was preparing dinner.

I put my duffel bag down and said, "Hi, Mom."

"Hi, son," she said and gave me a warm, motherly hug, the hug of a mother whose son has returned to her after he was lost.

Growing up, we rarely had family dinners. Thanksgiving, Christmas, birthdays. I don't think I'll ever have another dinner as meaningful, as special, as that first dinner. The only way it could've been more perfect is if my older brother Charlie had been able to come up from Atlanta.

After dinner, my mother took out a manila folder and handed it to me. Inside was a story of a mother's love, a stack of letters from every conceivable authority, American and Korean, and newspaper clippings an inch high. She had been doing her best to get me out of the service as well.

I read every letter and article. A few of the letters from the Ministry of National Defense were infuriating.

The first, sent while I was in boot camp—"We are not only supporting him in his barracks life by assigning a recruit who has spent a long time

261

abroad as his helper, considering the fact that your son is not familiar with the Korean language and culture…."

The second, sent about ten days after I had been sent to Daegu—"The MND has assigned your son to a permanent station in which he can display his talents and ability to his potential and fulfill his military service in health and for his benefit. As confirmed by the MND, not only has he improved his speaking and comprehension abilities to the point that there should be no inconvenience, he has also adapted well to life in the Army with the other young Koreans, and you may rest assured."

I then understood the phone calls during my first weeks in Daegu.

After Jason left and my mother retired for the night, I headed out to the garage to dig out my things. A violet nostalgia overwhelmed me as I rummaged through the junk that was my life, the artwork and the photographic equipment I'd never gotten around to setting up in the garage, the car parts and tools, the notes and books from college, the boxes of clothes and photos.

It had only been two years since I first left Seattle, and yet I found myself displaced from the person reflected in the mirror of my belongings. There was a familiarity but a foreignness to them, as if they were someone else's belongings, someone I might've known, perhaps relics of a past life. A strange melancholy overwhelmed me, replacing the nostalgia, and I packed everything away and shoved the boxes back into the corner of the garage.

After that initial period of adapting to life back home, the person I've become and the person I once was seemed to come to terms with each other at a comfortable middle ground, and it was almost as if I had never left. Almost. Things will never be the same, but it's also something I've accepted.

When I walk out of the station, I look up at the blue lettering at East Daegu Station. I'm reminded of the time I first arrived in Daegu, a little over a year ago. It certainly feels like much, much longer, like several lifetimes have come and passed, but somehow I'm almost back to where I started. The difference this time being that I left a first-month PFC and am returning a fourth-month corporal.

I jump into a cab, and it drops me off in front of the Chinese restaurant across from the rear gate. As I walk past the parade ground, the Signal Battalion, the Motor Pool, I'm reminded of my time as a miserable private, running around with my head up my ass, and a pang of fear hits. There's nothing to fear, but it's hard to separate the place from the memories.

As I near the HHC barracks, I see unfamiliar, petrified faces. The privates don't know how to receive me. The dilemma of being a private. Damned if you do, damned if you don't.

If you see a new face, you should just salute. If you fail to salute a superior and stand slack-jawed with your thumb up your ass, you're in trouble. If you salute a soldier and it turns out that he's from a different company, you just feel like an idiot. Embarrassment is preferable to ire.

They don't salute. Instead, the privates look to a PFC standing with them. The PFC looks at me, squints his eyes. I return the stare. As I walk closer, he continues to stare. What has happened to the discipline in the company? It's only when he can make out the tiny *bon* in the white triangle on my chest[61] that he stands up straight and salutes. The privates follow. Idiots, the lot of them. They should know better.

I choose not to educate them. I just nod and walk past. I hear a sigh of relief as I walk away, followed by questions in hushed tones.

"Who was that, sir?"

"I don't know."

I go up to the administration office and report my return to the company to the officer-on-duty. There are many privates running around, getting ready for the evening call, checking duty sheets, locking up rifles for the guys on night duty, checking the challenge and password on the bulletin board hidden under a flap of cardboard, reporting numbers for the roll. They all give me scared, furtive glances. They're curious but scared to look for too long.

"15th Squad is gone," the first sergeant tells me. "There's an empty spot in 12th squad. Report to Squad Room 12."

Squad Room 12 is also full of unfamiliar faces, save two. Sergeant Ho-se[62] is the squad *wang-go* and the two-*go* is Corporal Seung-gi, a dark-skinned, skinny kid who likes to draw cartoons.

---

[61] The unit insignia. *Bon* is short for *bonbujungdae*, Headquarters Company.

[62] Ho-se is a September 2003 serial number and one of the more fluent linguists in the company. During one of my first evening calls fresh out of basic training, one of the sergeants told Ho-se to speak in English with me. I tried to be as respectful as possible (although English lacks the levels of formality that Korean has), but after evening call, Ho-se took me to an empty squad room and proceeded to berate me in Korean for a good ten minutes. I couldn't understand what he was mad about, but I think it had to do with being caught up in my humiliating side-show. Needless to say, I didn't particularly like the guy.

"Welcome back," Seung-gi says.

"Thank you, sir," I say as I start unpacking my things in the empty locker against the wall. As I unpack, he gets up and sits on the ledge nearest my spot. He introduces the younger kids in the squad, the ones who are present. I feel bad for them. I remember the significance of an empty spot, the potential for a subordinate. They've now got another *gocham* instead.

"What happened to 15th squad, sir?" I ask once the introductions are over.

"It was disbanded last year. When did you go to Afghanistan?"

"July, sir."

"It was around that time."

"I see, sir."

It makes sense. The squad hierarchy of the 15th was too lopsided to be sustainable. It's too bad that I had to suffer through it without enjoying the fruits of the suffering. With all the sergeants in the squad getting discharged while I was gone, I would've been two-*go*.

"Hey, you remember Ballerino?"

"Yes, sir."

"He's gone. They let him out early."

"Is that true, sir?"

"Yeah. They had him go through some psychological evaluations and then they kicked him out."

"I understand, sir."

Good for him. I thought that Captain Jin would make Ballerino suffer until his discharge. I wonder about what I overheard once, that it was all part of some master plan to get out of the Army. Although it seems most of the others believe he was just gay, I'd like to think that he was some kind of genius that had everyone fooled and managed to escape the system.

The company is no longer the company I knew when I left for Afghanistan, and I'm no longer the same person I was when I was a private. Is it a result of rank? Is it that the shadow of Squad Leader Lee no longer haunts me? Is it that I finally understand how the system works?

"Everything is possible as long as you can get away with it." It was something the *gocham* used to say. The person I was didn't understand, but the person I have become is beginning to understand. Nobody's going to help me. I have to help myself.

D-312 (22MAR05): The Twins: Ju-uk and Hun-hee

There is a welcome face in 12th Squad. Private Ju-uk was one of two 15th Squad subordinates I trained before leaving for Afghanistan. It was after Beaver's discharge and the resulting flight of Jeong-hyeon and U-don. Sergeant Hyeon-seok, the Professor, was our new squad leader.

"We're getting a surprise today," he announced after dinner.

"It's Young Jin's lucky day," Sergeant Sang-jun chimed in.

While horrible surprises such as manual labor or *mishing* on a day of rest are commonplace here, nice surprises are a rarity. With our depleted squad, it was obvious that the surprise was a fresh fish to replace me as the squad's lackey.

Of my *donggi* in the company, I was the only one who hadn't passed on the role of *mangnae*, literally "the youngest," to a February or March private. This meant that I was still running around with the "younger" guys, scrambling in the mornings and relaying messages and carrying the squad's water bottle.

When the Professor returned to the squad room, not one but two surprises followed meekly behind. We got twins.

They certainly looked like twins. Both were the same height and build, tall and gangly, bespectacled with similar glasses frames, the same dark skin and thick hair.

"*Chungseong!* I'm Private Ju-uk, sir!"

"*Chungseong!* I'm Private Hun-hee, sir!"

Sang-jun asked if they were twins, and the two privates blushed, looked at each other, and stuttered in unison, "No, sir!"

Over the next two weeks, I took them under my wing like a mother duck, a mother duck with a handicap. I taught them their duties in the squad and the company, the words to the company and unit war songs, and other tidbits on how to survive that I had picked up the hard way. I don't know if they could understand what I was saying, but not once did they comment on my inability to put together a sentence.

When I told them I was accepted to the Afghanistan deployment, their faces betrayed feelings of shock and sadness.

"Private Chun, may I ask you a question, sir?"

"Go ahead."

"Do you really have to go on the deployment, sir?"

"Yeah," I said, trying to look sympathetic. "I'm sorry."

Ju-uk is now a month away from his promotion to corporal and seems much more at home in 12th Squad than I do. He plops down on the raised floor, apparently having just played basketball with the squad leader.

"Corporal Chun, when did you get back, sir?"

"I just got back. So you came here after 15th Squad got dis… dis… disappeared."

"Yes, sir."

"Where's Hun-hee?"

"He's in 4th Squad, I think."

"Where—"

"Sorry, sir. I'm going to wash up before the nightly cleaning."

"Oh, okay."

Feeling uncomfortable in my new squad but unwilling to draw unwanted attention from *gocham* out in the halls, I take out a book and read, facing my locker. The privates file out for the nightly cleaning, and when they return to clean the squad room, I try to help, getting up to straighten the uniforms in the lockers, but one of them rushes over. "Sir, I'll take care of it." At least these guys have some discipline. I decide staying out of their way is the only thing I can do for them, so I leave to use the head.

The privates are still cleaning the third-floor bathroom, so I walk down the stairs to the second floor, looking both ways once I hit the second-floor landing. The halls are quiet. I turn into the bathroom and bump into another conscript.

"Corporal Chun. When did you get back, sir?"

It's Hun-hee.

"I just got back today."

"It's good to see you, sir," he says and hurries down the hall.

As I empty my bladder in the freshly scrubbed urinal, I reflect upon my lukewarm reception in the company and by my former squad subordinates. I've been gone for eight-and-a-half months—six weeks pre-deployment training, six months in Afghanistan, and one month back home in Seattle. It's a different company now. Most of the *gocham* who tormented me are gone, my "fathers" are gone, too, and among the privates scurrying around are probably my "sons" as well.

I'm going to be a good "father," I tell myself, but I can't but help feel sad about the twins. Sure, I taught them during those first few weeks, but I abandoned them and didn't return until they came into their own. They "grew up" without me, and they don't owe me anything. I'll have to find a way to make it up to them.

D-286 (17APR05): Standby

I'm on standby again. Just as I had been when I first reported to the Headquarters Company last year. Limbo, the hell you endure before they assign you to the hell in which you'll spend your days typing, making instant coffee, and shredding paper.

But there's something different this time. The hell that's awaiting is me is the same, that's for sure. Although my spot at Mobilization has been taken over by more capable manpower, every other office at Headquarters is more of the same. What's different is this room. This room isn't a cage like the squad room last year, when all the company *gocham* came and mocked and gawked at me throughout the day. Or maybe it still is a cage and I've just become used to it. Either way, it's comfortable, and I'm left alone to read and write in peace.

I wake up for morning call, have breakfast, and spend the rest of the day in the squad room or taking long breaks at the PX. Occasionally there are calls for manual labor, and I'm expected to be there. If it's during the week, the call comes during the lunch hour, before the kids can run off to Headquarters.

There was the day we had to move in the new base commander—he has a refrigerator-sized safe we had to break our backs to take upstairs to his office on the second floor—and on Arbor Day, we had to plant a thousand trees around the base because they were the new commander's favorite. I don't mind manual labor when it's not in addition to other duties. I've always had blue collar in my blood.

A couple of days ago, the first sergeant had me take a bunch of privates down to the generals' mess to move around kitchen equipment and set the dining hall for some event or other. It was a different world—linen tablecloths and fine china and silverware and paintings on the walls. When we were mostly done, we went out back for a break. The smokers smoked and a handful of privates sat on plastic crates, huddled together. I sat off to the

267

side to let them relax in peace.

I was passing by the huddle on my way to throw away my Dixie cup, and all of them looked up at me.

"Corporal Chun," called one of the privates.

"What is it?"

"Would you like me to read your palm, sir?" It's Private Sang-hee, one of my "sons."

"I don't know."

"He's pretty good, sir," one of the more senior privates added.

"Okay."

I held out my hand and assured Sang-hee it was okay when he hesitated to take a hold of my hand. Sang-hee brought his face close to my hand, staring intently at the thatching of wrinkles on my palm.

"There's a girl you've had feelings for a long time, sir."

I blushed slightly and hoped none of them could tell. He went on.

"You've come close before but it never worked out. Am I right, sir?"

His words hitting too close to the mark, I avoided a direct answer.

"What makes you say that?"

"If you look here, sir," he said, pointing at the fine wrinkles at the base of my thumb. "There are two lines that look like they're touching, but if you look closely, they don't actually touch, sir."

I took back my hand and stared closely at the wrinkles he was talking about. There were indeed two lines that were separated at one point by a minute, almost imperceptible gap.

It's the late afternoon, and I'm heading back to the company after stopping by the PX for some ice cream. I had an interview for a position at a counseling center for conscripts that just opened up. There were only two of us that showed up for the interview, and I'm fairly positive the other guy got the job. Part of the job description was answering the phone, something I still can't do.

I don't mind not getting the job. The job seems like "honey," Army slang to mean something that's relatively easy, but I'd like to prolong my standby as long as possible. It's been over two weeks, and I've gotten used to this life of relative comfort. This is my honey.

The problem is the first sergeant. He's the one who sent me to the interview. My not having a place to go during the day is a problem for him

268

because it's now apparent that there's nowhere for someone like me to go. I'm an old, deaf, and dumb dog, only good for lying around the room.

Nevertheless, the interview was a bad omen. A sign that the good thing that I have is coming to an end. Good things never last long in the Army. I've been trying to stay under the radar, trying not to remind the first sergeant of my presence. I take the outdoor stairwell up to the third floor, peering through a crack in the door to make sure the hall is empty. It's worked for me so far, but now that the first sergeant has started to find a place for me in earnest, it seems I'll need to take some active measures.

When I get back to the squad room, I look at the pocket calendar I've taped to the inside of the front cover of my notebook. I have about ten months, three hundred days, left until my discharge. Thanks to the deployment, I haven't used any of my regular furloughs or weekend passes, which account for ten days per furlough and two days per pass, but I'd like to save them until the end if possible. I'm going to need to come up with something soon.

D-277 (28APR05): MSEL-able

I'm on a bus headed for the 50th Division to set up and run the camp for reserve-mobilization training. While the facilities are run down and it's a pain in the ass to herd reserves from place to place, I volunteered for the duty. It's a strategic move. Four days off-base means another four days without getting an assignment.

The bus is idling in front of the company. I slouch down in my seat and pull down the brim of my battle cap. I've put a private in the window seat to hide behind but I can only rest easy once the bus has left the base with the Second Army behind us.

With the hiss of the air-brakes, I let out a sigh of relief, slinking down a little further in my seat. There's a soft jerk and the bus slowly begins to pull forward. I've managed another week of freedom.

Before we make it out of the driveway, there's a hard *thud, thud, thud,* and the bus jerks to a stop. The doors whoosh open and a private from the administration office hops on. I peer at him through the crack between the seats in front of me.

"Is Corporal Chun on the bus?"

Damn.

I follow the private off the bus, watching it leave over my shoulder, and up to the administration office, where the first sergeant is waiting. Although I've been avoiding the first sergeant, I respect and like the guy. The first sergeant is actually a command sergeant major, the highest-ranked NCO, but he takes it easy, as if he's been through it all and nothing bothers him. It certainly looks as if he's had a life of hard work and hard drinking, the constant bags under his eyes sagging halfway down the cheeks on his dark, haggard face. Maybe I like the guy because he doesn't look like a soldier. Even if his uniform is cleanly pressed, the way it hangs on his rotund body makes him look like a drunk after a long night of inebriation.

"Corporal Chun, we haven't assigned you to an office yet, have we?"

"No, sir."

"Okay. Report to the Exercise Branch of Operations for a short-term assignment. They need a linguist. One week only."

"I understand, sir."

"Okay, head over to Headquarters."

"Yes, sir."

Since my return, I've been back to the Headquarters building, but only for the morning and nightly cleanings. It's slightly depressing to have to report there for actual duty. It's only for a week, I have to remind myself.

I pass by a private on my way up the stairs and ask him where the Exercise Branch is. Fourth floor, at the end of the hall, sir. Fourth floor? Mobilization is on the fourth floor. I walk down to the staircase at the other end of the hall so I won't have to pass by the office.

I find the door and walk in, and I see a familiar face at the computer.

"Corporal Chun. What are you doing here, sir?" Hun-hee asks.

"I didn't know you worked here."

"Yes, sir."

"The first sergeant told me to help out here. Short-term assignment."

Hun-hee takes me around and introduces me to the branch officers. Whereas the officers in the Construction Company had simian features, the ones here look like hawks—thick eyebrows which turn upward and bushy toward the ends; large, piercing eyes; pointy, slightly crooked noses; and thin, beak-like lips. As in the Mobilization Branch, the chief is a colonel, Colonel Kim, and has a separate room off to the back. He is tall and well-built and mean-looking; he looks like he might've been a boxer in his youth. In contrast, the senior officer in the branch, Lieutenant Colonel Lee, is round and puffy but imposing, like a decadent patrician.

There's a civilian contractor in this office as well, a skinny, middle-aged woman with a mass of permed curls surrounding her gaunt face. She says something to me I'm completely unable to comprehend. It takes a moment to realize that she's speaking in the thick Daegu dialect.

"You don't know *morakaneunji*, right?"

"I didn't hear you clearly, ma'am."

"*Aida.*"[63]

One of the majors takes me aside and explains what I'm here to do. He hands me two stacks of papers.

"You're going to translate the *mijeul* for the upcoming Amrokgang exercise. This stack is from last year. Study it and then translate the stack for this year."

"Yes, sir."

I look at the stacks of paper. The front page reads Master Scenario Events List, MSEL, pronounced like "measle." Each page of the stack has a possible scenario in the event of an outbreak of war. It doesn't look as if it's going to be too difficult. The MSEL from last year has the scenarios in both English and Korean, and comparing it with the MSEL for this year, the scenarios only have slight variations in time and place.

The MSEL translation isn't difficult, but it's very time-consuming. The initial week-long assignment was extended to two weeks, and again to a third week. I've finished the translation of over two hundred scenarios, over two hundred pages of North Korean spies and guerilla teams wreaking havoc across the South Korean countryside, starting labor strikes and blowing up chlorine tankers in tunnels along major supply routes. I thought that I'd be able to return to the company after the translation, but now they have me inputting the scenarios into a computer with a direct link with the US Army.

The computer terminal is located in the Tactical Operations Center, the command center for the operations of the entire Second Army. I've never

---

[63] She was a really nice lady, but I only understood 20 percent of what she said to me. Korea is not a big country but there is a considerable difference in the various dialects. *Morakaneunji* (Gyeongsang dialect) = *Mweorago haneunji* (Standard Korean), What I'm saying. *Aida* (Gyeongsang dialect) = *Anida* (Standard Korean), It's nothing.

gotten any kind of security clearance, and now I'm in one of the most sensitive areas of headquarters. Not that I would do anything, but it's sweltering hot in Daegu, one of the hottest cities in Korea, and the construction of the TOC is like a hot box. I'm stuck in a small, partially enclosed area off to the side, exiled here with an officer dispatched from the Navy who has no apparent duties here except to pester me.

"What're you working on?"

"I'm inputting scenarios, sir. The same as every other day."

"For what?"

"The Amnokgang exercise, sir."

He gets up and looks over my shoulder at the computer. The sound of his nose-breathing and the warm gusts of nostril breath over my shoulder are unnerving.

"You're good at English?"

"Yes, sir," I reply, too tired to be Korean modest or to go into an explanation of my situation.

He returns to his seat but I can tell he's thinking. At first, his interruptions were a welcome break to the monotony of data entry, but I've heard too many lectures about naval history and watched too many videos of naval battles. Please, leave me alone. Let me work in peace.

"Hey."

"Yes, sir."

"You ever ride a white horse?"

He's not literally referring to the animal that happens to be the color white or figuratively to cocaine but asking about my sexual experience.[64] I only know this because I was asked the same question on one of those long nights in boot camp and had to have Johnny explain it to me.

"No, sir."

"Why not?"

"I don't know, sir." I look at my watch and, thankfully, it's close enough to lunch to escape. I pack up my things, log off the terminal, and tell the lieutenant to have a good lunch as I hurry out the door.

---

[64] To ride a white horse means to have sexual intercourse with a Caucasian woman.

D-269 (04MAY05): Battle Simulation Center (BSC)

This "short-term assignment" is now going into its second month. After I finished painstaking task of inputting the scenarios into the computer, the Exercise Branch filed yet another extension so I could provide support for the exercise.

"Don't worry, sir," Hun-hee assures me. "The BSC isn't so bad. We'll technically be on deployment while we're there."

Because he called it a deployment, I expect the Battle Simulation Center to be off-base, but it's just down the road from the company. Technically, being on deployment is an advantage because it means no company guard duties and no roll call. We'll be sleeping in the barracks at the BSC and reporting to the Exercise Branch during the day. Having to wake up in the middle of the night and stand guard duty two to three hours every day or two is a part of life, but nonetheless draining, and something I'll be glad to do without.

Once we've moved the entire office from headquarters to the BSC, Hun-hee shows me another benefit of being on deployment. He opens up one of the majors' desks and produces a stack of small papers.

"What's that?"

"Here, sir," he says, handing me the stack.

The papers in my hand are weekend passes.

"We can go out on weekend passes whenever we want, sir."

"How?"

"We're on deployment, sir. The company doesn't know where we are and the officers don't come by on the weekends. And we have this, sir." He digs into the desk and produces Colonel Lee's official stamp.

When the exercise begins, the BSC is bustling with officers and conscripts from units across the rear area. The officers on deployment ignore the conscripts for the most part, unless they need something. The conscripts are here for "support," but I'm not sure what kind of support they're giving. All I know is that they're happy to be on deployment and rarely sleep. They also sleep in the barracks on the third floor, and I've chosen a spot as far away from them as possible in order to make sure I can get some sleep.

Hun-hee was right about being at the BSC. Amnokgang is a ROK Army-only exercise and, with the MSEL behind me, I don't have much to do. I have to physically be in the office during the days, and on standby at night, but I spend most of my time reading.

I'm sitting in the office during lunch one afternoon when one of the conscripts comes up to the office to ask if I can relieve him for a bit so he can eat lunch. I don't mind, so I go downstairs and sit at the desk in front of the entrance. I'm struggling with an autobiography of Che Guevara in Korean when the officers return from some meeting or another. I don't bother with standing and saluting them and they don't seem to notice me at all.

"What are you reading?"

I look up and a plump captain from the group has stayed behind and is staring down at me. I've seen him around. He's bothered me on occasion, and I've noticed that he's not well regarded by the others. He probably doesn't have rank among the other officers on deployment.

"I don't know. Just some biography, sir," I reply, giving him a brief glance before turning back to the book.

He reaches down and takes the book from my hands. He turns the book over in his fleshy hands, giving the cover a once over.

"Did you get this approved at your company?"

I didn't. All outside books are to be approved by the company commander and stamped but I never got around to it.

"No, sir. I didn't have the time."

"I don't think it would be approved. It's about a Communist, isn't it? The book is red."

The cover of the book is indeed red. A deep Communist red. I shrug and open the book up again.

"I might have to report this to the DSC." The DSC is the body charged with military security, akin to an internal-affairs department.

I've read of a German general who classified his officers into clever and stupid and lazy and industrious. Here are his conclusions.

      1. The clever and lazy are fit for the highest command.

      2. The clever and industrious are fit for highest staff positions.

      3. The stupid and lazy are fit for regular staff.

      4. The stupid and industrious are worthless.

There seems to be truth in this. Being stationed at headquarters, I'm surrounded by the clever and lazy, scheming bastards who have everyone beneath them do their work for them.

Major Jeong from Afghanistan was clever and industrious, and it seems to me that Colonel Lee here in the Exercise Branch is the same. Captain Jin, my company commander, is stupid and lazy and will get somewhere but not very far. Captain Park from Afghanistan was stupid and industrious, and nobody paid him much heed. This guy seems to be of the same ilk.

This captain is harassing me because he's relatively low-ranked and estranged among the rest of the officers on deployment as if they can smell the stench of failure on him. The way he's resorting to passive-aggression tells me that nothing will come of his pestering.

I give him a half-hearted "Yes, sir," and return to the book.

It's the last day of the exercise, and Colonel Lee has been giving me a hard time. I understand. The type of officer he is, he doesn't look favorably upon useless types like me. I personally like the guy. He minds his own business and works hard, rarely making me do trivial things the other officers are so good at doing.

Earlier in the morning, I was sitting at my desk reading when he barked something at me. I told him I didn't understand and he barked it again. I didn't understand a second time and he got fed up and got up from his perch and stormed over to the printer and picked up the print out. It was then that I realized that he was using the Korean *chullyeokmul* instead of the English bastardization *peurinteu* that most of the officers use when talking to me.

After lunch, I return to the office and just before I can sit down, Colonel Lee calls me over. As I rush over to his desk, I quickly run through the day to think of what I did wrong.

"How may I help you, sir?"

"Chun, I'm sorry about blowing up this morning. Sometimes I forget you're not Korean."

"I-it's nothing, sir."

The stutter is from shock this time. I'm shocked for two reasons. First, it's the first time I've heard an officer actually apologizing to a conscript. Second, it's a rare thing that an officer would consider a conscript's particular situation.

"Tomorrow, you're going out on pass, right?"

"Yes, sir." Hun-hee had already asked for permission the day before. It's safer to get permission in the event the officers come looking for you.

Colonel Lee pulls out his wallet, takes out a few bills, and holds it out toward me.

"Here. Eat something nice for lunch tomorrow."

"Th-thank you, sir."

After I return to my seat, I pull the cash from my pocket and count it. 11,000 won.[65] It might not be much to the layman but, even with the slight raises with each rise in rank, it's still equivalent to about a third of my paycheck.

D-250 (23MAY05): Corporal Ken and Captain Ryu

On Monday, I head down to the administration office to talk to the first sergeant. The exercise is over, and I'm not the type of fool who'll extend his own short-term assignment without someone making me.

"First sergeant, I...," I begin and realize that I don't know the best way to phrase my question.

"Chun, you're on standby again. The Exercise Branch has had you for too long. 'Short-term assignment,' my ass."

"I understand, sir."

"We'll find you a place to go," he says.

I disappear before he can think about it for long.

I'm walking back to the squad room when I hear someone call me from behind.

"Corporal Chun."

I turn around and see a welcome face. It's Corporal Ken.

I first met Ken a month before leaving for Afghanistan. I was washing the rags for the nightly cleaning when a private with a bright pink face as if it had been scrubbed with steel wool walked up next to me. Thinking that he needed to wash his rags, I scooted over and told him to go ahead.

"May I ask you a question, sir?" he asked.

"Go ahead."

"Are you the American, sir?"

Damn it, I thought. Months of being on display and I'm still getting pestered by the others about my nationality. And a private, at that.

"Yeah. So what?"

"Is it okay if we talk in English, sir?"

---

[65] With the exchange rate at the time, it was about ten dollars.

Another fucking soldier trying to get free English lessons, I thought. I was angry but for some reason I gave him my permission.

He surprised me with his fluent English. At first I thought he was like me, but he explained that his father traveled often for business and he studied at international schools until he went to the States to study at Washington University. In St. Louis. "I went to school in Seattle," I had to clarify. The Korean translation obscures the difference.

I stopped him to close the door. If any of the *gocham* heard us talking in English, we'd both get a beating. I promised him that we'd talk again and went off to clean the squad room.

Until I left for the deployment, we'd talk occasionally, always in a place where *gocham* weren't likely to frequent. After months of being shunned and ridiculed, it was comforting to be able to talk to someone and actually understand the conversation.

"Where've you been?" I ask. I haven't seen him since my return to the HHC. He seems to have gotten some sun.

"I just got back from Iraq. I left a couple months after you did, sir."

"I was wondering where you went."

"Are you going to work now, sir?"

"Nope. I'm on standby."

"Me, too. Do you want to get some coffee, sir?"

"Sure."

We head outside and I pay for two cups of vending machine coffee. He tells me about his experiences with the Zaitun unit in Iraq, flying in a MED-EVAC helicopter, the blood of wounded soldiers soaking his uniform. I share a little about my time in Afghanistan, but I don't have much to say. Aside from an occasional rocket attack, it was pretty much the same as life in Daegu. As we talk, a private walks by and stares because we're talking in English. I glare back and he skitters off in a hurry. It's good to have rank.

I'm now a fifth-month corporal—the Personnel Officer at the Korean Support Group made sure that my early promotion didn't follow me back to Daegu—halfway through the rank. We say that I've *ggeokkida*, which means I'm over the hill and practically untouchable unless I do something completely out of line. I think the verb means to be folded or to turn a corner, and as a symbolic gesture, I have the right to crease my shoulder rank insignia in half.

There were two big developments in the company this month. The first is that we're no longer the Headquarters Company. We've absorbed the Facility Engineer Team, a unit of about twenty soldiers responsible for maintenance work around the base, and are now the Support Company. I don't know who initiated the move, but it's meant that the remaining three squads of the third floor have had to move our entire furnishings, lockers and all, to the other end of the hall. Our new squad room is the same storage room in which I used to train Hun-hee and Ju-uk and in which I had the talk with Ho-ju about going to Afghanistan.

The younger guys have been grumbling because they now have more *gocham*, but the FET has it much worse. The privates there maybe had fifteen *gocham* before the move. Now they have ten times that number. I assure my squad that I won't let the move affect them much.

The second big development is related to Captain Jin, our company commander. He's no longer Captain Jin but Major Jin, and he's no longer our company commander. With the promotion, he's been assigned to a staff position somewhere else. Where is inconsequential. He's gone and that's all that matters. The last of my major tormentors is gone.

He's been replaced by another captain, Captain Ryu, but nobody's really seen him yet save the guys that work in the administration office. I grab onto Gang-san, a quiet, bespectacled private that works in the office, as we head down to the parade ground.

"Hey, Gang-san. How's the new commander?"

"He seems like a decent man, sir."

"You just being nice?"

"No, sir," he says, smiling enigmatically.

I'm inclined to believe him for the same reason we're headed to the parade ground. Captain Ryu has called for a day of athletic competitions, I'm guessing to create a bond with us straightaway. It's a good sign. As far as I know, we never had athletic competitions under Captain Jin. He didn't give a damn about our physical health. He didn't really give a damn about our mental health, for that matter.

I get my first sight of the company commander at the parade ground. He's a young guy, probably not much older than me, with sharp eyes and thick eyebrows. What surprises me is his smile because he's sporting one, and it looks genuine. Can we be so lucky to get a decent guy for a commander? Only time will tell.

I sit up in the bleachers for most of the competition, watching the privates run around and waiting for a nice breeze to pick up. Daegu is far too hot for optional physical exertion. I only get up for the last event, a relay race, because the captain announced that he'll award two members of the winning squad a weekend pass. This guy knows how to motivate conscripts.

D-222 (20JUN05): The GOP Incident

Private Seong-ik is sleeping. His head is resting on his pillow, his fleece blanket draped over his body. He's sleeping on his side. The lights are off and the curtains are drawn. It's just after lunch.

I unlace my boots and lie down on the raised floor. I'm not going to say anything. There's a part of me that wants to, a petty and juvenile voice that says that it's not fair. There's an even smaller voice that says that it's not the way we do things in the Army, and I'm repulsed by the fact that this voice exists.

Seong-ik is our *mangnae*, the lowest-ranked private in the squad.

This was unthinkable just a week ago. The unwritten but often spoken rules are that privates can only lie on their backs without bedding, and even then, only with permission. The use of blankets is a right reserved for corporals and sergeants, and control of the lights and curtains is the right of the highest-ranked. The petty and juvenile part of me still remembers Beaver not allowing me to lie down at all in the lull before breakfast.

Last night, the officer-on-duty had us watch the news until it was time for evening call. A good portion of the news was devoted to the Army. There were short pieces about a private who went to a hotel in Cheongju and hanged himself with his bootstrings; another set himself on fire; two trainees went AWOL after only four days of boot camp; and there was an incident in which the commander of a basic-training company made all of the trainees literally eat shit after an unsatisfactory bathroom inspection.

The reason why these stories were being broadcast—while sad, these kinds of stories are all too common in the Army—was the main story of the night, of the past week. There was an incident at the GOP[66] on the front lines on the border between the two Koreas. A Private Kim cracked and went

[66] General Observation Post. Commonly used in the Korean Army to refer to the front because these posts are along the border between the two Koreas.

on a killing spree, killing eight. He threw a live grenade in his barracks and shot several others, including the platoon leader. Then he went to his guard post and watched the line as if nothing had happened.

According to the newspaper, the private hadn't been physically abused, but he couldn't handle the verbal abuse, cursing, and overall psychological abuse at the hands of his *gocham*. I have my doubts about the absence of physical abuse, but only because I've read reports about it and seen plenty of abuse far from the front. But I have no doubt that even without physical abuse, verbal abuse and a hostile environment can drive a conscript to madness.

As a result, we've experienced a spike in mental education sessions and mental health questionnaires recently. The lower-ranked guys are happy because it means time away from their posts, and I'm fine with it because it means the first sergeant is occupied with more pressing matters than the corporal in his company without an assignment.

"How am I supposed to fill this out, sir?" Seong-ik asked me as we were filling out the questionnaires.

He was asking whether it was okay to answer honestly or not. My answer should have been, "Lie and say everything is fine." I've seen how honesty on questionnaires like this has only led to trouble, with Captain Jin when I was a private and with Captain Park when I was in Afghanistan. Honesty is not the best policy here. Honesty will get you doing laps around the parade ground with a forty-kilogram pack on your back or reciting passages from the field manual ad nauseam.

"Write whatever you want," I said, surprising myself. I was surprised by the fact that, against my better judgment, I still thought some good can come of a stupid decision. I was also surprised that I was willing to take responsibility because a stupid decision by one of my squad members might come back to bite me in the ass.

In the wake of the incident, all of the higher-ranked conscripts have been more careful. We've begun to see our subordinates as ticking time bombs. I saw a private throwing rocks at one of the stray dogs that rummages through our garbage the other day and instead of disciplining him for his sadistic act, I slowly backed away. Aggression toward small animals is never a good sign.

The Army is changing for the better. The way we do things is needlessly restrictive and does nothing but push the lower-ranked to the edge between contemplating suicide and throwing a grenade in the squad room. Now that I'm two-*go*, I don't see any need to oppress my subordinates when their actions have no bearing on my quality of life.

Things are changing for the better. It's just my luck that they're changing when they no longer apply to me.

D-220 (22JUN05): Master Sergeant Maeng I: Afghanistan Interview

I'm on the train to Ansan for another interview for deployment to Afghanistan. Another deployment would mean that I would return to Korea a full month after my scheduled discharge. I don't think I would mind much because, strange as it seems, Afghanistan is a much nicer place to serve than Daegu. Not that it matters. It's policy that a conscript can only do one overseas tour.

The important thing is that the first sergeant doesn't know the policy. Having an interview has meant that he couldn't give me an assignment on the off chance that I'm selected again. It has meant at least another week and a half of standby.

Ken is going with me. He enjoyed his deployment to Iraq and is hoping for a tour in Afghanistan. We're also taking Private Ho-geun, a quiet, skinny kid with thick eyebrows who's hoping for a chance to fill an administrative position like Ja-hong did.

Unlike the first time around, I manage to speak passably during the interview. My answers are short and to the point, but I don't get tongue-tied and rendered dumb like last year. Ken does well, too. The competition isn't very stiff this year. Once Ho-geun is finished, we head back to the city for dinner.

After dinner, we're walking to the train station when Ken stops abruptly.

"*Hyeong.*" He refers to me familiarly when we're not surrounded by other company members.

"What is it?"

"How about getting a drink before we head back?" he asks, pointing at a small traditional bar near the station. Bases are completely dry, and conscripts rarely get a chance to leave base, so soldiers on furlough or pass tend to head straight to the bar.

"Why not?" As the highest ranking of the three of us, I'm in charge and

I'm not a very responsible person. I'm also a drunkard but figure the hour-and-a-half trip down to Daegu will be long enough for us to sober up.

We have seven bottles of *heukju*, a traditional alcohol a bit sweeter and easier on the stomach than *soju*, and stumble drunkenly toward the station with just enough time to catch the last train that'll enable us to make the 2100 deadline for returning to base.

Inside the atrium of the station, I look up at the electronic schedule. Oh shit. The next two trains down are full and the next available train is almost two hours later.

"What are we going to do, sir?" Ho-geun asks.

"Let me think."

I walk over to the pay phones and call the company. Thankfully, it's Gang-san on the line. I tell him that we're going to be late, explaining that the interviews ran later than expected and we missed our train.

The thought of what will come is enough to sober me up on the trip down. All soldiers are to be on base by 2100 to be ready for evening call. It's a firm rule. We don't arrive at East Daegu Station until almost eleven.

We jump in a cab and tell the driver to step on it.

"Sure thing," he says and starts zipping down the quiet streets of Daegu.

Most taxi drivers speed, especially at night, but it shouldn't take more than fifteen minutes to get to the base for even the most law-abiding of drivers.

After twenty minutes, I lean forward to ask what's taking so long and he beats me to the punch. "Where did you say you wanted to go?"

I'm at a loss for words. Ignoring the fact that he could've asked twenty minutes ago, this guy is taking us for a ride. It's not uncommon for taxi drivers to take a roundabout route in order to hike up the meter, but this guy is a bastard. We're drunk and from out of town, but we're soldiers with not much money and obviously out far past our return time.

"Second Army Headquarters in Manchon-dong," I say, the annoyance apparent in my voice. "We're in a hurry."

"Got it."

It doesn't seem like he's got it. When I notice that we're driving down the same street for the third time, I speak up.

"Hey, you're driving us in circles."

"Sorry," he says in a very unapologetic tone. "I haven't been a taxi driver for very long and don't know the roads well."

When he finally pulls up in front of the main gate, it's past midnight. We're fucked.

As we approach the guard post, we're blinded by a blaring floodlight.

"Halt! Put your hands up!"

Eyes watering from the stinging light, we do as we are told. It's a good idea to listen to armed guards with clips in their rifles. It's standard procedure. There are stories of guards who earned award leaves by shooting drunken citizens who approached the gates, disregarding their warnings.

"*Hwarang!*" It's the challenge, but I can't remember the password. I'm still drunk. I look at the others but they don't seem to know, either.

After a few moments of extremely uncomfortable silence, the junior guard approaches.

"Who are you?"

"I don't remember the password," I explain carefully. I'm sure the other guard still has his rifle pointed directly at me. "We're re-returning to the HHC from in-in-interviews in Seoul."

The guard returns to the guard station and calls the company. After confirming our story, they let us pass. We hurry the rest of the way.

As we walk up the stairs of the company, we're met by the night watch, a private.

"Corporal Chun, you smell of alcohol, sir."

"I know. Who's the officer on duty?"

"Master Sergeant Maeng, sir, and he's not happy."

Damn my luck. Out of the rotation of noncoms that do night duty, Maeng is undoubtedly the nastiest son of a bitch out of the bunch, a rat bastard with a permanent sneer on his verminous features.

Before walking through the door, I give my face a couple of slaps although I know it will do nothing to mask the smell or the red in my cheeks.

"*Chungseong!* Corporal Chun and two others returning from deployment interviews in Seoul."

Master Sergeant Maeng doesn't acknowledge my report. Instead he sniffs in the air markedly, letting me know that he can smell the alcohol.

"Why're you so late?"

I lower my salute. "The interviews ran late and we couldn't catch an earlier train, sir."

"Don't fuck with me. You went to drink, didn't you?"

"We did drink, sir." There's no point in denying it. "But we only had a ffew drinks after we found out the trains were full, sir."

"You're lying. Tell the truth."

"It's the truth, sir," I say resolutely.

"You insubordinate little shit." He turns to Ken and Ho-geun and tries to get a confession out of them but they corroborate my story, just like we discussed on the way from the front gate. There's no proof to the contrary and the smell and drunkenness will be gone by the morning.

Maeng continues his interrogation, which turns into a lecture once it's clear we're not going to change our story. When he runs out of things to say, he dismisses us. "Get out of here."

"Yes, sir."

Outside the door, I assure Ken and Ho-geun that everything will be all right and head back to the squad room, exhausted and still drunk.

D-182 (30JUL05): The Best Laid Schemes of Mice and Men

I've used up one of my regular furloughs. One down, two left. I applied with the administration office shortly after the results from the deployment interview came out and I didn't make the cut. I figured that if I spaced it out correctly, the first sergeant would have no choice but to allow me to stay on standby.

I didn't have anything to do while out on furlough. Practically all of my friends from my first year in Korea have left,[67] so I spent my days taking long walks all over Seoul. My aunt thinks I'm a popular guy but all I did was wander around the busy streets, sopping up the real world and listening to my mp3 player.

One thing I did do was get a cell phone. My cousin Jay gave me his old phone, and I went down to the local phone store and had them set up my account. I don't know why I did it. I have no one to call, and getting caught with a cell phone on base is an automatic trip to military prison, a violation of communication security. I snuck it back with me anyway.

It's only after my return that I realize I went on furlough prematurely. I'm eating at the mess hall when I overhear talk of the upcoming UFL exercise. One of two joint ROK-US exercises—the other being RSOI, which I

---

[67] Most expatriates in Korea only stay for a year before returning to their home countries, just as I had been planning to do.

thankfully arrived too late for this year—there will be plenty of work to find for a linguist. I should have scheduled my furlough closer to the exercise. A stupid mistake, but I was in training for the deployment to Afghanistan this time last year.

While I'm walking back to the company, I run into Hun-hee at the PX and I get an ominous feeling.

"Corporal Chun."

"Hey, Hun-hee. What's up?" I ask while paying for my ice cream. I pocket my change and look over at him. He has a goofy grin on his face, the kind of grin that says that something good has happened so please ask me about it. "Well?"

"I'm going to Iraq, sir."

"Oh. Congratulations," I say half-heartedly. I'm happy for him, remembering when I got the news for my deployment a year ago, but this is not good news for me. "When are you going?"

"I leave at the end of next week, sir."

An unexpected opening at the Exercise Branch means a high possibility that I'll be called in to take his place. Officers like conscripts they're used to. I can already see my days on standby dissipating into a fond memory.

Unwilling to go down without a fight, I spend the next week trying to find a way to fill the opening with someone else.

I first stop by the administration office.

"Hey, Gang-san. Can you check if there are any linguists coming in anytime soon?"

Gang-san takes out a manila folder and leafs through the pages.

"I'm sorry, sir. There are none for at least the next couple months, sir."

I'm racking my brain for other possibilities as I walk back up to the squad room. I retreat into my corner, lost in thought. A train is coming, and it's going to hit someone. I'd like that someone to be someone else.

I'm brought back out of my distraction by the opening of the squad-room door. Like the angel staying Abraham's hand, it's as if heaven is providing me a suitable replacement to place on the chopping block.

"*Hyeong*, can I borrow some books?" Ken asks, not knowing that he has inadvertently stepped into my crosshairs. He's a prime candidate for sacrifice. Fluent in both Korean and English, he's the most capable linguist in the company in my estimation. And he's the only other linguist on standby.

"Sure," I reply and recommend a couple of books for him to read, barely able to conceal the sinister grin on my face. I have my sacrifice; all I have to do is bring him to the altar. It will require cunning and guile, but the promise of rest has sharpened my wits to a fine cutting edge.

The next day, I go to see Hun-hee after lunch.

"Hey, let's go get some coffee."

"Yes, sir."

I pull out two cups of coffee from the vending machine and hand one to Hun-hee.

"So, did you tell the office you're going to Iraq?"

"Yes, sir."

"How did they take it?"

"Colonel Lee wasn't too happy, and I had to have a talk with the chief, but they've accepted it, sir."

"Good." I take a sip from my Dixie cup and decide to get on with it. "So what're they going to do without you?"

"I don't know, sir. I'll have to find and train a replacement before I go, but I don't know if that's possible." He adds with a smile, "You could always come back, sir."

I ignore his last comment, pretending to think for a second before getting to the point. "You know, I hear that Corporal Ken doesn't have an office. He's handy with a computer and damn good at translating."

Hun-hee's expression tells me that he thinks it's a good idea. Having planted the seed, I crumple up my cup and toss it in the trash.

The next step is convincing the mark. I know that I won't have to go to Ken; he'll come to me. Word travels around the company. Everyone knows everyone else's business. I know that Ken will hear of the news before the administration office calls him up, and that he will come to me for advice.

I don't have to wait very long. While the guys are going about the nightly cleaning, Ken walks through the door.

"Hey, *hyeong*. I think I might be going to the Exercise Branch. You used to work there, right?"

"Yeah, just for a short-term assignment."

"How is it?"

I again pretend to think for a moment before answering.

"I think it'll be good for you. It'll be a good place to challenge yourself and make the most of your gifts." Ken is a different animal from me. He's very motivated and would rather work in a place where he can experience a degree of success rather than sitting on his thumbs, which I'd rather do. "Besides, there's the BSC deployment where you can go on pass whenever you want and you're not subject to the obligations of the company."

I play up the perks and avoid talking about the tedium of the work and translation. I can tell that he's thinking positively about the prospect.

"Thanks, *hyeong*," he says as he leaves the squad room.

No, thank *you*, I think to myself. It's a shitty move to sacrifice perhaps my only friend to make my life more comfortable, but surprisingly, I have very little trouble falling asleep that night.

Having heard that Ken is doing well at the Exercise Branch, I sleep well the rest of the week and the weekend, but on Monday, I'm told to report to the administration office to see the first sergeant.

"Orders have come out. You're going back to the Exercise Branch for another short-term assignment."

D-179 (02AUG05): Back Again

I'm getting ready for lights out when Ken returns from the latrines, the standard issue baby-blue towel draped around his neck and toothbrush in hand. I've cracked open a book and am reading when he interrupts me.

"*Hyeong*, how do you do it?"

"Do what?"

"How do you not go crazy in here? It sucks for me, but I'm sure it's much worse for you."

I shrug. "I don't know. I try not to think about it."

This "short-term assignment" is turning out to be much worse than the previous one. The work on the MSEL was the same, but working in the TOC was even more torturous. It was bad enough in May, but Daegu in August is unbearably hot and humid—it's as if the sweat is already hanging in the air—causing the Navy lieutenant to pester me incessantly out of sheer madness.

Now that the exercise has started, things have only gotten worse. Unlike the ROK Army-only Amnokgang, this exercise is slowly chipping away at the little self-worth I've regained since leaving for Afghanistan.

I'm no linguist. I've been in this hell for twenty months, and I still can't put together an intelligible sentence, much less translate reports about the strategic laying of pipelines or placement of Patriot missile systems into Korean. Translation from Korean to English is manageable if I have ample time and my trusty dictionary; translation from English to Korean is an impossibility. I'm constantly being derided throughout the night shift, which builds to a head when it comes time to wrap up with the video teleconferences with the Joint Chiefs. It's the same feeling of a year and a half ago, when I was a lowly private fresh out of basic, sitting at the duck restaurant after RSOI.

I haven't been sleeping well, either. The conscripts deployed from other units are determined to make as much noise as possible, blasting the boom box and jumping around on raised floors at all hours. They also harbor open antagonism toward me, which I don't understand. I only know that it's spearheaded by a corporal from the Signal Battalion whom I have never wronged.

"You know, you sleep like someone with a lot of stress," the naïve young lieutenant who can't speak English but is an Interpretation Officer told me the other day.

I didn't know exactly what he meant and I was too tired to ask.

I'm walking out of the American PX truck parked out in front of the BSC, taking a bite out of a microwave mini-pizza, when I run into Ken talking to a private in a US Army uniform. Not one to make new friends, I give Ken a quick grin and head toward the entrance of the BSC.

"Hey, *hyeong!*"

I swallow my bite of pizza and reply, "What's up?"

"This is Private ———. He's a KATUSA."

I greet the private and he returns the greeting sheepishly. I'm guessing he doesn't know how to communicate with conscripts from other units. I don't know if there are multiple KATUSA units on American bases or not.

"So, you're a KATUSA? Lucky."

"Yeah," the private replies, his eyes glued to the floor.

"It must be nice, being able to use the Americans' D-FAC."

"No," he says, "I hate American food. I wish I could have rice and kimchi."

Damn. I'm sick and tired of rice and kimchi. I've been frequenting the PX truck as much as my time and finances can allow, and I've been rummaging through the trash bins at the American mess tent for the cans of Chef Boyardee the Americans are always throwing away.

I stick around while Ken and the private talk for a little while out of courtesy and excuse myself, wishing the private luck with the rest of his term of service.

The office is empty. The officers are still at lunch, and Ken's outside talking to the KATUSA. I sit down at my computer, put down my mini-pizza, and crack open the book that's sitting on the table.

I read, look up words in the dictionary until I can understand the sentence, and write a translation in the small space between the lines. This is how I've been spending my break and meal times and a few hours of my sleeping time while the support conscripts are raising a ruckus to prevent me from sleeping.

The book is *The Lighthouse Keeper* by Cho Chang-in. A Korean book. One of the first books I was able to read cover to cover although there was a lot I didn't understand. The book is about three hundred pages, a heartwarming story about the relationship between a son and his elderly mother.

I'm translating the book for a competition. Another small blessing of the exercise is that Ken usually gets his hands on an English newspaper from the American soldiers after they're done with it. I was flipping through the pages when I came across a notice for a translation competition held by the newspaper.

I'm doing it for the prize money. Five grand for the grand prize and half that for the runner-up. I've been running low on funds lately, and the prize money would be useful for my remaining passes and furloughs. I've sent almost all of my deployment money back home to pay off my debts, credit card bills, and school loans, and have been getting by on my measly thirty-dollar-a-month salary.

It's nearing the end of the exercise and the deadline for the competition, and I've only managed a rough translation of about half the book. It's why I grabbed a mini-pizza for lunch, and I didn't want to waste time talking to the KATUSA. I've spent the majority of this past month translating, and I don't want it to be for naught.

The process has also been difficult, being on base. With no internet access, I've had to sneak out on passes to sit in an internet café and contact the publisher and the author for permission. They were surprisingly supportive. The problem is that, even if I manage to finish up the translation, I'll have to be off-base to submit it to the newspaper.

I've been watching Colonel Lee all day, waiting for a moment he's not scowling. When I see my window of opportunity, I approach his desk.

"Colonel Lee, sir."

"What is it?"

"I… I was wo-wondering if it is possible to go on a short fur-furlough after the exercise ends, sir."

"What?" The scowl has returned.

"A-a furlough, sir. I… uh… I've been working on a translation for a contest during my free time and need a fu-furlough to submit it, sir."

Colonel Lee's silence is unnerving. It feels like everyone in the office is staring at me and I feel very small. I'm sure everyone in the office knows about my incompetence during this exercise, being unable to translate into Korean and to interpret for the chief.

Long moments pass in silence before Major Jeong comes to my aid.

"Sir, Sergeant Chun has been working very hard throughout the exercise."

Major Jeong is one of the good ones. He transferred to the Exercise Branch at the beginning of my re-assignment and we worked together on the MSEL.

Colonel Lee considers the statement and gives me a hard stare. "Okay," he says gruffly. "I'll let your company know and you leave after we finish things up here."

"Th-thank you, sir."

Colonel Lee is one of the good ones, too.

There is no rest or relaxation during the furlough, my time devoted to finish up the translation. When I head out for the train station on my last day, I still have seventy pages left unfinished, having spent most of the time typing up the lines I scrawled between the lines of the pages.

As I walk from the subway station to the train station, I pass by a post office. I also spot a trash can nearby. Holding the stack of papers that is my translation in my hands, I struggle with what its fate should be. It's unfinished, and what's finished is rough and unedited. I take a step toward the trash can. But I've worked tirelessly on this piece of shit through the mental and emotional anguish of the exercise, and it seems a shame to just throw it away. Fuck it. It'd be a waste not to turn it in, and besides, I did my best.

I walk into the post office, stick the translation and my copy of the book into a manila envelope, and send it off to the Korea Times.

D-138 (12SEP05): The End of Responsibility

My dealings with the Exercise Branch are over. There are no more exercises until after my discharge next year. I'm also now a sergeant, automatically promoted at the 19th month, and it will be difficult to place a sergeant with two regular furloughs remaining in an office. I had my sergeant insignia stitched onto my uniform before I left for my furlough.

My first morning back, I head to the administration office after breakfast to talk to the first sergeant.

"First sergeant, may I ask you a question, sir?"

"Corporal, no, Sergeant Chun. What is it?"

"I would like to be the company's manual laborer, sir." I've come prepared this time.

The first sergeant thinks for a second, the deep wrinkles in his dark face becoming more pronounced. "Okay. Stand by in your squad room until the boys need help."

"Yes, sir."

Most conscripts would consider me a fool. Why give up a cushy office job for spending the workday digging holes and moving furniture? Perhaps it's just me, but I always hated walking to Headquarters for unpaid overtime while guys from the other companies were out playing soccer or lounging around the PX. Besides, I was never cut out to work in an office.

I wouldn't mind doing manual labor every day, but my choice was the right one. The highest-ranked conscript in the administration office is my *donggi*, and unless the task requires a lot of hands or Captain Ryu is overseeing it, I'm left to be on effective standby permanently. I spend my days in the squad room with the lights off, hiding in my corner with a book.

This is the beginning of the good life. I've somehow managed to shirk all responsibilities. The highest-ranked of a squad of ten, I should be squad leader, but I took care of that during the exercise. I stopped by the company to pick up my laundry, and Seung-gi tossed me the green epaulettes that grace the shoulders of the squad leaders.

"Here you go, squad leader," he said with a smirk.

I took the epaulettes with me back to the BSC, tried them on in the mirror, and decided never to wear them again. While they are a sign of status, I'd rather not have to attend the regular squad-leader meetings and be held responsible for my subordinates' actions.

291

The next time I stopped by the company, I got a hold of the next in line, Yeong-min, a March corporal. A tiny kid with Coke-bottle glasses, he's displayed signs of short-man's complex. At barely five foot six, I'm short, but my inclination toward indolence has always overpowered my desire to prove my masculinity.

"Yeong-min, can I talk to you for a second?"

He was barely able to hide his eagerness behind a mask of decorum and humility.

I then went to see the first sergeant.

"First sergeant, now that Sergeant Seung-gi is getting dis-discharge, I don't think I should be squad le-leader. Corporal Yeong-min would be g-good, sir."

He didn't even have to think about it, my pathetic display of incompetence at a level already expected of me.

I'm fully enjoying my status as the deadbeat uncle who occupies the guest bedroom and does nothing all day. There are times when I feel a little sorry when I see some of the privates getting called out for overtime day after day with little time for rest, but they'll have their turn when they become *wang-go*. On the days my conscience acts up, I head out to the PX to buy snacks for the squad.

For the most part, I keep to myself and let the kids play. As long as they don't interfere with the tiny bit of happiness I've managed to find, they're free to find their own happiness. There are a few of them that snore and grind their teeth at night, but I don't hit them or force them to sleep in the bathroom, as I've heard happens in other squad rooms. Perhaps it's the result of the leisure of a man with no responsibility.

We got a fresh fish the other day. He sits in the squad room at attention like a good private should do. I've told him to take it easy several times, but he doesn't listen, and I'm not going to force him. I remember what it was like to be a private, and I know time is the only thing that will bring him comfort.

I'm in my corner reading a book, and the private is sitting at attention when Ju-uk enters the room a little early for lunch. He plops down next to the private.

"Private."

"Private ———!"

"You adapting to Army life well?"

"Private ———! Yes, sir!"

"Things are tough here, aren't they?"

The private hesitates. Privates shouldn't hesitate but I did my fair share when I was one. I guess it's still too early for him to know a trap when he hears it.

"You're supposed to say 'No, sir,' dummy."

"I understand, sir," the private says contritely.

"You see Sergeant Chun over there?"

"Yes, sir."

"You have no right to complain in front of him." I stop reading and listen. "He's had it harder than anyone else. You know he's an American?"

I glance at the private and he's eyeing me with curiosity, which annoys me. I hated the attention as a private, and it still bothers me now. I return to my reading.

"He couldn't even speak when he first came here. Nobody's had it harder."

"Y-yes, sir."

I'm surprised that Ju-uk still thinks that way. Even I don't think that way anymore. Sure, I'm reminded every day that even after twenty months, I still can't speak fluently enough to carry a decent conversation, but I guess I've come to accept it as my lot.

"Try harder from now on, got it?"

"Yes, sir!" the private responds, straightening his back.

D-101 (19OCT05): Fortune Favors the Bold

It's been a quiet weekend, and I'm reading in my corner when I hear an unfamiliar twittering from my locker. I fish out my cell phone from its hiding place under one of the bracings of the locker and flip it open.

It's a text message from my cousin Jay. I read it and flip the phone shut. I flip it open again and read it again. I can't wrap my head around what he's saying.

Hyeong, you've won a prize for your translation. Congrats!

A disbelief and joy wells up in my chest and rises up to my temples,

293

numbing my ears. How is this possible? I didn't even finish.

A bittersweet thought crosses my mind, that they've only chosen my translation because I'm a soldier and an American-Korean soldier at that. Hell, for what amounts to seventy months' pay, I'll take the equivalent of a pity fuck.

The day and the next pass in a euphoric trance. No taking the slow train to Seoul or sleeping in internet cafés for the remainder of my service. I can buy all the snacks and instant spaghetti I want. I only snap out of my trance when I get a second text message from my cousin.

They want you to call them as soon as possible. Here's the number....

Why would they want me to call? Are they second-guessing their decision? That would be cruel but not unexpected. I head out to the pay phones, bracing myself for bad news.

"Hello?"

"Hello. Is this Mr. So?"

"Yes, how may I help you?"

"This is Young Jin Chun. My cousin told me to contact you."

"Ah. Yes, yes. Congratulations on winning the prize."

"Thank you, sir."

"We were wondering if you would be able to attend the awards ceremony next week."

I exhale a deep sigh of relief. The prize money is still mine. I have no need for awards ceremonies and am saving my furloughs for the end of my service. They can just mail me the check.

"I'm sorry, sir, but I don't think I'll be able to make it. As you may know, it's not easy to get permission to leave base."

"I understand. Congratulations, once again."

"Thank you, sir."

The next day, the entire company is out at the Officers' Club, cleaning the entire building and setting up things for some ceremony the Army Commander will be attending. There are monstrously obese flies like bumblebees buzzing around everywhere, and after we've cleaned all the windows and mopped and finished setting up the banquet hall, the officers have us chasing the flies with wooden slats with tape on the end of them.

294

Captain Ryu is walking around, inspecting the job we're doing. I've worked with him a couple of times since becoming the company manual laborer, and he seems like a genuinely decent person, the kind of guy you wouldn't expect to be a soldier. Seeing him here and setting up the ceremony, I get an idea and decide to try it out. I wait until after he gives his approval of my window-cleaning skill and make my request.

"Captain Ryu, I have a question, sir."

"Go ahead."

"I t-talked to my cousin yesterday and he told me that I won a translation prize from The Korea Times, sir." I make sure to avoid the phrase "text message."

"Congratulations, Chun," he says heartily, giving me a pat on the back.

"Well, sir… there's going to be an award ceremony next Wednesday. Would it be po-possible for me to go to Seoul for a day to attend, sir?" Requests have to be made small and unassuming.

"Sure," he says. "Why don't you take a couple days? Just tell the office to put in the paperwork."

"Yes, sir."

As he walks off, I'm dumbfounded. What an immense difference between Captain Jin and Captain Ryu. Over the next couple of weeks, Captain Ryu allows me to interview with the newspaper and even gets a jeep to take me there. Captain Jin had threatened me with jail for talking to the press. Of course, the natures of the interviews are different, but I have a feeling Captain Ryu might have let me interview even with bad press.

The night after I return from the awards ceremony, I open up the envelope with my check and am slightly disappointed to see that it's less than I expected. I won the runner-up prize,[68] and it turns out the tax on awards is thirty percent. The bastards.

The next morning, I'm shocked when I pick up a copy of the *Defense Daily* and see an article about my winning the prize, mostly because I never gave them an interview.

The reporter chose to completely fabricate the entire story, saying that I voluntarily entered the military "out of a love for [my] fatherland despite having American citizenship," and that "I was only able to win this award

---

[68] There were no grand prize winners for literature in 2005. I was one of two runner-up prize winners, the other prize shared between two people working as a team.

because I am serving in the military in Korea." One particular quote makes me laugh out loud: "[My time in the Army] will be an absolutely unforgettable fond memory in my life."

Let them say what they want if it'll get me an award furlough. Being used is nothing new to me. I was called into the Public Relations Branch, and the officer in charge of civilian news coverage patted me on the back and told me the news would be reported to the Army Commander in the morning briefing.

"You'll probably be getting good news later today," he said, hinting that the Commander would be sending down orders for an award furlough through the chain of command. An award furlough from the Commander of the Second Army is good for ten days.

I wait the rest of the day and the next and the day after that before I realize that the Commander doesn't give a damn about a lowly sergeant. I'm surprised that it doesn't affect me as much as I thought it would. If you want something, you have to go out and get it yourself. And that is what I do. The next time I work with Captain Ryu, I ask for an award furlough and he gives it to me.

D-72 (17NOV05), D-42 (17DEC05): Finding Young

I'm lying on my back in the mud, my arms outstretched on either side and my legs together straight up in the air, or at least as straight as I can get them. One. I sway my legs to the left about sixty degrees. Two. I bring them back up. Three. I sway my legs to the right about sixty degrees. Four. I bring them back up. We do this countless times, and our backs are taut like guitar strings about to pop, and our stomachs are burning as if there's acid dripping on them, and our legs don't seem like they'll ever straighten out, and when it seems as if it's over, the *jogyo* trick some private into counting the last number, and here we go with another set of thirty.

There are fourteen other drills, but this one is the most tiring—not to mention the *jogyo*'s favorite—and we cycle through them all day in between rappelling off towers or traversing gorges on ropes or running obstacle courses, jumping and climbing on logs and tires. This is ranger training. At the end of the day, I've been yelling so much I've given myself a migraine.

We drag our beaten and weary bodies back into the barracks and collapse at our respective spots. Five days of rigorous training and the gas chamber, and we've reached our limits. I pull out my sleeping bag to use as a pillow, and my head hits hard where I've hidden my cell phone. I reach in and pull it out, careful to hide it close to my body as I flip it open and see that I've gotten a text message. It's not from my cousin. It's enigmatically signed "the person you miss most in the whole world." It's Jen.

Apparently, she's back in Korea. As we text back and forth, me on my side, huddled toward the wall with my phone nestled in my hands, and her, on the outside but somewhere close, I get a warm feeling in my chest. It's the same feeling I felt when I got her postcard in Ansan before I left for Afghanistan and whenever I logged on to the internet in the MWR in Bagram and saw there was an email waiting for me. But something is different this time. I think it's almost as if, all those times before, I never let myself expect anything because I was in here and she was out there and things weren't going to change anytime soon. It's as if I was in a slumber and now, with the end in sight, I'm beginning to wake up and remember what it is to be an actual person.

The Army has done its best to make me lose myself, beginning with that first day in basic, by taking away my name and my identity, and it was necessary to surrender myself in order to survive those long, frustrating days.

When I was out on this last furlough, I was walking through the subway station, and I noticed a dark figure shadowing my movements about ten feet to my right. Every step I took, he took in perfect unison. It was unnerving, but I kept my head down and kept walking until a large column obscured him from view. When I passed the column, he was gone without a trace. I looked around, but he was nowhere amongst the throng of people heading wherever they were headed. I took a few steps back past the column, and there I came face to face with him. It was a mirror. The dark figure was me. I couldn't recognize myself.

Had the Army truly taken away who I am? Who I was, I should say. I looked hard in the mirror and realized that it had been a very long time since I had truly looked at myself. Perhaps this was the reason I couldn't fit in when I was home.

In Afghanistan, Major Jeong had commented to Sergeant Luvaas that I was almost American. A few months later, he commented to Captain Bang that I was almost Korean. I didn't have the leisure to think about what that meant back then. America, my home, the place I consider home, considers me American as long as I'm not in Korea. Even then, when I was home, I was reminded that I'm not completely accepted every time I was asked where I was *really* from. Korea, my captor, only recognizes me as Korean with regard to the Army. I only have a citizen-registration number on Army documents. I can't use it to get an ID card or a passport.

It's an issue I've struggled with my whole life, and it's now that I realize that I don't give a damn anymore. All I can do is try to regain who I am as an individual as best I can, and I have a couple of months left to do so. Many of the ways I've attempted so far can earn me a trip to military prison— bringing in a cell phone and mp3 player and buying a set of civilian clothes and sneaking them in under my uniform—but I've learned enough about the machine to get away with it. I've done these things for no apparent reason, having no one to call and no one to meet, but Jen has given me a reason.

Over the next month, we text when we can and try to set up a chance to meet. I put in my request for my second furlough at the end of December so I can spend Christmas with her, Christmas being a holiday for couples instead of families in Korea, but she tells me that she might not be in country, so I head back to the office and put in a request for a weekend pass for the next weekend.

On the night before my pass, I get a message with bad news after lights out. She's been snowed in at her aunt's house in Gunsan, somewhere in the vast countryside. I try to message her back but fall asleep with no word, the phone nestled in my hand.

When I'm outside the gates the next morning, I check my phone. Still no word. Hoping that she'll get back to me soon, I head to an internet café in the area around the rear gate.

Sitting in front of the computer, I cradle my head in my hands and think about what to do. I had planned out things for a rendezvous in Seoul, and it's all going to be for naught. There's no reason for me to even to be out on pass if I can't meet her. Before I know it, it's nearing time for lunch.

"What should I do?" asks one voice.

"You took this pass for her, didn't you?" responds another voice, a voice I'm unfamiliar with.

"But I don't even know where Gunsan is."

"You're sitting in front of a damn computer. Look it up."

I open up the browser and find that Gunsan is in Jeolla Province on the western coast, nearby Jeonju.

"Wait. But it's snowing, and if she can't come out, what guarantee do I have that I'll be able to get to her?"

"Don't be a chickenshit. Just get to Jeonju and march the rest of the way if you have to. This is your last pass, and you took it for her."

Convinced by the bold, foolhardy second voice, I set out for the bus terminal and buy a ticket to Jeonju.

The bus ride is long and uncomfortable. I'm reminded of the bus ride down to Jeungpyeong, now almost two years ago. The cold is coming in despite the closed windows, and the heaters beneath the seats are on full blast, making me a shivering, sweating mess. The bus is moving at a snail's pace through the mountains. It's snowed and the roads are narrow with steep drop-offs. I sleep as best I can, waking from time to time to check my phone. Still no word.

After making it safely to the bus terminal in Jeonju, I change into my civilian clothes and find another internet café to try to figure out exactly how I'm going to get to Gunsan. I'm heartened when I find out it's only around fifty kilometers away. But what do I do when I get there if I can't get a hold of her? The second voice doesn't know either.

I guess it's time to give up.

No, it's not, says my phone. It's Jen.

"You're in Jeonju? Why? How?"

"I took the bus here. To see you."

After I get her to calm down, we set up arrangements to meet in Gunsan. I head to the intra-provincial bus station and get on a bus for the last leg of my trek. An elderly man with a weathered, droopy face sits next to me and I turn my head toward the window because of the strong smell of fish that I assume comes from a man who lives on the sea. I wipe away the frost from the window and watch as the sun sets over the farms and wheat fields.

It's late when the bus pulls into the bus station in Gunsan, almost midnight, and bitterly cold. I only have on a long-sleeved shirt and a thin jacket and stand shivering in the cold as I wait for a taxi. My uniform is in a paper shopping bag, but I don't want her to see me in my uniform.

As the taxi heads to the coffee shop we arranged to meet at, I notice that the streets are dark and empty, with only a handful of couples huddled together as they walk beneath the lonely street lamps.

The coffee shop is empty save for a couple in the corner who read a magazine together. I take a seat against the wall and wait. I take out my journal and am writing when the bell hanging above the door chimes.

On the inside, on base, time seems to flow so slowly but when you try to remember what existed during that time, there is nothingness. As I watch Jen walk through the door, time seems to slow down, but every moment in every second is full of beauty. She gives me an unabashed smile when she spots me and comes over to my booth.

She sits next to me and we talk for what seems like hours, but not more than twenty minutes can have passed. She's in Gunsan to get away from her parents, who are still mad at her for quitting her job at the UN against their wishes.

"What should I do?" she asks.

"About what?"

"About my situation, my parents, my life."

She always does this. I have a weakness for girls who pretend to lean on you when you know damn well that they can take care of themselves even if you aren't around. I start to think of an answer when she interrupts my thoughts.

"You know, I still have that message you sent me."

"What message?"

"You know, the one telling me that you'd marry me and make everything better."

I used to do that, too. When I couldn't think of anything practical, I'd at least try to get a cheap laugh. It was my usual answer when she came to me with one of her problems. I wonder if I've lost my sense of humor while in the Army.

I haven't had dinner yet, so we leave the coffee shop in search of a place to eat, but it's past midnight, so we duck into a dive bar not too far away.

"The cook's gone home for the day," the bartender says. "All we have are nachos."

I get a whiskey and Coke, Jen orders a cocktail, and the bartender goes off to get our drinks.

Once I have some nachos and a few drinks in my stomach, I decide to set in motion plans I had spent the last month planning for Christmas in Seoul. I call the bartender over.

"I don't suppose there are any bars with live music in the area, are there?"

"You're in luck," she says. "There's one across the street."

300

I pay the bill and we walk across the street in the snow.

This bar is also completely empty except for the lady working the counter. We take a table in the middle of the place and order a couple of shots of whiskey each. It was only a short distance across the street, but we need to warm up, and I need some liquid courage.

With the whiskey still burning in my stomach, I get up and approach the counter.

"Excuse me, would it be okay if I played the piano?"

"Knock yourself out," the lady says curtly and disappears behind a curtain into the kitchen.

I walk back to our table and hold out my hand.

"What's this?" Jen asks.

"Come on."

I take her over to the piano and sit down in front of the keys. I blow into my hands and give them a good stretch and play a few warm-up chords. It's been a long time since I've played and just as long since I've sung. My fingers stumble over the keys, and my voice cracks as I fumble through my serenade.

She's smiling. She smiles as I tell her that how I've felt about her for the past month, how I've felt throughout my deployment, how I've always felt about her. She sits next to me on the piano bench and takes my hand in hers and doesn't let go until the taxi stops in front of her aunt's house.

I watch as she goes inside, stopping briefly to wave good-bye. There is a sadness to see her go and a different sadness that she had to go. Her aunt had her cousin call repeatedly until we could no longer ignore it.

I spend the rest of the night sleeping in front of a computer in my third internet café of the trip, but I'm happy. Today is my birthday, my second in the Army, and it almost feels as if I'm again the man I was two years ago.

D-24 (04JAN06): Master Sergeant Maeng II: Farewell to Arms

The company is having an early dinner today in the officers' mess hall. Before us are platters of actual food, not the ordinary chow they serve in our mess hall. Good cuts of fatty pork belly steamed a nice brown, blocks of steamed tofu swimming in the run-off from fried kimchi, fresh vegetables, and rice that's not completely dried out. But what has the room buzzing is something more unattainable to the common conscript—alcohol. Arranged neatly in the center of each table are green glass bottles of soju.

As far as I know, this is the first time conscripts have been allowed to dine in the officers' mess, and it's thanks to Captain Ryu. He's called this dinner to celebrate the merger of the Headquarters Company with the Facility Engineer Team, but the real reason for the dinner is to put us all in one room and make us get along. There have been gripes on both sides, and Captain Ryu is hoping that good food and a fair amount of social lubricant will accomplish his goal.

I consider the dinner also to be my farewell party. I have a few weeks left, but I've saved my last furlough and have scheduled it so that I return the day before my discharge. I don't drink with anyone from the FET. Instead, I drink with my squad for a while and then go out in search of my *donggi* and others close to me, and finally in search of bottles that haven't been completely emptied.

All around are drunk and raucous conscripts. For many of them, this is the first alcohol they've had in months. Having built up my tolerance close to pre-Army levels from my recent streak of furloughs and passes, I'm still thirsty when Captain Ryu and the first sergeant tell us we have to go to sleep. It's four in the afternoon, and they want us to get enough rest to show up for work tomorrow morning.

Unsatisfied, I call over Ken and Corporal Byeong-hun, a junior linguist, and tell them to meet me in the corporal's squad room in fifteen minutes. They also look thirsty, and I have a plan.

I stroll across the street to the PX and head straight to the alcohol section. The section is normally like a strip club—look, but don't touch—reserved for officers and conscripts going on furlough with valid orders. I pick up a few bottles of strong liquor made from wild strawberries and grain and walk up to the counter.

The private working the register is at a loss for what to do. The PX clerks are from the same company, making me their *gocham*, and they know me well because I stop by regularly. The corporal behind him steps in and rings me up. He nods and I nod and there's an understanding. He'll figure it out, ringing it up as a purchase by an officer or a conscript on furlough. I leave the PX in and with relatively good spirits.

We drink with the lights dimmed so as not to disturb the others sleeping around us. None have the rank to complain, but the soju from before seems to have had its effect—the sleeping soldiers do not stir or give any indication as the three of us drink and talk and laugh.

After draining every last drop from each of the bottles, we hide the empties in the bottom of the trash cans, carefully covering them with balled-up tissue and candy wrappers. It isn't long before the officer on duty barges through the door. It's Master Sergeant Maeng. He gives me a cold look when he sees me sitting on the raised floor. I've long forgotten the bad blood between us, but I guess he hasn't.

"Why aren't you sleeping?"

"We wanted to talk for a little longer, sir," I offer.

He doesn't answer but lifts his vermin-like nose in the air and begins to sniff. He continues to sniff as he walks down the center aisle straight toward the trash can. He bends down and knocks off the lid of the trash can, digs through the trash, and produces the empty bottles. He finally has his evidence.

"Go to sleep," he says with a sneer on his face. "Things aren't going to be nice in the morning."

Ken and Byeong-hun are worried but I assure them it'll be okay and send them off.

The next morning, I wake up with a magnificently skull-splitting headache, all fire and brimstone behind my eyes.

"Sergeant Chun, wake up, sir. It's time for morning call."

I slip a hand out from under my sleeping bag and wave the voice away. The second time someone tries to wake me up, I tell him to tell the sergeant-on-duty that I'm sick.

I sleep until after lunch, when Ken stops by to tell me there will be a disciplinary committee. My head is still pounding and I wave him away.

The disciplinary committee is held the following morning after breakfast. Even after a second night of sleep, I'm still suffering from my hangover, struggling to focus my eyes as I stand along with Ken and Byeong-hun in front of the first sergeant, Master Sergeant Maeng, and a handful of other noncoms in the first sergeant's office. The office is absurdly small—I surmise that it must have originally been a storage closet—and I find it amusing that they've gathered so many noncoms to sit lined against the sides of the room, their knees practically touching in the middle.

The first sergeant reads off a summary of our offenses—disobeying orders, purchasing alcohol, consuming alcohol, disrupting others after lights out, and so on—and follows with a string of threats, which I respectfully ignore through the buzzing in my head.

"What do you have to say for yourselves?"

Ken and Byeong-hun look to me, and I speak up.

"It was all my idea, sir. I or-ordered Sergeant Ken and Corporal Byeong-hun to drink with me." It isn't a noble gesture. It's the truth. Besides, I only have a couple of weeks left.

The first sergeant asks Ken and Byeong-hun if it's true and they confirm my statement.

"As punishment, Ken and Byeong-hun are having two days cut from their final furloughs. I'm cutting three days from your final regular furlough because it was your idea. You have a problem with that?"

"No, sir."

"You don't have that much time left. You'd better stay out of trouble."

"Yes, sir."

"Get out of here."

I salute and he waves it off. As I leave, I notice that Master Sergeant Maeng is sneering again. He might have won this round, but it's not over yet.

I stay out of sight, steering clear of the administration office for the next week. When I feel like enough time has passed, I talk to my *donggi* in the administration office and make sure I show up for one last manual-labor task, waiting around in the office so the first sergeant notices that I'm around and working.

When he shows up, I give him a hearty salute.

"Oh, Sergeant Chun," he says, gives me a pat on the back, and walks into his closet of an office.

I approach Gang-san, who's sitting in front of his computer, typing up a report for the first sergeant.

"Hey, have you heard anything about my punishment lately?"

"No, sir," he says and smiles a knowing smile. "I don't think the first sergeant even remembers, sir. I don't think he'll notice that I've misplaced the paperwork." He opens up a thick folder and pulls out my paperwork and sticks it somewhere in the back.

A few days later, I leave for my final regular furlough as scheduled, without the loss of three days. After I report my leave, the first sergeant pats me on the back and says, "Have a good time."

I will, sir. I will.

Afterword (D+3,285)

I was discharged the day after I returned from that final regular furlough. Captain Ryu shook my hand and patted me on the back, and then I took my last walk down that road past the Motor Pool, signal battalion, and parade ground toward the rear gate. I didn't look back once, even after I crossed that invisible but very real line that separated my life as a soldier and my life as a free man. I looked up and saw the sun shining and knew that everything was going to be fine.

All these years later, I still have an occasional nightmare about the Army. It invariably deals with being drafted for a second time, and the fear and bewilderment and frustration are as vivid as they were at the start of the ordeal. The surreal nature of my dreams does nothing to convince me I'm only dreaming; if anything, it enforces the delusion of the reality at that time. There was a time when I'd wake up in a cold sweat and compulsively scour the dark of my room, my eyes furtively darting across every corner until my fear-addled brain could process that this non-Army reality was the true reality.

Those two years were the only two years I lived as a Korean. As I was getting discharged, I was told that, according to Korean law, I had to cancel one of my citizenships. I also had to take care of the matter so I could clear up my "illegal overstay" and return home to Seattle. As I cancelled my Korean citizenship, I was told that I could get it back whenever I wanted because I finished my military service. The magnanimous bastards. Since then, the government has begun to recognize dual citizenships but I still have yet to feel a need to request it back.

Perhaps my luck is changing. Had I been accepted to that second deployment, I might not have been able to write this memoir. I heard, after my discharge, that the interpreter for Intel/Ops during that deployment was the unfortunate victim of a suicide bombing at the front gate while picking up local nationals to operate the construction equipment.

I still live in Korea, an expatriate and an ex-patriot, and I can't give a clear reason why. When I returned to Seattle, I couldn't settle back into my former rhythm. I was always a beat behind wherever I went. I can't say whether it was a result of the Army or whether my experience only made it painfully clear, but I returned to Korea to start over. A benefit is that most people don't ask about my experience because it is a fact of life here. An additional benefit is that the drinking culture here is very liberal, and God knows I could use a drink.

Nothing ever materialized with Jen. I actually had a chance, not too long ago, but as with most things in my life, I screwed it up beyond repair. Perhaps Sang-hee read my palm correctly, and the two lines that came close but never touched were me and Jen. Even now, the lines are still there at the base of my thumb, but the gap is much more pronounced. I remain close with Ken and see Seok-bae, Ho-ju, and Richard, a conscript that worked at the administration office when I first reported to Daegu, on occasion. I've lost touch with Jeong-su, and I still wonder what happened to Johnny.

To my knowledge, everything written in this book is true. I've left out many episodes and changed some inconsequential details, some for the sake of the story and some at the request of the person involved. Certain names have been changed for the same reason. Any other discrepancies are due to a faulty memory ravaged by time, age, a strong desire to forget, and liberal amounts of alcohol.

Glossary

AB: Air Base

ACAS (Army Consolidated Administrative School): The base where the deployment unit completed its pre-deployment training. Located in Yeongnam, North Chungcheong Province.

ACU (active combat uniform): Standard Army uniform, fatigues.

Amber Alert: A status given over the Giant Voice alerting soldiers on Bagram AB of some sort of danger, usually in response to a rocket attack. Not to be confused with the alert for missing children.

AWOL (absent without leave, *talyeong*): Being absent from one's post or duty without official permission.

B-hut: Short for "barracks hut," a temporary structure for sheltering troops, usually made of plywood and covered with a tent.

BSC (Battle Simulation Center): The building in the SROKA Headquarters in Daegu where simulations for war exercises are overseen.

Bu ik bu, bin ik bin (富益富貧益貧): Literally, "the rich get richer, the poor get poorer."

***Bulchimbeon*:** A nighttime patrol of the barracks.

***Byeonbi*:** Constipation.

***Byeongshin*:** A (physically) disabled person, used as a slur to mean moron or idiot.

***Chijil*:** Hemorrhoids, a million-dollar condition.

Chocopie: A snack cake akin to a Moon Pie, manufactured by the Orion Confectionary Company.

***Chungseong*:** Literally, "loyalty." A general catchword for the Korean Army, used when saluting.

Commuter soldier (*sanggeun yebiyeok*): A conscript who is allowed to commute to his post from his home.

Conscript: A person enlisted compulsorily. The conscript ranks are private to sergeant.

D-FAC: Dining facility.

***Donggi*:** People who started at the same time and are therefore one's peers.

ENDEX: End of Exercise

***Eohakbyeong*:** Linguist, similar to Translator or Interpreter but with less responsibilities.

Eopdeuryeo buchyeo: The call to assume a physically demanding position as punishment. The positions are usually either a maintained push-up position or a tripod position balancing on one's head and two feet.

"Father" (***abeoji gunbeon***): Conscripts in the same unit who started one year earlier. They are responsible to take care of their "sons" to a certain extent.

FET (Facility Engineer Team): The unit that is responsible for maintaining on-base facilities.

Furlough/leave (*hyuga*): A vacation. Conscripts get one ten-day furlough upon promotion to the next enlisted rank in addition to a five-day furlough on the 100th day of service.

Gakgaejeontu: Individual combat training.

Ggalggari: A padded, collarless jacket to be worn under the field jacket.

Ggul: Literally, "honey," used to indicate a duty that is relatively easy.

Giant Voice: The public announcement system on Bagram Air Base.

Gocham: A senior conscript.

GOP (General Observation Post): Often used to mean the front area in general.

Gwangdeungseongmyeong: Name and rank, to be given when addressed, touched, or even looked at with intent by a higher-ranking soldier.

Gyogam: Drill instructor, an officer tasked with educating recruits.

Hagwon: A privately run after-school academy for over-worked Korean schoolchildren.

HHC (Headquarters, Headquarters Company): The unit comprised of conscripts who provide support for the headquarters.

Hojeok: Family register, the basis for citizenship in Korea.

Hoju: Head of the household, the eldest living male in a family.

Hoju bongeoji: Base (residence) of the head of the household.

Hyeong: Literally, "older brother." Often used as a term of affection for an unrelated older male by a younger male.

Jeongshingyoyuk: Literally, "mental education."

Jeontu shiknyang: Combat rations, MRE (Meal-Ready-to-Eat)

Jogyo: Drill sergeant, a conscript tasked with training recruits.

JSA (Joint Security Area): The portion of the Demilitarized Zone (DMZ) where North and South Korean forces face each other.

JSA (Joint Smoking Area): The designated smoking area on the Korean compound on Bagram Air Base.

***Jumindeungnokbeonho*:** Citizen Registration Number, the Korean equivalent of a Social Security Number.

K2 Rifle: Manufactured by Daewoo Precision Industries, the standard service rifle of the ROK Army. Basically a copy of the M16 with a side-foldable buttstock.

KATUSA (Korean Augmentation to the US Army): Conscripts who serve on US Army bases as support for the US Army.

Kevlar: Body armor

KPD (Karzai Protective Detail): Protection detail for Hamid Karzai.

***Mangnae*:** Literally, "the youngest." Used to refer to the squad member with the least seniority.

***Michinnyeon*:** Literally, "crazy bitch." Squad Leader Lee's favorite term of abuse for his squad.

***Mishing*:** A thorough scrubbing of the facilities with toothbrushes.

MMA (Military Manpower Administration): The government body that oversees conscription.

MND (Ministry of National Defense): The government body that oversees national defense. Similar to the Department of Defense in the US.

MOS (Military Occupational Specialty): A four-number code to identify a specific job of a conscript.

MSEL (Master Scenario Events List): A list of simulated events to be used during a war exercise.

MWR (Morale, Welfare, and Recreation): A US Army facility on Bagram Air Base with video rentals, a movie viewing area, and an internet café, among other things.

NCO/noncom (*hasagwan*): Noncommissioned officer.

Notice of Suspension of Departure (*chulgukgeumji tongjiseo*): A notice from the Ministry of Justice that informed me that I was barred from leaving the country.

***-nyeon*:** Bitch

***Ochim*:** Permission to sleep until lunch, usually given after a conscript is forced to do overtime past midnight.

Officer-on-duty: An NCO that oversees company affairs overnight.

***Oppa*:** Similar to *hyeong*, but used when a younger female addresses an older male.

Overtime (*yageun*): When regular duties extend past normal working hours, unpaid.

Pabyeong: Deployment

PRI (Preliminary Rifle Instruction): Training that involves holding one's rifle in one of three specified stances, often used as punishment.

PT (Physical Training): Usually a jog around the base.

PX (Post Exchange): An on-base store that sells snacks and basic necessities.

Reveille: A bugle call used to wake military personnel.

ROK: Republic of Korea

S1: Personnel (staff)

S2: Operations (staff)

S3: Intelligence (staff)

S4: Logistics (staff)

Sekjeuksigong gongjeuksisek (色即是空 空即是色): I still don't know exactly what this means, but I heard that *sek* most probably doesn't mean sex.

Sergeant-on-duty: A higher-ranked conscript that assists the officer-on-duty with company affairs overnight.

"Son" (*adeul gunbeon*): Conscripts in the same unit who started one year later.

SROKA (Second Republic of Korea Army): Since re-structured and re-named Second Operational Command, the army in the rear area, the lower half of the peninsula.

Ssibal: Fuck, fucking.

-*saekki*: Literally, "young child/animal." In a curse, equivalent to "bastard."

Sugohaetda: "You've toiled," but something akin to "Good job."

Suha: The guard procedure of issuing a challenge and verifying a password response in order to distinguish whether someone approaching a guard post is friend or foe. Similar to "flash" and "thunder" used on D-Day in Europe. Literally, "who and why."

TOC (Tactical Operations Command): The operations center of a unit.

Two-*go*: The second-ranked conscript in a squad.

Unjeonbyeong: A conscript whose MOS is driving.

Wang-go: Literally, "king *gocham*." The highest-ranked conscript in a squad.

XO (Executive Officer): The second-ranked officer in a unit, in charge of administrative operations.

Yeongchang: Military prison

Conscript Ranks
PVT: trainee, *hullyeonbyeong*, no insignia
PV2: private, *ideungbyeong*, one bar
PFC: private first class, *ilbyeong*, two bars
CPL: corporal, *sangbyeong*, three bars
SGT: sergeant, *byeongjang*, four bars

NCO Ranks
SSGT: staff sergeant, *hasa*, one-bar chevron, point down
SFC: sergeant first class, *jungsa*, two-bar chevron, point down
MSG: master sergeant, *sangsa*, three-bar chevron, point down
SGM: sergeant major, *weonsa*, three-bar chevron, point down, with a star on top
WO: warrant officer, *junwi*, gold diamond

Officer Ranks
2LT: second lieutenant, *sowi*, one diamond
1LT: first lieutenant, *jungwi*, two diamonds
CPT: captain, *daewi*, three diamonds
MAJ: major, *soryeong*, one flower
LTC: lieutenant colonel, *jungnyeong*, two flowers
COL: ("full-bird") colonel, *daeryeong*, three flowers
BG: brigadier general, *junjang*, one star
MG: major general, *sojang*, two stars
LTG: lieutenant general, *jungjang*, three stars
GEN: general, *daejang*, four stars

Units
Squad: *bundae*
Platoon: *sodae*
Company: *jungdae*
Regiment: *yeondae*
Battalion: *daedae*
Brigade: *yeodan*
Division: *sadan*
Corps: *gundan*
Army: *gun/gundae*

Made in the USA
San Bernardino, CA
28 April 2020

68922287R00177